ADVANCE PRAISE

"This gorgeously written book is more than a memoir; it is a celebration of holy moments nestled in the ordinary trajectory of a life: prophetic callings and fallings in love, echoing emptiness and luminous epiphany, magical encounters and a reverence for trees. It is a beckoning, a heartsong, an invitation to discover the face of the divine in each other. This is a magnificent book!"

—Mirabai Starr, author of
Caravan of No Despair and *Wild Mercy*

"Writing with stunning insightfulness and unprotected candor, Bill Glenn invites readers to become rapt companions on the journey into his psyche, heart, and soul. *I Came Here Seeking a Person* is a deep and fascinating book worthy of the great Thomas Merton, whom Bill considers his mentor."

—Ron Hansen, author of *Mariette in Ecstasy*,
professor at Santa Clara University

"Beautifully written, captivatingly expressive, this book is genuine literature. A central figure in the gay community and its response to AIDS in San Francisco, Bill Glenn reveals an aspect of gay experience that few tend to consider—the spiritual. Here is a stabilizing lesson, sorely needed amidst the divisiveness of today's world.

—Daniel Helminiak, author of *The Human Core of Spirituality*
and *Sex and the Sacred: Gay Identity and Spiritual Growth*

"In a long line of compelling spiritual autobiographies, starting from Augustine through to Merton, Bill Glenn's deeply interior story of his life and times is a moving witness to what many of us saw, felt, and ultimately, by the grace of God, survived. How often does one get to sit down and spend a big swath of time with a sharp mind and an open heart, with a man who can tell not just his own story but the story of a whole generation, and do so from the inside out, with grace, insight, and wisdom? Not often. Bill's book is such a gift."

—Robert Hopcke, author of *A Guided Tour of the Collected Works of C.G. Jung* and Jungian analyst

"The person has been magnificently found, and most thoughtfully shared. In this compelling spiritual autobiography, inspired by Augustine and mentored by Merton, our courageous and generous guide, Bill Glenn, helps us see our own process in finding ourselves through God and others. I sat silent in gratitude that my soul brother, Bill, and I are so synchronized in our life treks. I believe you will experience the same joyful recognition."

—Brian McNaught, author of *On Being Gay*

"*I Came Here Seeking a Person* is not a book for wimps (the coward within). This powerful narrative will nevertheless resonate with our inner wimp while calling it to see the bridge to a greater reality—our unity as human beings on this planet. Thank you, Bill Glenn, for being who you are and for shining the light of unity on us one and all. This profoundly powerful memoir reminds us that separation is an illusion and unity is our true source of light—clearly visible only to the eyes of the soul. Reading this book lifted my spirit while clearing my mind. *I Came Here Seeking a Person* is a deep meditation on the meaning and purpose of the life we live and share. This is a must-read for every spiritual traveler!

—Robert Thompson, author of *A Voluptuous God* and former president, Parliament of the World's Religions

I CAME HERE SEEKING A PERSON

A Vital Story of Grace

One Gay Man's
Spiritual Journey

WILLIAM D. GLENN

Paulist Press
New York / Mahwah, NJ

Library of Congress Cataloging-in-Publication Data
Names: Glenn, William D., author.
Title: I came here seeking a person : a vital story of grace : one gay man's spiritual journey / William D. Glenn.
Description: New York / Mahwah, NJ : Paulist Press, [2022] | Includes bibliographical references. | Summary: "This book presents the profound if seemingly counterintuitive graced moments in one's life and their capacity for transformation, individuation, and living in graced presence"— Provided by publisher.
Identifiers: LCCN 2022018998 (print) | LCCN 2022018999 (ebook) | ISBN 9780809156146 (paperback) | ISBN 9780809187751 (ebook)
Subjects: LCSH: Glenn, William D. | Catholics—United States—Biography.
Classification: LCC BX4705.G5569 A3 2022 (print) | LCC BX4705.G5569 (ebook) | DDC 282.092 [B]—dc23/eng/20220805
LC record available at https://lccn.loc.gov/2022018998
LC ebook record available at https://lccn.loc.gov/2022018999

ISBN 978-0-8091-5614-6 (paperback)
ISBN 978-0-8091-8775-1 (e-book)

Published by Paulist Press
997 Macarthur Boulevard
Mahwah, New Jersey 07430
www.paulistpress.com

Printed and bound in the
United States of America

For Scott Hafner
Lifeguard Extraordinaire

Part of the proceeds from the sale of this book will
be used to further the works of
The Trevor Project, Los Angeles, California
and
Insight-Out, San Quentin, California

If You Seek a Heavenly Light

If you seek a heavenly light,
I, Solitude, am your professor:

I go before you into emptiness,
Raise strange suns for your new mornings,
Open the secret windows
Of your innermost apartment.

When I, loneliness, give my special signal
Follow my silence, follow where I beckon:
Fear not, little beast, little spirit,
(Thou word and animal)
I, Solitude, am Angel
And have prayed in your name.

Look at the empty, wealthy night
The pilgrim moon!
I am the appointed hour,
The "now" that cuts
Time like a blade.

I am the unexpected flash
Beyond "yes" and "no,"
The forerunner of the Word of God.

Follow my ways and I will lead you
To golden-haired suns,
Logos and music, blameless joys,
Innocent of questions
And beyond answers.

For I, Solitude, am thine own Self:
I, Nothingness, am thy All.
I, Silence, am thy "Amen."

—Thomas Merton

CONTENTS

Contents

ACKNOWLEDGMENTS

I'm grateful to have so many to whom I can express my gratitude!

To my partner of forty-one years—and my husband of twelve, a very long engagement indeed—Scott Hafner. I express my abiding gratitude for your steadfast love, healing kindness, generosity, for wrangling with me and amply employing good humor as you did so, for the home we have created—a place of welcome for family and friends—and in important ways, a respite for this highly extroverted introvert. You have encouraged me to be true to my Self, and to my journey—always. You made me a dog lover: Phoebe, Maude, and Sophie. My mother's sage advice was not to *bleep* it up with you because it would never get any better—as good advice as she ever gave.

To Ida Rae Egli, my early editor, for your insight, clarity of both purpose and prose, and for your interest in matters of the Spirit, a totally unexpected gift!

To Fr. Mark-David Janus, CSP, the president of Paulist Press, for finding this book worthy of the Paulist imprint.

To Paul McMahon, my editor at Paulist Press, for your kindness, erudition, spirituality, literary eye and style, care for the text, sense of flow, and patience.

To Tom Hall, my senior English teacher at Prep, who saw in me the slight glistening of a writer and modelled for me what it meant to be *a man for others*.

To Richard Smith, SJ, longtime editor of *Review for Religious* who asked me to write criticism for the *Review* whilst in my midtwenties, at St. Louis University, for your early confidence in me.

To the professors who honed my critical thinking skills at Creighton: Eileen Fogarty, Richard Shugrue, and Robert Shanahan, SJ; at St. Louis University: Sr. Elizabeth Kolmer, John Wilson, and John Carlson; at the University of San Francisco: Larry Palmetier; at the Jesuit School of Theology: Joseph Powers, SJ, Anne Brotherton, and Robert Egan; and at the Pacific School of Religion: Mary Donovan Turner, Sharon Thornton, Michael Mendiola, and Karen Lebacqz.

I have been provided teachers at every turn: my students at Marquette University High School and Mercy High School, San Francisco; the clients who brought and then bared their souls in my office throughout my years as a therapist; the clients and staff of both the San Francisco AIDS Foundation and Continuum; my several teachers among the incarcerated men at San Quentin State Penitentiary; and my colleagues and friends at the Morris Stulsaft Foundation, Horizons Foundation, and the Graduate Theological Union. I have been an eager, if at times a recalcitrant, pupil.

I had two readers, with sharpened red pencils, who read the entire manuscript and offered keen critical insight and, on occasion, courageous correctives: Brian Glenn Jr. and Sonny Manuel, SJ. From different eras, disciplines, and perspectives, they were remarkably in sync about what was needed to make this a better book. Brian would often say, "Billy, I think you need to unpack this *whole* sentence." Sonny, was less reverent: "Billy, who talks like this?"

I had several multi-chapter readers whose generosity was of great value: Liza Boyer, Ray Pickett, Bob Hotz, Joyce Glenn, Jenn Grace, Doug Dunlap, Mary Osborne Dunlap, Brian Glenn Sr., Bob Hartnagel, Dominic Longo, John Glenn, and David Kundtz.

A remarkable group of gifted writers read several chapters (several read the whole slog) and offered generous endorsements prior to publication. My gratitude to Brian McNaught, Chris Glazer, Nick Carter, Bob Goss, Robert Hopcke, Mirabai Starr, Jim Bretzke, SJ, Bernie Schlager, Ron Hansen, Bob Thompson, Dominic Longo, Kittridge Cherry, Toby Johnson, Jacques Verduin, and Sonny Manuel, SJ.

For many years, I wrote for the blog "A Voluptuous God," created by my friend Bob Thompson. Annually, I would include a list of "Books and Media, Soulful and Spiritual." Many readers, while encouraging me to write more, asked me to share even more books! Thanks to Judy Haney, Judy Langford, Bert Thelen, Jack Farrell, John Blegen, Kathy Hurley, Jack Price, Jane Nordli, Tim Huerter, Susie Laird, Larry Colton, Mike Gale, Tom Burke, Dick Hafner, Pat Boyer, and Michael Mullen.

And, unequivocally, my gratitude to two gifted therapists: Mario de Paoli and Gordon Murray, and four gifted spiritual directors: Don Driscoll, SJ, Peter Fleming, SJ, Michael Park, and Richard Smith, and my earliest mentor, Tom Shanahan, SJ. You each led me to the entrance of the interior where, upon entering, I discovered the vast, often dark chamber in which the soul resides.

To my extended family, your spacious love has allowed me to flourish, and your often unsolicited observations keep me humble!

To Jimmy, my bookish, worldly Foreign Service Officer brother, a confirmed European, and spouse to Waltrud.

To Diana, my singing, second mother-to-all, caretaker *extraordinaire* sister, and spouse to Richard (deceased).

To Lisa, my fashionista, doting grandmother sister, and spouse to Tom.

To Joyce, my justice-seeking, cookie-baking, friend-to-all sister, and favorite fun aunt to our brood of nieces and nephews.

To Greg, affectionately known as Doc, lifelong Prepster, dedicated teacher, inveterate lover of the Grand Tetons.

To Brian, my family-centric brother, friend to Santa, mirthful but exacting gardener, and spouse to Pennie.

To John, my *bon vivant*, Big Red diehard brother, fundraising genius, and family sustainer, who is spouse to Sonya.

To Liza, my sister-cousin, bright counselor, confidante, friend to Corita, and spouse to Harry.

To Admiral Michael Glenn Mullen, USN (Ret.), my wise, deeply moral, injustice-smashing cousin, spoused to Deborah, and a renowned *Wounded Warrior* advocate.

To the Hafners, welcoming me for the past four decades, whose collective integrity and generosity have been an immense gift.

To Scott's and my thirty-nine nieces and nephews and their spouses and children, who are our utterly unexpected and enduring treasure.

And finally, some persons I came here seeking, and found...

To my lifelong friends, Art and Jo Moore, faithful, with bawdy humor, solace, and our ongoing conversation to solve the world's problems. We just need a little more time.

To my friend Grace Myerjack, a contemplative Maryknoll nun, who has taught me the proper name of the Divine, Love, still showing me what it means to be a human being.

To my friend and nephew, Brian Glenn Jr., intuitive conversation partner, psychic doppelgänger, source of immense joy, for whom no subject is taboo, there are no limits to the search, and there is nothing humor cannot lighten.

To my friends Richard Howard and Robert Hotz, though you have never met, you bookend my life with your fully engaged Ignatian charism, lovely care for me, first in and then out of the Society, my dear *compañeros* of so many decades.

To my friend Mark Cloutier, my California mainstay, model of forgiveness, sharing our mutual love of Jung, sacramentality, strategies for justice, all with ample humor.

To my friend Adele Corvin, on whose family foundation—caring for kids at risk—I sit as a trustee. At ninety-nine, you lead the board with panache, treat all as your equals, the doyenne of the generous Jewish philanthropic community in San Francisco.

To my uncanny friend Dominic Longo, synchronously connected, who came late into my life, but thankfully not too late, in an ongoing, seemingly inexhaustible conversation, an intentional transformer and bold instigator, we hold in soulful mutual regard.

Acknowledgments

And to all my dearly departed, yet alive in me: Larry Tozzeo, Steve Swanson, Michael Foley, Randy Harvey, Steven Baker, Ken Kamman, Philip Justin Smith, Peter Fleming, SJ, Jane Glenn Mullen, Rita Coffee, Sr. Eileen de Long, RGS, Joseph Mary Powers, SJ, David Smith Fox, Michael Kelly, my mother-in-law, Mary Hafner, my mother, Ginger, and my dad, William Fay.

INTRODUCTION

As a child, I felt myself to be alone...because I know
things and must hint at things which others apparently
know nothing of, and for the most part do not want to
know. Loneliness does not come from having no people
about one, but from being unable to communicate
the things that seem important to oneself, or from
holding certain views which others find inadmissible....
It is important to have a secret, a premonition of
things unknown. It fills life with something impersonal,
a *numinosum*. A man who has never experienced that
has missed something important. He must sense that
He lives in a world which...is mysterious....For me,
the world has from the beginning been infinite and
ungraspable.

—Carl Jung, from *Memories, Dreams, Reflections*

The title of this memory book—these notes from the interior, this
accounting of a life—comes from my teacher Thomas Merton, a
mid-twentieth-century Trappist contemplative, man of letters,
interreligious seeker. I regrettably did not meet Thomas Merton,
who died when I was twenty, but I came to know him through his
writings, as I have come to know so many of my great teachers,
often years after their deaths. Several years ago, in a Merton-
centered text, I read, "I came here seeking a person." When I
went to retrieve the citing, it was not to be found! I wrote to the

International Thomas Merton Society, of which I am a member, but it was not in the database. Nonetheless, I persisted in quoting the phrase, knowing I had read it! Perhaps Merton's spirit whispered these words to me, unbeknownst to my conscious self. The sentence sounds so "Mertonesque," although also quite Jungian for it contains its own truth, the simple declaration any of us might well make—*I came here seeking a person*.

A year later, while thumbing through my liner notes in Mary Gordon's *On Thomas Merton*, there it was, quoted from Merton's trenchant *My Argument with the Gestapo*, written before he became a Trappist:

> "Did you not come here only to write?...No, that was never my purpose. I came here looking for a person."

"I" generates a threefold declaration—a triptych—where each panel represents a segment of the declaration. The triptych is an art form used as an altarpiece in the Middle Ages. It usually depicts a sacred event, for example, the Annunciation, which is painted in the larger central panel, with the complementing side panels embellished with characters germane but not central to the action in the main panel. The three panels are intended to be appreciated together. In the case of the Annunciation, angels and *putti* might adorn the side panels.

This quote, "I came here seeking a person," implies a journey—a having come from, a journey embarked on alone, and a journey with a purpose.

On the left panel of the triptych, one might picture the I. Only the I. In the most significant and profound ways, the journey is traversed alone. As Carl Jung's opening quote instructs, being alone is not a depressive condition but rather an existential reality, one concomitant with and necessary to the spiritual journey. Earlier in my life, of course, my response had been *Yes* to almost everything. But then, somehow, I heard, off with you. Go off, alone, all the while sensing I am never truly alone.

Our interior journeys, not unlike Merton's, have no road map, no regularly updated internal GPS. There are few rest stops.

And while it seems that we are not exactly driving the vehicle, neither are we on autopilot.

On the right-side panel of the triptych, one might imagine a specific here: this place—this psychological, emotional, spiritual as well as physical place, the economic and social location in which one finds oneself, one's historical landings, one's here and now—this moment, this now. For Merton, his arrival at the Abbey of Gethsemane outside Louisville, Kentucky, a serene wooded and meadowed expanse—where he remained for nearly thirty years—became his psychological, emotional, spiritual, physical, and social *here*. His here might include the Abbey, his cell, the hermitage he built, his stall in the choir, his typewriter, and his complex internal makeup.

The center panel—perhaps twice the width of the two sides, as the medieval triptychs were—is the most intriguing, for it depicts a person. Who might this person be, and to whom am I addressing my declaration? As I have discovered, there appears to be a triptych within the triptych: three distinct persons represented within the center panel.

I would surmise for Merton, after his arrival at Gethsemane, that he sought a similar encounter as I have on my journey, and as you might as well. An encounter with his self and then with the others with whom he filled his life, for he was truly no hermit. Centrally though, and finally, I feel sure he sought the One, the person whose proper name is ever unknown: Jung's *numinosum*; Meister Eckhart's *compassion*; and Martin Buber's *Thou*.

For Merton, for me, and perhaps for you, I came here seeking a person.

The *I* is both problematic and solutional for me. I was admonished at the family dinner table to cease using the "perpendicular" pronoun, as my dad would often say, with a further quip about my ever-present ego. But that was not to be the whole nor final story. My own journey, my own *here*, has seen so many departures and so many arrivals: Omaha, Los Angeles, the Twin Cities, Pine Ridge Lakota Sioux Reservation in South Dakota, St. Louis, Milwaukee, Berkeley, San Francisco, San Quentin, Sonoma County, with many diversions across this nurturing, magnificent planet. The *I came here* also suggests many homes and other residences where I have done my seeking.

For Merton, correspondingly: Prades in France, Long Island, New York, Oakham and Cambridge in England, Columbia University and Greenwich Village in New York City, St. Bonaventure College in Upstate New York, Gethsemane Abbey in Kentucky, beloved Whithorn, California, and finally, Bangkok, Thailand.

You have your own journey, too, but for me—and I suspect for you—I have been seeking a person.

The immediate person is this I, this self, this inhabitant of the body whose fingers are typing these words. From unknowing into innocence through masquerade and *persona* to some partial stripping away to disclose some chip of the mosaic at the still center, this journey continues. Parents, siblings, friends, companions, soulmates, the Beloved: I have been seeking you since I first traipsed home from first grade with my new friend, Michael; and ever since, I have been seeking *you*. My favorite Jesuit word is *compañeros*...companions, for it captures what I have been seeking. And, blessedly, I have so often found *you*, my companions.

Being a monk with the vow of silence, Merton had scores of friends, who often came and visited him, and hundreds of correspondents, including many of the luminaries of his age: religious, political, literary.

My journey, now in its eighth decade and with the horizon brighter and more compelling each day, has been a long, complicated, blessed, and most human journey. It has been marked by patterns and threads, and genetic, familial, and cultural traits so deeply ingrained that only great investigation has exposed their many animating sources. My life journey has been one long seeking. I have been seeking a person, yes; and yet, I have been seeking this person, this self, or, as Carl Jung dignified with a capital *S*, this *Self*, denoting the inner presence of the divine.

I have come seeking the Divine, earlier from without, and of late, within. I am still seeking You, the absolutely personal and utterly cosmos inhabiting, Divine You. I no longer know your name, though I am drawn to Doris Grumbach, the literary critic, who calls you *The One Whose I Am*. That seems correct, apt, and sufficient. I am yet seeking this sacred Self: unfathomable resident of the soul, the divine within, the vivid center of my interior life, the creative force that animates all the life of the cosmos— the One, the Thou, the You Whose I Am.

So, like Merton, I come seeking a person, a triptych of persons: my Self, you, and You.

When I was a boy and so early on in my journey, I took one passage from the Gospel of Matthew as my personal obligation: "Be perfect, therefore, as your heavenly Father is perfect" (Matt 5:48). That passage was to be a prime motivator for the first three decades of my life. And scratches of it remain, of course, so deeply did it get etched. That instruction is oxymoronic, for perfection for us mortals is impossible. It also creates a perfect double bind, by description, a situation in which a person is confronted by two irreconcilable demands, out of which a decision is purportedly to be made. The dilemma is horrific. Yet the dictate to be perfect seemed so clear and necessary. For me, a double bind to be conquered! Or so I thought and tried to will.

My plan for perfection had many files: spiritual, behavioral, sexual, familial, and as a man in the world. Basically, in my thoughts, words, and deeds. Yikes! This goal demanded a thorough mortal inventory with almost every breath. It became the heart of my early spiritual journey. It required a scrupulous posture, yet one so revered and rewarded by the law and culture. For me, its use-by date came and went.

What softened my perfectionism over time, and allowed my journey to commence, thankfully, along with so much else, was what I was learning from manifold sources:

from intuition, epiphany, synchronicity
from revelation, grace, and inner knowing
from presence, seeing, and sacrament

via annunciation, and contemplation and healing
via counterculture, ritual, shamanic wisdom, and
    meditation
via connection, curiosity, insight, and silence

from the prophets, the mystics, the Psalter
listening to the wild: mountains, trees, desert
the Pacific, fauna, the garden, and the night sky

in dance, running, and massage
via the Enneagram (a One), Myers-Briggs (INFJ),
    Celtic spiritualty
all within the immensity of the cosmos

That's a partial list, for there are influences that cannot be fully discerned nor named. But much of the above has worked—together—to free me from my perfectionism, my need for dogma, my attention to the rules, my hidden anger, my sophisticated defense system, and the masquerades I have—and still—employ. From *the all of it.*

Teachers often counsel budding authors to "write what you know." The memoirist Anne Lamott says, rather, "Write what you have always wanted to read." I have taken to heart Lamott's advice. I have written what I have wanted to read—and what I want to share with you; perhaps your journey shares similarities to mine.

I have been writing this book for forty years. I took a course as a young Jesuit—in 1977—titled *Spiritual Autobiography.* I got my first introduction to Carl Jung, Nikos Kazantzakis, and Fyodor Dostoyevsky, among several others. The professor, my dear friend Joseph Powers, SJ, assigned us the task of writing our own spiritual autobiographies. My response:

This writing I have begun a multitude of times in my mind, at night when I have tossed to and fro the third time and I want to tell everyone who I am so I can sleep in peace. I have tried a thousand tacks, always falling off when I realized it would not be pure and that I and it would fall short of definitive, would not be the release of the forbidden knowledge that separates man, this man, from freedom and life to its fullness. I too have thought it quite presumptuous to write MY autobiography...with a real note of pride and almost arrogance. When faced with beginning the narrative, the arrogance departs. And the gnawing inside, the seeking permission—but from whom?—returns. I am twenty-nine years old, not even middle aged, let alone wise or ripe of having attained the charm which seems to come with forty, if one is not too afraid. I have been afraid. I think most others are, too, and I think they want to stay that way, and I say I don't, so my arrogance returns. I want to write this damn thing, because I have an audience within that pant after my heart.

That spiritual biography did not get written.

I have looked for the book Lamott suggests I write, the one I have wanted to read. I could not find this book at any bookstores. I could not find this book because it had not yet been written, for I felt too self-constrained to write it.

And yet, here we are, me writing this sentence and you with this book in hand. Miraculous! And who are you, dear reader? Perhaps you are the other person I have written this book for, maybe even the only other one. That's how Jung has shaped me to think. But the truest answer would be in the final sentence of my twenty-nine-year-old's awareness: I have an audience within, one that is panting after my heart.

I write this book for you who have intuitions you have been told to ignore. For you, who harbor a flame of the holy inside but have no one with whom to share it. For you, who feel lonely and have not yet found your others.

I write this book for you who have been told to accept the division society offers you—your integrity or mere belonging. For you, who know things but have been told you don't. For you, who have had epiphanies that changed your life but that you nonetheless have been told to doubt their veracity.

I write this book for you if you have been traumatized and keep getting triggered, long after you were told to get over it; if you were told you were an intrinsically disordered person, but you've come to know that as an insidious lie told for the benefit of the teller. For you, if you have had double binds placed on you that entwine your heart with barbed wire.

I write this book for you if you feel like a fraudster. Or feel unworthy. Or have been asked, *Who do you think you are?*

And finally, I write this book for me. To share with you that which I have come to know, that which I have had the grace to witness and perceive in the chance that it might have value for you on your sacred journey.

I started to have a certain awareness as a child. In bed, at the age of six or seven, reading a book on the saints, reading about Little Nell of Holy God, whom I somehow knew, I was aware of a presence (though I had not that word). I knew things the way a child does, and I knew that I could not tell anyone—anyone being my parents—knowing they would not understand. And the next morning, I was again just a kid in this large family. But the awareness persisted.

My life has been shaped by many people, by forces and ideas and ideals, by movements, and by the phenomena of what it means to be a man in a body with the exact dollop of DNA I inherited.

I have been shaped by the Glenns, now numbering some three dozen, including my siblings, their children, and now their grandchildren, an array of greats tagging behind, along with my very present deceased parents.

I have been profoundly shaped by Scott Hafner, my husband. The inextricable intertwining with him over forty years cannot be fully comprehended, only marveled at, to feel gratitude and humility.

Being a male and the great-grandson of Irish and Danish immigrant farmers who met well-established English landowners, intermarrying with them over three generations, shows up on my Ancestory.com print out. Catholicism, primarily, with blushes of Celtic paganism and queer intuitions, brew to form a pot of spiritual complexity. As do my gender and ethnicity, which have given me economic, cultural, and educational privilege.

I am a product of an intellectual and spiritual tradition embodied first, and variously, by stellar men—Merton, Teilhard de Chardin, Jung—men who stood tall in the Western world prior to women having the necessary access to share their wisdom in the worlds of spirituality, cosmology, politics, and psychology. Of course, there were notable exceptions, but they were exceptions to an ironclad rule.

My life, from the age of thirteen, when I entered the polished terrazzo halls of Creighton Preparatory School, until this moment fifty-eight years later, has been profoundly impacted by the Society of Jesus, the Jesuits.

These privileged, often wise, forceful, erudite, generous, sometimes arrogant, occasionally scurrilous, and now and then highly manipulative, but humanly holy men educated, formed, shaped, and often nurtured me, and sometimes not, but deeply marked me for life with their terms:

> man for others, preferential option for the poor
> the *magis* (the greater good), the discernment of
>   spirits
> *memento mori* (remember your death), *compañeros*,
>   contemplatives in action, inculturation, and *cura*
>   *personalis* (care of the whole person)

The Jesuits have formed me into a man, one fully engaged by and in the contemporary world. Their influence will be seen throughout this text.

The other great collective that has shaped me are all who have been embraced by the many ways a person can be queer. My life was changed in a single stroke by words uttered by the late Harvey Milk, whose mantra was simply "Come out." My coming into this great gay collective at twenty-nine resulted in me being recognized, welcomed, embraced, enjoined, tutored, witnessed, wounded, acclaimed, invited to serve, and immensely blessed. These queer ways have formed me as a conscious and conscientious man in the contemporary world. These queer ways have intimately braided with and have often become indistinguishable from the spiritual and psychological influences that have shaped me. As more gay men—and of course women and trans folx, too—have come out of closets, these dynamics are slowly being understood as gifts to the larger culture. They include:

an insightful wit and bawdy humor—a celebration of
     the body
a piercing of the false fronts of culture—a radical
     acceptance
a recalibrating of the masculine—a free expression of
     the anima

an awareness of the soulful heart of pleasure—a
     challenging of the patriarchy
an aesthetic marveling—a mastership of feng shui
an occasional acidity of the tongue—camp and drag

an irreverence, solidarity, and political
     consciousness—a deep knowing
a justice-seeking anger, and profound suffering and
     joy

Happily, these dynamics are available to all persons who make their interior journey. The influence of the universal gay culture and its progenitor, the "queer" culture, will be evident throughout the book.

I have been shaped by the men and women of every imaginable way of being in the world who came into my psychotherapy office and sat opposite me in the leather chair, or into the Quonset hut on the windswept campus of San Quentin State Penitentiary, or the outpatient chemical dependency program at Summit Hospital in Oakland, and allowed themselves to be the most human of beings in my presence. They allowed me the grace of sitting with them, sharing silence, words, and a courageous exposure of vulnerabilities and woundings, and of course dark humor, tears, sometimes anger, and the hope that comes when humans are genuine in each other's presence. To honor their anonymity, I will speak little of these immensely potent years.

In these pages are shared peak moments from my life, turning points, epiphanies, and intuitions. I have recounted the presence of an inner voice. Our lives are filled with these. I have had moments of bright light, infused with sufficient shadow to create a whole.

This is not a diary or a journal, no full accounting. It is a collection of major moments and significant encounters with the *yous* who have shaped me. It is a book accentuating patterns and rhythms. My hope is that you become cognizant of similar patterns in your own life, patterns particular to you and your way of being in the world, patterns with underpinnings lodged in your soul, sometimes even irrefutable truths that guide you, if almost imperceptibly trustworthy, reliable, but often challenging to uncover and receive.

I write as one man, not as any who have influenced me. I write for no other Glenn, no other Jesuit or ex-, no other psychotherapist, no other married person, no other gay man. While our experiences are utterly unique, they may contain masterly collective patterns. No one is accountable for what I have done with the love or wisdom they shared with me. My defects of personality are primarily of my own making, to tame and, when possible, convert into loving energy. I am yet an incomplete work in progress.

I have come to know we are not alone, even when companionless in the desert. And, we can be alone, even amid those we love. This mystery, this paradox, and our responses to it surely accompany our journey.

I came here seeking a person, and I still do. I, now and in part, seek this person with you as my unknown *compañero*.

1

POLIOMYELITIS

The question is not how to get cured, but how to live.

—Joseph Conrad

ON OCTOBER 20, 1952, we boarded the flight—a prop plane bound for Los Angeles—at the small Omaha Municipal Airport in the company of a woman, Marie, whom we had only met the previous day. My father referred to her as my aunt—a word that had no meaning to me—and I could see that she and my father had strong affection for each other. I sensed that she was a safe person to be with, albeit a stranger. My sister, Diana, who was five and a half years old, and I, having just turned four, were being sent away from home—although the full import of that could not yet be realized—with this strange woman to somewhere other than the only place we knew, our house on North 61st Street.

Several days earlier, my younger sister, Lisa, who was two and a half, had also been sent away, very sick. A few days later, my mother also went away—also very sick, though how sick I did not know. Lisa had been misdiagnosed with pneumonia, and the hospitals were filled with children suffering from poliomyelitis, the contagious virus that had already hospitalized many in Omaha. In 1952, polio was in its last epidemic surge, infecting Americans without favor. Dr. Jonas Salk's salvific intervention was yet two years away. Lisa, having just pneumonia, was sent home. But she was soon rediagnosed as having contracted polio, as had several neighbors on our street, and was sent to the local Children's Hospital as her legs deformed under the aegis of this paralysis.

At the time, my mother, who was only thirty years old, had five children—four were five years or younger, another one seven months in the belly—and a few days later, she also developed severe symptoms. She was rushed to St. Joseph's, the local Catholic hospital, where she, with her not-yet-born baby, was immediately placed in an iron lung, a contraption of Rube Goldberg-proportions that breathed for its inhabitant. Hermetically sealed save an opening for her head, which lay still on a short, pillowed palette of a head rest, she looked at her world through a diagonal mirror placed a few inches above her eyes.

Lisa and Mother were now both hospitalized, Mother in danger of losing her life, not to mention the life of her unborn baby, and Lisa alone in a ward with scores of other children, with a two-year-old's total lack of comprehension, but not instinct. With my dad at home were my older brother, Jimmy, who was bright, self-contained, and slow to express any needs, and an aptly named younger sister, Joyce, who was not yet two, and almost never cranky then and still now a source of joy for the family. My maternal grandmother, just fifty-eight, residing nearby and in perfect health, thought she just might be able to manage the toddler during the days while my father worked and spent the evenings going from St. Joe's to the Children's Hospital several miles away, visiting his now likely dying wife and ever so slowly improving baby daughter.

On October 16, with a crew of firemen standing by (for reasons that now nearly seventy years later seem a mystery), her ob-gyn opened the iron lung just long enough to take the seven-month-old baby—by Caesarean section—a boy to be named Gregory John (the John named for that beloved doctor, John Grier) from her womb to a waiting incubator where he would live for the first two months of his life. They then closed the iron lung, and my mother's caretakers resumed their vigil, pinning saints' relics to the iron house in the hopes a miracle might save her life. The Madames of the Sacred Heart and the

Sisters of Mercy were in her camp, and faith was the coin of the realm for this family.

Two weeks into this impossible regimen, my father, William Fay Glenn, was diagnosed with cancer of the inner ear. His Omaha doctors recommended going to the celebrated Barnes Hospital at Washington University in St. Louis to have it surgically treated, so he dutifully travelled southeast, now splintering our once intact family into five places.

Gregory, in a nurse's arms, and my mother, Virginia Anne Mary Westergard Hogan Glenn, looking up at him from her supine position, were snapped by a photojournalist for a newsworthy story on the poliomyelitis epidemic that appeared above the fold on the front page several days later in the Omaha daily newspaper, *The World Herald.*

With Dad in St. Louis and Mother in the iron lung, it was decided that Diana and I would go and live in California with two of my dad's sisters and their families, and his mother, Bessie, my other grandmother, in residence with one of her daughters. Diana and I carried copies of that *World Herald* with us to California on the plane to show the relatives what was happening back in Omaha.

We spent the fall, winter, and early spring in California. At first, we were situated with my Aunt Jane, Uncle Jack, and their three sons on Kraft Avenue in Studio City, out in the then sparsely populated San Fernando Valley. Diana was enrolled in kindergarten at the local parish school, and I, too young, floundered in a strange house with three roughhousing boys claiming some of what had been their territory.

Staying with my boy cousins proved impossible. I had a doll, perhaps a gift upon departure from Omaha, a little boy doll, whose visage I remember yet. One day these cousins, two of whom were older than me and perhaps confused by seeing a boy whom they did not know having a *boy* doll of unknown provenance, substituted the said doll for a football in a game of indoor tackle; the doll's head flew off. I was distraught, and my aunts quickly moved me from one safe house to another.

I landed with my Aunt Marie, a single mother with two children. She also provided a home for her mother, Bessie, in her small frame house in North Hollywood. My faint memory of my grandmother is that of a distant woman who alternated saying the Rosary with watching her favorite soap operas, a pattern that would last the rest of her life. Since Grandmother, at sixty-two, was unwilling or unable to help maintain the household, Marie had a housekeeper and cook called Coco, with whom I bonded. One of my clearest memories of my six-month life on Bosworth Street was Friday breakfast. Coco brought fresh doughnuts at the end of every work week, sugared and glazed, and chocolate milk, something that was rarely experienced in Omaha. For me, these constituted a feast, and, having no real competition for them when Coco put them out, I had my fill.

Those months seemed like forever, though from the perspective of adulthood, they mostly remain a blur of images in an internal landscape devoid of vitality. I can recall a Christmas tree, and the night my aunt's ex-husband dropped by (when I refused to look at him and instead drew my pajama top over my head to shield my eyes!), sleeping in a twin bed with my cousin Stephen, and vague memories of Sunday Mass at St. Jane Frances de Chantel Church in North Hollywood.

By mid-spring, my mother had recovered to the extent that she could leave the iron lung. The damage to her lungs and upper musculature was severe and permanent. She would eventually receive years of physical therapy and recover the use of her legs, but would spend the rest of her long life compromised in her breathing and in the use of the necessary muscles for full movement of her upper body. Lisa, too, survived, and while hobbled to some degree by the effect of the virus on her legs, would ultimately have surgeries to restore them to nearly normal use.

Greg, in so many ways the miracle baby, survived and soon thrived.

Diana and I returned to Omaha in the company of a stranger, who had been solicited to accompany us on our return flight, perhaps in late March or early April. I remember my dad picking us up at the airport and observing the remnant snow along the roads back to our home on 61st Street. In that brick and clapboard house, a reunion was waiting for us. We were the last to return home. Lisa made it out of the hospital first, and then several months later, miracles apparently intact, my mother and Gregory got home. Mother had lived through this ordeal. The iron lung had done its work. The medals and relics, not for us to know. Now in a wheelchair, her very life was a source of immense joy and gratitude. Gregory was undoubtedly fed formula at whatever clip he could take it in. Dad had beat the cancer, which remained in full remission for the rest of his natural life.

The family, to which I had returned, now included Elizabeth, an elderly Black woman (my youngish grandmother had apparently found it all too much to deal with two children at home) who would provide additional care for us as my mother convalesced. I recall feeling overwhelmed as we entered the front door, seeing my mother in that metallic chair, frail and looking nothing like the woman who I had remembered leaving the previous October. Though I recognized others, I ran straight to Elizabeth, who wrapped me in her thin body and held my small hands in her long, elegant fingers. We were home.

I have been a therapist now for a long time, working with women and men and girls and boys to decipher the encoded mysteries of their childhoods to grasp more sufficiently their current lives. The work, as we call it, is both for them to make of their childhoods what they will but also to make of them the foundation for a more secure life—a less scary, more meaningful, more their own life. Our lives are comprised of memories and experiences, many embedded in the active unconscious, and for me, far beyond those of the winter of 1952 to 1953. Although my own therapeutic work as a client has given me insight and creative ways to manage and live my life, the full meaning of those long-ago events from that dark winter has in many ways eluded me. I have wanted to know what that little boy experienced, what he felt, what got encoded, what he thought was happening, how he interpreted the trauma of those fast and furious episodes that split our family into so many parts in a matter of days that took him—me—from a secure family of seven to a foreign land with strangers masquerading as family, affectionate though they may have been, and finally, to return again, to family that somehow also resembled strangers masquerading as family. The developmental psychologist in me knows that this experience for me and for all my family was profound, and some parts of its effects I have come to speculatively appreciate. That it dovetails with my subsequent life is perhaps no accident. The search for the elusive parent, for the reconstituted family, for a place for my young, and no longer young-at-all, self. Those concepts—stranger, family, masquerade, home—would mark my journey for the rest of my life. They also are threaded through the journey about which I write in these pages.

2

ON BEING A GLENN

It never takes longer than a few minutes, when they get together, for everyone to revert to the state of nature, like a party marooned by a shipwreck. That's what a family is. Also, the storm at sea, the ship, the unknown shore...and the fire you light to keep away the beasts.

—Michael Chabon, *The Yiddish Policeman's Union*

MICHAEL CHABON DESCRIBES the Yiddish version of the Irish as "the all of it," a phrase that captures a reality—family—difficult to separate into its several parts, and confirmation that the whole is greater than the sum of its parts. It's a particular skill to see each part, each one, each person discreetly, and to tease out oneself from the whole. That has been my task since I first emerged from the mass of Glenn. When did this all begin? Long ago, within my family, in a different time and place.

Listening as a therapist for more than thirty years as a confidant and sometimes confessor, and as a member of three families, I have come to understand family as a system of great complexity. There are family units into which we are born and that we then most often re-create, spend considerable energy trying to understand, feel closer to, and extricate ourselves from—all at once. We idealize family, then necessarily tear down those idealizations. We love our families, and as often, loathe them, if unconsciously, both in the aggregate and in the particulars of our unique family. We acquire an immense load of traits, habits, biases, prejudices, likes and dislikes, even dreams from our families. We enact the various necessary stages of human development on the platform that was offered at birth, one from which we cannot escape for some other, better venue. We are loved by a particular human family, in all or in part, or sometimes not; we are recognized by them or ignored; we are praised or damned, even if faintly; we are projected upon, and we project; for some, we are asked to carry unconscious family material and tropes into the world—the archetypical hero—or we are assigned an archetype to play out our existence on both the family stage and the world's. Shakespeare, so insightful, enacted his perennially wise and startlingly true family dramas and tragedies of archetypal characters—Lear, the Macbeths, or Hamlet, Cordelia, and her darker sisters, Regan and Goneril—on the stage at the Globe! No accident.

Like you, I come from a family. For years I have described it as a large, mid-twentieth-century, midwestern, Irish Catholic family. Somewhat accurate. With our parents, ten of us at the dinner table in that large English Tudor house on 57th Avenue in Omaha, Nebraska, where we had moved as a sense of triumph, I suspect, after defeating polio. We were only there altogether, at the table, for a few years, from John's birth in 1960 to Jimmy's departure for graduate school in the late '60s. My mother had children over a seventeen-year period, so there were comings and goings from 1943 until 1982. Seven years later, in 1989, my father died, followed seven years later by my mother.

Omaha is not really in the Midwest, as often characterized; rather, it is on the Great Plains, a land topographically, agriculturally, and politically different from Illinois and Wisconsin, the true Midwest. Omaha is the westernmost industrial city of the United States, back in the day having plants in large numbers, slaughterhouses, meat packing plants, and breweries, plus insurance, higher education, and medicine, which all employed large segments of the population. Two hours west, in that very wide state, the real prairie begins, and it is a most beautiful sight, though coastal eyes have a difficult time focusing on its inherent majesty. The Sand Hills form its heart, so big that Massachusetts, Rhode Island, Connecticut, and Delaware could all fit within its borders. Omaha, the city in which I was raised until I graduated from Creighton, the Jesuit university, is a hilly city with a lush canopy of trees over its many neighborhoods. I moved away fifty years ago, but in so many ways, paradoxically with Thomas Wolfe's axiom in mind—that we cannot go home again—I do, and often, though we have a five-day rule when visiting.

To say we are Irish is only half correct. In our house, with my father's second generation Irish dominant personality, you would have thought my mother's English and Danish DNA had been obliterated during conception so that we came out all-Irish. We knew our father's extended family in eastern Iowa, Connecticut, and Los Angeles, but had only brief encounters with my mother's extended family, though the Berrys in Kansas City were not so far away. Her ancestor Charles Carroll had signed the Declaration of Independence, with the flourish of Carrollton; that his brother, John Carroll, a former Jesuit, had been the first Roman Catholic archbishop in the United States, and after whom my brother, John Carroll, is named, mattered, even as we have come to know these illustrious forebearers held slaves. But being Irish was seismic in our family story; the Danish, not at all. Years later, as adults, my mother purchased little strings of the Danish national flag, red with white dissecting lines forming a cross, to adorn our Christmas trees, to remind us that we were also Danish and that it was the Danish King Christian who had worn a yellow Star of David when the Nazis invaded in 1940, as did his countrymen, so that the Jews of Denmark could not be distinguished by that shaming symbol, and thereby most all saved from the Shoah. I took special pride in that knowledge, and those tiny flags still grace our tree each December.

We were Catholic, if not catholic. My mother had converted—from what is not quite clear—while a student at Duchesne College of the Sacred Heart, where her agnostic father had enrolled her to keep her from a certain forest ranger in southern Illinois, whose acquaintance she had enjoyed.

We were educated by the Sisters of Mercy at St. Margaret Mary's School and attended Mass at the serenely beautiful stone parish church. After grade school, we were separated: the boys went to Creighton Preparatory School; the girls to Duchesne Academy or Marian High School. For college, more of the same: the boys were educated by the Jesuits and the girls by the Madames of the Sacred Heart, though my youngest brothers, Brian and John, each attended one the University of Nebraska's then two campuses, formerly regarded by the local church as occasions of sin.

My mother's first husband, another Irishman, Jim Hogan, was a navigator in the Army Air Corps (the precursor of the Air Force) whose plane was shot down in the South Pacific in 1944. My mother, a widow at age twenty-three, lost her great love. My eldest brother, Jimmy, age one, lost his dad, who, from all accounts, was one swell and loving man. When my parents met soon after the war, they married not long afterward and became a family of three. But that would quickly change: Diana was born in 1947; I followed in 1948; Lisa in 1950; Joyce in 1951; and Greg, known affectionately as Doc (nicknamed for a nursery rhyme character) in 1952. Five kids in six years. Six kids in nine years. Eight kids in all. Brian and John were born in 1957 and 1960, respectively.

My father, typical of many husbands during these years, was the breadwinner and did not engage much in the tasks of childrearing. My mother, who had been raised by very disengaged parents with only one brother as a sibling, somehow figured it all out. Lisa and Joyce are Irish twins, so called for they were born within the same twelve-month period, in their case not quite eleven months apart.

Beginning in 1952, polio became the defining trope of our lives. Like many who are compromised by polio, my mother accommodated her disablement, compensating by using her glutes and thighs and quads and calves in a complicated set of maneuvers to accomplish her tasks at home—and, in a quite remarkable fashion—move on with her life, and ours. We children accommodated polio and its many complications, too. My sister Diana, an extremely able and gifted girl, took on the large task per the archetype of the eldest daughter, and helped raise this family, particularly the three, in succession, younger boys. My mother never fully regained use of her body. Her musculature was deeply compromised, she could not easily lift her babies, nor effectively navigate her environs. Her lungs were depleted. She had a very large heart from which emanated love, intuition, and faith, offering up wisdom steadily acquired from her compromised condition.

We all learned to cook, clean (to my mother's exacting specs), iron, do the wash, take care of younger children, make our own enjoyments, fight, whine, tattle, make up. We ate as a family nightly, except Saturdays, when my dad would grill steaks in the aptly named log cabin room's stone fireplace in the basement. He and my mother would have what were not yet called date nights while the kids ate hot dogs in the breakfast room above.

We lived out the liturgical year, as did so many Catholic families of that time. I was deeply drawn to it, particularly the rich sacramental expressions of the divine-human connection. I found praying—of course, these were the prayers of a child—consoling. My mother would lead evening prayers—her prayer list was seemingly endless, including the recently deceased, especially if they were clergy, who would then be petitioned for specific graces. The list of saints to whom we prayed was equally long. Mother loved St. Anne (her middle name), and Blessed Rose Philippine Duchesne was the jewel in the center of her prayer diadem.

The religious pattern was intricate: daily Mass in grade school, weekly Saturday afternoon confession, grace before meals, the Rosary, holy candles (to light during Nebraska's tornado season), holy water fonts in each bedroom for making the Sign of the Cross upon entering, devotions of those particular saints and their feast days (St. Jude, patron of hopeless cases and my eventual confirmation name, was my one true). Contemporary Orthodox Jews and observant Muslims are no more extreme than we were in the way faith and life were indistinct. The habit-wearing Catholic nuns and contemporarily draped Muslim women might be indistinguishable. In essence, we lived in a Catholic world.

Through early adolescence, my faith answered my questions. With the onset of puberty, that assurance—simple and given—began to change. I would eventually find teachers who spoke to me with a different authority, ones that would be distinct from my parents and the church, our formidable foundations.

Mother was no slave to dogma and its many enforcers. Her life had taught her too much. She could spot a phony as he crossed under the lintel of her front door, or as they preached at the pulpit of the parish church. A particularly unctuous priest would come around to enjoy an after-dinner drink with my parents—uninvited—and, seeing him pull his car into the driveway, my mother, feigning exhaustion, hightailed it to her bedroom. She did not suffer fools. And she fostered individuality in each of her children. As I entered a Jesuit high school, these many forms on which I had staked my life imperceptibly began falling away. Crushed by their own weight. Some readers, no doubt, may have similar stories.

As I would later learn in graduate school, and while engaged in my own therapy, and even later experienced daily as I sat in the clinician's chair, siblings can have seemingly diametrically opposed memories, and views, of the same family events or of the same parent. Family dynamics are such that one child can completely miss what another child is experiencing, and another can ardently defend the offending parent as being incapable of what the other bears in her psyche and body. We can deny the favoritism shown a sibling in a household with no favorites! We are taught—all of us and very early—to figure how to get our needs met, and to obviate whatever might occlude fulfilling those needs.

A significant marker for me from an early age, and yet present at this late age, and the most baffling, powerful, and complex aspect of my life, is that I, for reasons beyond my ken, have the capacity to see into others deeply. This is no accomplishment. It is, in truth, a complication. I perceive, the more apt word, people I am close to, and people I am not. Intimates, and sometimes, awkwardly, strangers. Folx who want to be seen, and those who don't. The perceiving's source, I understand, is an aspect of my strong sense of intuition. Bill Ball, the wunderkind artistic director of the American Conservatory Theatre in San Francisco, was quoted one day in Herb Caen's column in the *San Francisco Chronicle* as saying, "I trust my intuition at all times, in every situation, with all people." His words struck me as revelation, so much did they correspond to my own sense of intuition and its presence. I had never had such external confirmation. As I look back at that little boy's seeing, I observe how it unfolded and affected the whole of my life. I have known I did not merit this ability, nor did I ask for it. It has remained a significant marker in my life, and while it has been a gift, it has also been a burden.

From early on, I sensed masquerades. Masquerades we all have, some of us several, each fitting the occasion. I saw with acuity my father's masquerade. Back then, I knew little about his woundedness, an awareness that came more gradually. I did not have adequate language to express what I had come to know. But the very act of seeing that which, of course, I did not realize was not what everyone else was seeing, drew a sharp rebuke from him. I have come to understand, as the result of my own inner work, that he *saw* me seeing him. He was aware, perhaps unconsciously, that I saw him with some depth, and what I saw discomforted him greatly.

As I came to learn much later, the one *seen*, if made uncomfortable, must inflict the same or a greater level of discomfort on the *seer* as he felt in being seen. The one seen uses this defense to allay the pain of being seen, and to forestall any such future engagement. This dynamic, understood by contemporary psychology as *the scapegoat complex*, was brilliantly chronicled by Sylvia Brinton Perera, a Jungian analyst, in her eponymous book. When I first encountered her book thirty years ago, I felt that she was writing to me, about me, to assist me in coming to understand the dynamic that had remained confusing to me since that early age. Once a child is scapegoated, others within a family system understand this, if unconsciously, and some, to gain the approval of the goater, pile it on. Mostly, my sibs seemed oblivious to this dynamic, initially played out behind the closed pocket doors of our library, and subsequently, in my psyche.

As a result of this early dynamic, my father became a complicated and dark presence in my life. Even when young, we would have confrontations, usually during my parents' cocktail time in the late afternoon. On myriad occasions, my mother would report to my dad on the children and, if there had been trouble, I was usually identified as the cause, most often with my sisters, who surrounded me in the family constellation. In these moments, I would hold eye contact with him, regarded—I sensed—as a brazen act. No defense I might offer was tolerated. I came to be known as the troublemaker, the back talker (though one sister could give me a run for my money on that score). I was remembered as the one who almost threw the big glass ashtray from the marble table at Dad, something that would have killed him! That these early encounters with my dad occurred during the two-hour cocktail time, in which children were banished from our parents' *lounge* is no accident. My parents drank every night, for years, pitchers of martinis, later, ice-filled tumblers of Scotch and Bourbon.

Over time, the offenses incorporated into me, so that I became the embodiment of the offense, the onerous disharmony in a complex household of both necessary rules and rituals that ultimately served my dad's comfort and were vital to his self-image. I, unwittingly, and later, more consciously, did not support this regime. And I would do the forbidden: I would defend myself and let my dad know that it was ultimately not about me. That would set him off, for there was no contradicting him. Regardless, his masquerade—*persona* in contemporary psychology—remained relatively intact. And, as I came to know well, alcohol helped keep his shadow material at bay.

This dynamic with my father was by no means my full reality while growing up in my family. With ten of us, there were stories and laughter and games and celebrations. But as I was to later learn, intermittent punishment is the most effective form of controlling behavior, and my memory retains these encounters as the most significant markers of my childhood. Of course, there were countless others, but these stand out, and it is around these that the work of my life—personally, professionally, spiritually—has evolved.

By high school, as I developed my own mind and began to discipline my will, as puberty took hold of my body and eros began its complex and complicated journey through my psyche, I began to disengage emotionally from the family. I withdrew, increasingly, from potent family dynamics and found larger places to inhabit. In retrospect, I came to realize that the effects of these powerful childhood dynamics, for good or ill, are permanently ingrained on a child's malleable psyche. To defend myself from *the all of it*, I put on weight, acquired several neurological symptoms and patterns and dysfunctional behaviors to manage the shame and extremely low opinion of myself that gradually emerged.

I was drawn to books at an early age and read mostly by the light of a flashlight back in the little boys' room where I was consigned with two younger brothers until I began high school. We were not a Hardy Boys or Nancy Drew kind of family, but we had plenty of Lives of the Saints and other Catholic subculture offerings. My outside reading, as I entered adolescence, involved a search. Salinger's *The Catcher in the Rye* was a perfect fit, right down to Holden's pimples. The first book on interiority to entice me was Dag Hammarskjöld's subtle and spare *Markings*, published after his tragic death. The beloved Pope John XXIII's sweet and pious diary, *The Journal of a Soul*, inspired me. Then, gratefully, Thomas Merton entered my life with the autobiographical *The Seven Story Mountain*. Erich Fromm's *The Art of Loving* helped me connect my nascent inner self with the outer world, where I sought some key to the burgeoning love I felt inside for other boys. Alas. James Baldwin, however, who would become a constant companion over the course of my life, led me back inside, and with *Giovanni's Room*—how I ever found this book still totally amazes me—to the hidden boy I was, and in some ways, still am. I also developed a clear aesthetic. I loved drawing, art, and design. My mother observed that most boys don't iron their polo shirts—no?—but I—of course—did. And the most vital pattern that exists to this day emerged early, regardless of how rumpled another's polo shirt might be: having friends.

The pain-filled relationship with my father—on hiatus during my years as a Jesuit seminarian; so proud was he of having a son in the Society of Jesus—never quite left but only went underground. I cannot know how much of my motive for entering the Society was to gain my father's approval; if unconsciously, it certainly played a part. As pleased as he was when I entered, he was equally chagrined when I left after nearly ten years. Our previously strained dynamic returned, though altered by our ages. I no longer talked back, no longer defended myself, and was no longer able to be sent to that mythical mailbox. Now, I knew I saw what I saw, and came to trust what I knew. I offered that *seeing* on those occasions when others intuited this part in me and would ask me to share what I had seen in them, with them. But from my dad, who I knew wanted none of this from me, I kept my emotional distance.

The one who did want to know what I knew and see what I saw was my mother, who had never doubted who and how I was. She had come to understand what transpired between me and my father, even her own role in it. She had her own, sometimes similar, dynamic with him, though she didn't have sophisticated psychological defenses or the physical stamina to challenge him directly and effectively. In fact, her acquiescence was a sine qua non to her managing her compromised health and her vital relationships with her children, and later, her grandchildren.

During my first year in the Jesuit novitiate, my parents came to St. Paul, Minnesota, for Parents' Weekend. We had, as would become our custom, a large gathering in my parents' room at the local Holiday Inn after dinner at the novitiate. There were many Jesuits there, with some of their families, and several of my siblings. The drinks flowed. At one point in the evening, my mother beckoned me to follow her out of the room into the long hallway of the hotel. As soon as the door was shut, she began to cry. I held her fragile body in mine as she wept. At some point, she stopped, looked up into my eyes, and said, "I can't do this without you."

We both knew what she meant. I froze. I did not know what to do. Should I leave the Society to go back home to be a buffer for her, to absorb her complicated pain? Or was I allowed to live my life on my terms? What was my duty? And why would she ask this of me?

But I knew the answer to the last question. By being scapegoated all those years, some of the disdain and disgust I had absorbed might otherwise have been directed elsewhere, including at her. That night, I could only console her. I became aware—painfully—I could not save her, nor anyone, try as I might.

My dad was a proud yet wounded man. He did good in the world. He had a beautiful aesthetic, he enjoyed the company of others (with a Scotch in his hand), had an ultra-devout religious life. He loved jazz and passed on that love to me. He could be very sentimental. I often remember his delight on Christmas Eve when his large brood, and later our spouses and kids, were gathered in my folks' home, awaiting the arrival of Santa. It was as if he was a boy again, sweet, accessible, innocent. And it is lovely for me to recall the joy he took in his garden, and his mastering the art of feng shui, and his keen interest in politics and the state of the world. Those, too, he transmitted to me, even if our politics ultimately differed.

Clearly, from my reckoning, he had suffered some wounding of unaccountable proportions in his own young life, the parameters of which I could never fully know. He was trained—by family, religion, farm, cultural masculinity, war—not to show his vulnerabilities, his fears, and in obeying cultural norms so deciduously, he paid a great price, as did those who accommodated him. We know the thread of wounding that goes through many generations before it eventually fades, much of it unintentional, some of it unpreventable, all of it scarring.

My dad never spoke of his father, long dead, except to say that he was a good man. There were no details, no stories, and no additional attributes. There was nothing about family life or relationships. Nor did his sisters speak; they would respond simply that he was a good man.

A most significant—and utterly unexpected—moment for me with my father occurred near the very end of his life. It was during my husband, Scott, and my Christmas visit home in December 1988.

The previous summer, while driving on Folsom Street in San Francisco, on the feast day of St. Ignatius, I had received strong intuition: *You cannot stay in the shadow of the Church.* The communication was simple, and again, life altering. It was not that you don't have to, nor that you might not want to, nor you shouldn't. Rather, that you cannot.

I had lived in her shadow, in various ways, since early childhood. The Church was in my bones and in my blood. It was how I knew, and in many ways, what I loved. It had gotten my peasant forebears through centuries of oppression at the hands of their English overlords, and its rituals, both genius and profound, had made sense of the very act of living. But its contemporary shadow—the scalding black and white sex-and-gender-obsessed world of the then papacy—was not a place of growth, of air, of light, nor of hope. I had known this for some time, against what I had wanted to be true.

I had recently turned forty and my dad would turn seventy-five the next January, two momentous dates in our lives. I decided to write him a letter as a Christmas gift—he had no material needs and he ably supplied his own wants. I wanted to express my gratitude and share some traits that I had received from him, now that I was turning forty: my own aesthetic, love of politics, music, gardening, parties, even the foundations of a faith life. In that Christmas letter, I included a paragraph sharing this new awareness on my spiritual journey, the necessity of leaving the shadow, acknowledging that my path was complicated, and would somehow be divergent from his as I walked as faithfully as I might. I left the sealed letter on his desk in his study. Scott and I left for a day of Christmas shopping. Upon our return in the dusk of the late December afternoon, as we entered the house, I could see that my mother, sitting in her chair, was agitated. She merely said, "Your father is pretty upset with you."

I knew immediately. I knew that brief paragraph in the gift-letter would not be regarded as such, for I had shared that after working hard to stay within the precincts of the Church, I had now found it impossible to know how to remain.

I sat down on the hearth in the family room, a fire glowing behind me, and waited for my dad. He soon entered, immediately saw me, and sauntered up to me. I rose to receive the moment. He started jabbing the air between us with his index finger and in a raised voice, now scratchy with age, said: "You always think you know so much. You think you know more than the pope!" (Hmmm.) Though he was so upset, I knew it was necessary to hold my place.

What I said next came from within where our deeper truths lie, perhaps dormant for decades. As he air-jabbed, I started, in a strong, unquivering voice, hands down but staring at him: "Stop!" A few moments passed. I continued: "You will never talk to me like this again! And you will never talk to her"—pointing to my mother sitting nearby, who was rapidly making the Sign of the Cross—"nor any of my sibs like this again. Ever!"

I sensed he was shocked and shaken. I was kind of shocked, too, and quite evidently shaken. He turned and skulked away, back to his study. The air in the room was extraordinarily electric. My mother rose, visibly shaken, and approached me. We hugged each other for a long moment. I then withdrew to the basement suite where Scott had earlier retired, wisely knowing that his absence would be a wise move. Though still shaking, I was at peace. I did not see my dad again that evening.

The next day, Christmas Eve, the highest of holy days in our family home, climaxing with the arrival of Santa—generously played by my brother Brian—nary a word or glance was spoken between me and Dad. Though the family gathered, we avoided any real contact. The following morning, Christmas, my dad was sitting in the living room reading the *Omaha World Herald*. I walked down the step and over to him and extended my hand. He took it in his, and I wished him a Merry Christmas. He returned the sentiment.

The next morning, Scott and I flew back home to California.

I was sad, but not regretful. I felt a necessary exchange had taken place.

My mother called some days later and said no one had ever spoken to him like that, and she added, so forcefully, and telling him the truth. She thanked me for my courage.

It was what I had come to know. Listening to my mother since my late teens, I felt I spoke for her, too, though his treatment of each of us differed profoundly. What characterized so much of these interactions was a trivializing of the other—our opinions, our wants, our desires, and what we knew because of living our individual lives, each of us having encountered suffering and grace. This was also true for several of my sibs, though not all.

It took me decades both to work through my relationship with my dad and to come to understand what was possible and what was necessary to embrace so as to finally forgive him. To see him as a human being, doing, as we all do, the best job he knew how to do to get through, using the tools he had been given and those he had acquired, to live a life, complicated by the nefarious and dusky disease of alcoholism, but one that we ultimately shared.

Perhaps in that Christmas Day handshake, he forgave me, too.

The healing professions have learned so much during the past forty years about family dynamics and family brokenness, about addiction, about trauma, about good and/or good enough parenting.

I have no knowledge of the effects four years on an LST (Landing Ship, Tank) in the South Pacific during the Second

World War had on my dad, nor how living in the theatre of war, so far away from loved ones, how loneliness and fear and perhaps even hopelessness might have gripped him, as it did so many of those who returned from that war alive. After my aunt Jane Mullen died, her daughter, Mary Kate, while going through her mother's things, found a cache of letters tied with a ribbon in her highly scented cedar chest, letters my dad had written his mother and father, and his sisters, from his billet on a navy ship many thousands of miles away, over the long three years of his wartime service. Mary Kate forwarded them to me and my sibs.

The letters were astounding. Through reading them, I experienced a different man from the father I had so long known. What emerged from the light blue onionskins in my hands was a tender, docile, and loving young man who missed his family deeply. *This* young man exhibited a vulnerable and deeply devout self of which I had only hints later in his life. I was seeing some other man, whose brilliant devotion to his family and to his faith were the opposite of shadow. I felt so grateful for this unexpected gift, a eureka moment in my relationship with him, even though he had now been dead several years.

How my dad, and countless other dads, some of whom I knew, handled his locked-up feelings was unknown, if ever felt. For I know both anecdotally and in the literature that there were traumatized, psychically wounded doppelgängers masquerading as husbands and fathers in households on every street in America.

Given the major strides in clinical education over the last few decades, we now know that alcoholism is a disease and one that affects the whole family, everyone, no exceptions. I share this disease with my father. It creates a raft of defenses in its enablers and subjects—we alcoholics ourselves—that we employ to make sure it is undisturbed. I have also come to believe—having spent a career working with addicts of all stripes—that it is often the most gifted, and emotionally sensitive, who resort to the balm of alcohol and other drugs to ease life's exquisitely experienced pains.

Alcoholism is only one of many toxicities that infect families. Dogmatisms, false and poisonous notions of the masculine and the feminine, tribalism, disparities in wealth and health, diminished civic engagement, the atomization of home life, and the bones of caste. Nonetheless, enormous change is occurring, if sometimes at a pace we think glacial. Thankfully, we have mental health practitioners, feminists, the civil rights community, gay persons, political activists, liberation theologians, and mystics seeding widespread religious, cultural, and political turf.

I see my brothers as beautiful, fully engaged fathers and teachers. My sisters have lived lives they carved from ancient models, sometimes revising them wholesale. I see my in-laws and my own spouse similarly: some come from homes marked by trauma, others less disordered, all living lives of intentionality and service. In my siblings, I see some of their wounds and acknowledge their amazing courage in addressing them. Through it all, perhaps because of it all, there dwelt a loving family on 57th Avenue in Omaha, Nebraska, a long time ago.

Several months after that Christmas confrontation, my brother-in-law Richard, a surgeon and at that point my dad's consulting physician, called and asked if I would come back to Omaha to be present when he shared the dreadful news that my dad was suffering with metastasized lung cancer. Of course, I said yes.

My mother, my sister Diana and her physician husband, and my dad were all in the family room, not an unusual gathering. Dad knew Richard had medical information to share with him. At one point, he asked my dad to join him back in my dad's study. He gave him an accurate, if foreboding, prognosis.

We stayed with my dad that afternoon and evening, and over that Memorial Day weekend. It was a good if painful visit, knowing my dad's time was short. Monday afternoon, following the annual Glenn family Memorial Day picnic and softball game, as I was preparing to depart for the airport, I saw my dad sitting in the soft soil in his garden, planting his snapdragons. I went over to say goodbye, and he insisted on getting up, we hugged each other, and made our adieus. We both teared up, knowing what was to come.

I did not see him again. He died in early August as I was nearing SFO to board a flight to Omaha with the hopes of seeing him one more time.

My mother survived him by seven years. We deepened an already abiding and lovely relationship in those years. She had asked me to eulogize my dad, which I gladly did, and when she died, my sibs asked me to eulogize her. I particularly spoke of the remarkable love of my sibs, who with their spouses had been so devoted to her. Her last years she suffered from post-polio syndrome, as undoubtedly my sister Lisa has as well. While Mother grew weaker in body, her spirit remained strong, if at times cantankerous. My sibs and their spouses, most of whom live in Omaha, took care of her basically 24/7 for two years.

I got a call in the summer of 1996 in which my sibs, some of them, asked me to come to Omaha and tell her this routine had grown too taxing, that she would need to leave her home, too big for the family to care for in addition to caring for her. They thought that she could hear this from me, one not engaged in her caretaking, and also acknowledging that Mother and I shared a mutual understanding that would allow her to hear bitter news from me.

I arrived on a Friday, planning on staying through the weekend. On Saturday, while enjoying morning coffee together, she said, abruptly, "Why are you here?" Taken aback, I said because I wanted to see her. She countered me: "You never come in August when it's so damn humid! No, you're here for a reason." She was intuitive as well. I said I wanted to talk to her about something. She initially inquired, and I began to share with her, she stopped me and said, "I can't talk about this now." The *this* had not yet been fully articulated.

The next morning, she asked, "What do you want to tell me?" I proceeded to share some challenging perspectives: she would need to leave this house, her home, the site of a lifetime of family gatherings. She could either move into a small apartment with Joyce, my sister who had moved back home to live with her after Dad had died, a more manageable arrangement, or the feared word, she could move into assisted living. "With Joyce!" she said without hesitancy.

She took a few months to get her affairs in order, and in the late fall, after dispersing the effects of three-quarters of a century of living, she put the house on the market. Her beautiful home sold quickly. She and Joyce moved into a lovely apartment in mid-November, in time to decorate for the holidays. The extended family celebrated Thanksgiving in this new place. Scott and I looked forward to joining the family for Christmas. But within days, her health deteriorated, and she was hospitalized shortly thereafter.

Soon, my sister Diana called in the middle of the night and told me it was time. Boarding a flight in San Francisco at dawn, I called the hospital after arriving for my layover at Denver International and was told that my mother was still breathing. Mid-air between Denver and Omaha I called again, this time from the plane's phone to the nurse's station at Bergan Mercy. I was sitting in the window seat, with—thankfully—the middle seat empty. The empathetic nurse shared with me that my mother had just passed. I turned to the cold pane and wept, silently.

Most of the family was downstairs getting coffee in the commissary at Bergan Mercy Hospital, and while our youngest brother, John, was cradling her head, she drew her last, always labored breath. She did so on the Feast of St. Nicholas, a holy day celebrated by her ancestors in northern Europe. She always made special this day by sending us each *Little Christmas* gifts, as the feast was known. I now refer to it as the feast of *GingerNick*, combining her nickname with that of her Christmas patron.

When I arrived in Omaha—Scott was to follow the next day—I went directly to the mortuary, but her body had not yet arrived from the hospital. When the undertaker, a longtime family friend, came to let me know I could see her, he asked if I wanted him to accompany me. I found the question weirdly absurd, but politely said, "No." I was shown to the door of the embalming room, entered, and beheld a sight I could not have imagined. Mother lay on a concrete slab, appropriately draped from her neck down, utterly, and finally, at peace. I drew close to her and bent over to kiss her forehead. My only words: "You are so beautiful."

I had no memory of her body as anything but mangled. But in death, the paralysis had released its grip, and she was, in all ways, in repose. She *was* beautiful. I was so grateful to be with her, alone, surrounded by a presence that was ineffable and surrounding us with such peace.

3

BEYOND THE PALE

Even if our efforts of attention seem for years to be producing no result, one day a light that is in exact proportion to them will flood the soul.

—Simone Weil

ONE MIDWINTER MORNING in 1996, while sitting at my desk early at Continuum, the AIDS agency in San Francisco where I served as executive director, the phone rang. The caller identified herself as an assistant to the First Lady, Hillary Rodham Clinton. She asked if I would attend a "Community Leaders' Tea" at the White House scheduled for later in the month.

After my initial startle, and my impulse to check to see if this was a friendly prank, I said, "Why, of course!" As you might imagine, I was honored, very excited, and understood this as an obligation.

Fast forward five years to midwinter in 2001. My friend Robert Hotz, the president at Creighton Prep, the Jesuit high school that I attended in Omaha, Nebraska, where my younger brother Greg has made his career teaching, called me one morning and asked if I would return to Prep and speak to the faculty about my experience of being a gay student there in the mid-1960s. He asked, too, if after sharing my story, I would suggest what I thought Prep might do to assist its gay students.

Again, I felt honored and understood this as an obligation. However, this time, I was not excited. The heart-pounding this invitation generated was intense. The hand that held the phone was trembling!

I hadn't been at Prep in thirty-five years. I had been to its gym for an occasional Christmas Midnight Mass, and I had been at the track watching my brother John and my nephew Brian practice football, but I had never really stepped foot in that building since graduation in 1966. In so many ways, it was the belly of the beast for me. And several weeks later, there I was.

In considering what to say to these women and mostly men teachers at this privileged school, I wanted to say *one perfect thing* that would forever change the way all gay students are treated, but there is no one perfect thing to say. Instead, I would tell them who I am, relate some of my experience at Prep, and what I have come to know and believe were ways to serve all their students better, particularly those who were gay.

After graduating from Prep, I spent four years at its mother institution, Creighton University. In 1970, I joined the Society of Jesus where I served the next ten years in a variety of ministries, most satisfyingly as a scholastic teaching and counseling at another prep school run by the Society of Jesus.

I shared with them that I had been in recovery, having become sober in 1978. Shortly thereafter, and for a multitude of reasons, but none of them because I did not greatly value Ignatius's vision, I left the order. As a fellow educator, I shared some of my years in Catholic school administration, my subsequent work as a psychotherapist, and particularly, my work through the AIDS epidemic.

As I was preparing my remarks for this talk, I was aware that I was not the fifty-two-year-old man that I appeared to be. I was again the sixteen-year-old boy, a sophomore of 1963, a gay boy, thrown back in time. I reexperienced my old life, with feelings and memories that echo within and still haunt me.

I was somewhat of a soft boy, and Prep was no place for sissies. After a difficult freshman year, I begged my parents to transfer me to the local public high school. That request, to my father, was ridiculous. Little did he know how ashamed and deeply isolated I felt inside, while a student in this revered high school. During sophomore year, as *eros* bloomed, I lived in fear that I would be exposed, living in dread that I would be discovered as this despised thing whose name I did not know, but whose negative associations I could see and feel all around me and mostly deep inside me. All was not bad, of course. I had good friends and some wonderful teachers: both Jesuits and laymen.

At Prep, and perhaps paradoxically, my nascent faith deepened as it grew pale. I encountered Jesus in a new way. I was introduced to rudimentary Ignatian wisdom—incomparable combination of a psychologically grounded spirituality that honored intuition and insight and a contemplative posture that fostered the religious imagination and presence. At Prep, I made good and lasting friendships as I developed my first forays into critical thinking.

But Prep was a difficult place for a deeply closeted gay boy. Prep then strongly exemplified the dominant culture's values that were better suited to molding boys into narrow and constricted men.

For example, during my freshman year at the Prep homecoming football game at Rosenblatt Stadium, I was sitting with a friend when two thugs-in-training from my homeroom approached. One said to the other, "This is the one," and proceeded to cuff my collar and pull me up out of the bleachers. The other sucker punched me, then threw me back into my seat, and walked away, scornfully laughing. They imparted the knowledge I dreaded: "We're on to you." I lived daily with that fear, believing that somehow I deserved what I got for being the one whom they were all on to.

They were strutting like punks, but they were also the kind of minor celebrities that high schools produce. They were both touted athletes, but with what we would later identify as toxic masculinity, part of the fabric of the dominant culture, perhaps unconscious, and nonetheless encouraged.

In my sophomore year, I fell-in-swoon like nigh all high school boys do, though unlike my friends, I was not falling for a girl. I was falling for a boy, one who sat a row away from me. It felt overwhelming. I was excited, alarmed, and scared. There was no one with whom to share these feelings, to even acknowledge that the feelings existed. I felt then the beginnings of what I would feel profoundly for the next fifteen years: I was alone in this—alone I believed I would always have to be, with no language, no community, no symbol nor myth, no conversation, no dialogue, no hope.

What I did acquire at Prep, and in the world in which I lived, were the messages the dominant culture proffers. I came to believe during puberty's final onslaught that I was beyond the pale of grace. I came to know that I was unacceptable in the eyes of the world. All our culture's words and notions and judgments came home to roost in me, a sixteen-year-old gay boy that the world, let alone his parents, could not know. But primarily, I grew to believe that I was unacceptable as a human being in the eyes of God. And in the truest sense, I did not know why, for this thing that had visited me was not of my making nor at my initiative.

The more I prayed to be changed, which was the heart and concentrated content of my prayer, so deeply aware that I had not chosen this but came to know it was visited upon me— somehow—because of my sinfulness, I regarded my not changing as God's further judgment on me that my prayer, and my life, were insincere and somehow beyond the pale of believability. I was not available to the strands of grace everyone else seemed somehow to merit.

The One I called God and my dear companion, Jesus, previously the source of such great succor in my life, were taken away, or they left, or I could not find them. It seemed that they had abandoned me to the despair of myself because this person I had become, through no wish of my own, could manage no change, could not desist either my feelings nor my desires, no matter how hard I fought them, or prayed to be delivered from them. In the end, I felt alone.

This is the terror for queer boys and girls: that we are alone. We suffer without the comfort and love of a mother or a father, of friends or even the odd solace of the cosmos. No one with whom to share this terrible fate: we believed all the culture's heinous images, holding our young selves responsible for this sick and perverted condition. There is no symbol to transform the experience, no story to context it, no person to explain it who could take the onus of bearing it away.

I wonder who would wish this on their enemy, let alone their child, or their friend? But this is what happens to gay boys and girls in this culture. Even as the culture changes, this continues to happen. And, in many parts of the developing world, it is far worse.

On the inside, I experienced a circular existence of guilt, shame, expiation, inescapable and from which there was no relief. On the outside, I straightened up and hyper-developed a good boy image to appear, in others' eyes, as *one of you*, knowing all the while I was not nor ever would be.

In the summer of 1978, a dozen years after graduating from Prep, and twelve summers after discovering the warmth and relief of Scotch whiskey, I got sober. One month later, for the first time, after so many years of my own hiding, I came out to myself. I was thirty years old.

As I continued with my story that morning at Prep, I found the teachers most attentive, a response I had not anticipated. But I came to sense that at least some of them knew who some of the gay boys in their classes might be, and they had some sense, I suspect, for the cost to these boys of carrying these secrets in a world that would judge them, and more, even in the Ignatian world of Creighton Prep. They probably knew, too, who some of the adults among them were, their colleagues and friends, good men but men-in-hiding, carrying a version of the weight I was describing, too late, in their estimate, to come out and live a fuller life.

I told them that I vowed with the conviction only a reformed drunk can muster, never to live in fear again, and at whatever cost, I would be myself, as I was being with them that day.

They got that my story is a version of every gay boy's coming out story, and these stories will continue until the dominant
culture—of which they are indeed a part—which suffers exquisitely from its own homophobia, withdraws its enormous and
blinding sexual shadow. These women and men, as teachers
everywhere are, are charged with protecting the spiritual and
psychological health of their students, along with their fine academic preparation and socialization.

From sophomore year to the age of thirty, nothing was
worse than being gay. But, as Providence would have it, I now
understand this biological, psychological, and spiritual dimen-
sion of myself, my gayness, as the source of enormous grace and
wisdom. I think some may have been startled when I said that
I am deeply grateful—most likely in inverse proportion to my
previous disdain—for being gay, for the grace of this path, for the
deep freedom coming to terms with this gift has given me, and
for the work my interior journey provides. And I realize that my
compelling and demanding companion, Jesus, of course, never
left at all. The overwhelming thrust of the Gospels, Jesus's ministering in the margins to the unrecognized and dispossessed, is
no longer just a model for me but an outward sign of grace, a sacrament. So, my story comes, though skewed, full circle. I am yet
that fourteen-year-old boy who came to Prep in 1962 to learn
how to become a man.

I concluded my remarks at Prep by offering some sug-
gestions to the faculty, premised on the following truths. First,
I invited them to remember that all queer kids, and most gay
adults, believe they are damaged goods, and as a correlation, all
gay kids, and many gay adults, feel and are isolated and alone.

Second, in response to being asked what I had needed to
hear at Prep in 1962 and what young gay Prepsters need to hear
today, I offered these three thoughts:

You are created exactly as God intended you to be.
You are not damaged goods, nor sick, nor evil.
You and the love you provide are essential,
    mysterious grace in God's plan for the world.

Finally, I expressed my gratitude and admiration for having received me so graciously, for inviting me to tell my story, and for having the grace and courage to host and attend this gathering.

Prep, in taking this initial, bold step, would not be the same going forward, nor would I. Those crusty faculty, often bearing tender hearts behind the seasoned facades that teachers acquire over time, had unwittingly healed an old wound in me, and I am yet in their debt. They are slowly doing the work of making this school a graced place for every student who enters those doors each day, those boys whom they assist in becoming men for others.

Bob Hotz, who showed courage in inviting me to speak, continued to educate the Prep community, which eventually met unforeseen roadblocks, as homophobia, presenting itself as wisdom, gained the advantage. Nevertheless, our friendship flourished, and he and his husband, Walt, are our regular companions and trusted friends.

Several years later, my friend since kindergarten Jim Cleary called and asked if I was going to attend our fiftieth Prep high school class reunion. I hesitated. He said that his wife, Quindrid, couldn't go, and I knew Scott couldn't either, so Jim said, "Why not be my date?" He could not have known how gracefully and gratefully that remark landed. I said, "Of course, I'll be your date!"

On the first night of the reunion, we met at Jim's hotel to do a pre-brief of the weekend to come. He asked if I was trepidatious about seeing anyone. I had moved away from Omaha forty-six years earlier by that point, and so much had happened to me, as undoubtedly so much had happened to each member of our large class of 235 boys. We were now in our late sixties. I shared with Jim the story of the encounter at Rosenblatt Stadium so many decades ago. I said I did not look forward to even eyeing the man who sucker punched me. Jim clearly understood. We proceeded to the Irish bar for that evening's festivities, and I saw so many old friends, both women and men. Many of the Prep boys married women from the girls' schools, and others from Creighton University. I knew almost as many women as I did men.

I did see the person who sucker punched me. I suspect that, if he did see me, he hadn't a clue who I was. I'm also sure that he had little memory of that night at Rosenblatt in 1962. That former bully, now an old man, had been typed in life, too. He had perhaps moved with the trajectory life had suggested, maybe not finding an off-ramp to move beyond the toxic masquerade he, and so many boys, are required to wear. I had been shown so many off-ramps, grateful for them, but knowing that none of this can be taken for granted.

The final night of the reunion, we gathered at a large restaurant for a sit-down dinner. The Alumni Director of Prep made some opening remarks and announced that "the wine this evening had been provided by Bill Glenn and his husband, Scott Hafner, from Scott's family's Hafner Vineyard in Sonoma County, California." That was a full circle moment I could never have anticipated sitting in my homeroom with an undeniable and so problematic crush on the boy in the next row back in 1964.

At dinner, Bert Thelen, my high school counselor, later Jesuit provincial, and the first human being with whom I shared my dilemma as a sixteen-year-old, and now, like me, a former Jesuit, was an honored guest at our table. We had a wonderful meal, many sweet reminiscences, and much laughter. Bert wrote me subsequently that being together that night, with this warm group of friends, including my friends from boyhood, Jim and John Brownrigg, and Bill Laird and his wife, Susie, and several others, fifty years later, was like sharing Eucharist. Was not like but rather *was*.

4

MARCHING TOWARD
JUSTICE

Girls and their dates still got dressed up to go to the
Apollo for amateur night, but by 1968 pretty much
every representation of hope in the country had been
put up against a wall and shot.

—Ann Patchett, *The Dutch House*

AS WE GRADUATED high school, many of my friends and I
matriculated at Creighton University, a Big East basketball power,
a university with five professional schools as well as a large
undergraduate enrollment. Few in our crowd went away, as many
were first-generation college-goers. Having a fine university in
our city precluded, for many of our parents, any need to go away.
A few of us went to the University of Nebraska, Lincoln, a few
entered the Jesuits, a select few went farther afield: Notre Dame,
Marquette, or an Ivy League. But most of our various posses
drifted down California Street and began college in the fall of
1966, the very last year the formerly intact, postwar, middle-
class, patriarchal, business-as-usual life of most Americans
passed basically unchallenged. Except for the civil rights
struggles that had been going on for a full century. Nonetheless,
America in 1966 was seemingly one culturally cohesive place.

For me, that was about to change, in unanticipated, large, and life-altering ways. Sometimes, the change was instantaneous; other times, it would emerge more fully years hence. One day, I held this opinion, and then, seemingly suddenly, I changed my mind. I began college in a button-down oxford shirt and khakis, but in no time had acquired bell bottoms, sandals, and a poncho. I spoke standard English upon entering, but slowly acquired the patois of the lefty college subculture. In 1966, my friends were white, but soon, with the segregating patterns of the larger culture being slowly dismantled on campus, I was part of a slightly more multiracial crowd. In high school, I didn't drink and the thought of drugs never entered my mind. Summer after high school graduation, I found alcohol and, in time, smoked my share of weed and hash. My friends were no longer all my age and soon ranged from graduate students to youngish professors.

The late adolescent I was—in the process of cohering a personality—had taken rudimentary steps toward a moral self, the foundation of an individual identity, and a deeper awareness of my spiritual being. As humans, we can and do get waylaid at any stage, but the developmental processes reach an initial conclusive step in late adolescence and early adulthood. Our development does not stop—far from it—but future growth depends on these initial and fundamental stages being encountered and consolidated. Throw burgeoning eros in the mix and it can be combustible—for me, very.

What political radicalization occurred in my life began in my sophomore year, as morality and politics jelled within me and gave me a foundation for my life as a citizen, both of the United States and of the world community. Changes in my consciousness only deepened as I grew older; these included thinking about war, race, social equity, religion, sexuality, culture, art, friendship, and family.

In my freshman year, I belonged to the College Republicans; in my sophomore year, before I was eligible to vote, I became an officer in the College Democrats. I entered Creighton with a kind of blind fealty to the Roman Catholic Church—a particular Roman Catholic Church—and by sophomore year, I was walking around campus with an ever-present internal conversation about the relevance of verities of religion. I was in military drag in mandatory ROTC as a freshman and organizing antiwar demonstrations the very next year. With an enormous amount of work, we succeeded in eliminating mandatory ROTC for males on campus.

I blossomed as a student at Creighton, as my affinities became my intellectual pursuits: history, literature, and political science. Finished were the unnecessary burdens of mathematics and the hard sciences. Senior year, I was invited into an exciting select seminar on the New Left and eagerly enrolled in courses on Black history and studio art, where I created what I thought were very avant-garde, found-object sculptures. Creighton went from an orderly campus in 1966 to—within two years—where we were shutting this place down over the Vietnam War, parietal visitations, the Biafran War, mandatory ROTC, the racism suspected of predicating many course syllabi, to whatever was deemed of utmost importance to that increasingly large and powerful cohort of radicalizing students, of whom I was an active and grateful participant.

Universities were also undergoing stages of growth, moving from shepherding an elongated adolescence to a more mature recognition of the agency of students. New methodologies of teaching, research, and communications flourished. It was all exhilarating and exhausting. Not all students joined this loose movement for social change, but we were a potent cultural and political force, and this change-soaked milieu affected us mightily. The movement introduced me to the bulk of my college friendships—with dormies—students from all over whose experiences and ideas challenged and stretched me. I was so clearly ready.

I dropped out of college in my sophomore year to work on behalf of Senator Eugene McCarthy's insurgent antiwar presidential campaign. His staggering numbers in the New Hampshire primary led the beleaguered—and on campuses, despised—President Lyndon Johnson to leave the race and not seek reelection. Three weeks later, Dr. Martin Luther King Jr. was assassinated in Memphis and an even darker cloud covered the

American landscape. The wanton slaughter of this young, Nobel Peace Prize recipient and humble leader pulled back the nation's racist cover that he had given his life to exposing, redressing, and working to eradicate through his deeply Christian articulation of the possibilities of love.

In this tumultuous year, the McCarthy campaign, manned mostly by young people, was also highly motivated with a singular concern: to end the war in Vietnam. I became a leader for the Nebraska effort, meeting highly dedicated people, idealistic and somewhat naïve, like me. Ultimately, we lost in Nebraska, but the national campaign plowed on. When I was subsequently invited to join that national effort and go on to work on the primary race in California, my parents strongly discouraged me from doing so. Their argument—that I could lose my college draft deferment permanently—was compelling. I was among the *selecti quidum*, holding my privileged college student deferment.

In June, Senator Robert Kennedy, the scion of the celebrated Massachusetts clan, while also campaigning on an antiwar platform for the Democratic nomination, was assassinated in Los Angeles. A man of immense charisma, he had worked to suture the gaping wound left by King's murder with his focused and physical engagement with African Americans. With his horrific murder, the pall increased. The nation's bonds were loosed. Hope, an elusive quality, had been greatly dimmed by these two—archetypally connected—assassinations.

I travelled in late summer to Chicago to work at the McCarthy campaign headquarters at the Democratic National Convention. After working days in the McCarthy delegate reception room in the storied Conrad Hilton Hotel, I ventured, with tens of thousands of others—young people much like myself—onto the streets each night. On the Wednesday night of that convention week, a march had been organized to protest the provocative actions inside the convention hall—the equally storied McCormack Place. As we gathered in Grant Park and began to march down Michigan Avenue, we were shortly met with the terror of club-wielding Chicago police. Suddenly, from closer to the front of the long march, we saw smoke and lights and heard what sounded like gunshots. We felt the sting of tear gas in our eyes and nostrils, and the fog of war that was created by Mayor Richard Daley ended in mayhem. Many marchers were beaten by baton-wielding police, a fate I escaped. That night, after a year of working for peace and a changing politics, after a season of slaughter in both the United States and in Vietnam, and then this, I went back to the home of my friend Timothy Mahoney, where I was bunking up, and wept. What was happening was beyond my imagining. It was a wake-up call to my burgeoning sense of the demands of justice and to what life seemed to be inviting me.

That fall I quickly reenrolled at Creighton so as not to jeopardize my student deferment—being the fortunate son that I was. My friend Jim Cleary had left the university and joined the United States Marines that year, and his girlfriend Phoebe Mullen and I took him to Eppley, Omaha's airport, to farewell him. Though a conservative then and still today, he asked me to promise, as we embraced on the tarmac (still possible in those days), to keep up my antiwar work so that he might make it home, a promise I easily made and made good on.

That same spring, good friends and I—both Black and white—found ourselves in another riot not exactly of our own making. The segregationist governor of Alabama, George Wallace, famous for standing in the door of the Administration Building of the University of Alabama to prevent the first two Black students from enrolling, was pedaling his gospel of hate—in the wake of the King assassination—as a candidate in the same primary election. He came to Omaha and held a rally inside the Civic Auditorium. Organized by my friend Michael Walsh, we marched down from campus to protest his racist presence in our city. We entered the auditorium and made our way to the top-tier bleachers to avoid the larger crowd seated on the arena floor. We heckled his profane and inciting speech, and he, feigning his fake rage, to be replicated by an equally pugnacious demagogue in the twenty-first century, invited his partisans to attack the Communist sympathizers—us! As his followers grabbed their metal folding chairs and proceeded up the narrow concrete stairs toward us, we rushed down another sets of stairs, trying to high-tail it out of the building. We were caught at the double doors by his vitriolic mob and escaped, with folding chairs banged on our heads and backs as we made our frightening exit. Not severely injured, we had the shit scared out of us that night. Nonetheless, two weeks later, Wallace was back, and this time, hosting a smaller event at the local Holiday Inn on 72nd Street. Our small cohort of good troublemakers, as the beloved John Lewis might have characterized us, drove out to the Inn and made our appearance. We were denied admittance by the Omaha police, wary of having a second such combustible event, so we chanted our antiracist feelings from the parking lot instead.

One night the following year, I asked Jerry Lewis, the president of the Black Student Union and a fellow undergraduate with whom I was friendly, to explain institutional racism—a then new concept to me. This understanding was fast emerging on campus, in political groups, in upper-division classes, and in seminars in American history, my major. I wanted to know more. One Saturday evening in a nearly empty Brandeis Student Center, Jerry sat me down (I weirdly remember Glen Campbell singing *Wichita Lineman* in the background as we began our conversation). He spent the next several hours tutoring me with fervor, commitment, and generosity, in the nefarious and subtle ways of racism, unconscious, cultural, historic, and institutional. Jerry had an elegant mind and was a generous young man. I knew I was being given a gift of significant import. I look back on that evening as a seminal piece of my own cultural education.

Many of us same good troublemakers—to utilize John Lewis's moniker—mounted a campaign on Creighton's campus to end the university's practice of requiring all male students to enroll in two years of ROTC, a fertile training ground for the fodder that second lieutenants became during the Vietnam War. Many men continued with the four-year program, graduated, and went directly to Fort Riley for training to lead squads of infantrymen into battle. Ending this mandatory practice was both a political and a freighted moral issue. There was a post–World War II sensibility that gave Creighton, and so many other universities, certain standing for having this program. We did not aim to end ROTC, only to make it optional. Over the course of the school year in 1968 to 1969, we organized and marched and petitioned and—with the winds of change at our backs—ultimately succeeded when the university's board of trustees endorsed our at-one-time radical idea. I will admit I was an inept soldier. One afternoon, when doing the necessary training of cleaning my M16 standard-issue rifle, I had my index finger in the bolt breech and accidently pulled the trigger, which slammed into my finger with the full force of a shot bullet. It mangled my fingertip, which quickly ballooned with engorged blood. I ended up in the ER. The doc punctured my nail bed with the end of a Zippo-heated, fully opened paper clip to release the bloody pressure. I remember the treatment being worse than the mishap.

As it did for perhaps millions of other Baby Boomers, the *annus horribilis* 1968 shifted everything. We would not again view war or racial injustice or power structures in quite the same way. I don't march so much anymore, though I have out of moral necessity in the last few years—the two great People's Climate marches in New York City in 2014 and in Washington, D.C. in 2017, the Women's March (being a friend of the community) in 2017, the marches after the murder of George Floyd in the summer of 2020, including a moving meditation-in on the plaza in front of City Hall in San Francisco, the destination of so many marches the past forty years. Marches are not the core of social change, but I have come to see them as essential—in our political culture—to citizens' empowerment and to developing a sense of solidarity. The march over the Edmund Pettis Bridge inspired by Martin Luther King Jr. and led by John Lewis and Hosea Williams—three intensely bright lights in the firmament—in Selma in 1965 changed the world and is still changing the world. Martin Luther King Jr.'s often repeated quote cannot be repeated enough: "The arc of the moral universe is long, but it bends toward justice."

When I was young, I presumed change would come quickly, for so many people had worked so long and so hard for it. Now, in my final quarter, I appreciate the wisdom of Dr. King's words in a way that eluded me as a youth. As we experienced in the summer of 2020, the immense work of dismantling the edifice of institutional racism, and the power structure that upholds it, and many other injustices and abuses, is ever ours to be doing. But bending has been done, in some ways significantly, and bending will continue. All of us riding the crest of that arc are pressuring its movement to just ground.

As we have seen in the aftermath of *the most secure election in modern American history*, forces increasingly alien to liberal democracy and to the complexion of a diverse America, forces grounded in racial resentment and a *faux* masculinity, empowered by the imbalance in our democratic structures, are loosed on the land. I suspect more than marches will be required to vanquish this revived poison.

The experiences I had in 1968—and the friends I made, some lasting a lifetime—grounded me in a politics of justice and a humanist philosophy that have dictated my choices since. They have led me to surmise the only possible construct for a theology of a loving God would be a God of justice. For love is predicated on justice, and only truly flourishes when justice is (being) established. Leo Donovan, SJ, the former president of Georgetown University, eloquently prayed at President Biden's inauguration in January 2021, to a *Most Holy Love*. Perhaps I would add, less elegantly, a most holy love grounded in a most holy just order. I suspect Fr. Donovan would not mind. The prophet Micah is often postured as containing the essence of a life of faith: "Do justice... love kindness, and...walk humbly with your God" (Mic 6:8). This simple and highly complex wisdom of a desert people of several millennia past has a most contemporary feel in this present moment. My many life concerns for peace, for racial equity, for the other, for a restored and vibrant environment, for a principled regard of our democracy's Bill of Rights, all grounded in justice, were forged on that Creighton University campus in that fateful year.

So many wise professors each invited me to take this life with utter seriousness and with enough humor and joy to keep my balance. And to be in this for the long haul.

During my college years, I kept my life of desire utterly hidden from all others, mainly from myself. The closet was claustrophobic, but I deemed it necessary, as I continued to internalize the culture's horrific posture toward me and my kin. I sublimated desire, with the predictable psychological effects that such sublimation renders.

5

VOCATIO IMBROGLIO

Give me only your love and your grace. That is enough
for me.

—St. Ignatius Loyola

I WAS FLYING to New York for the second time, the first having
been two years earlier during sophomore college winter break
to spend some time with my friend Michael Walsh, his family, and
particularly his brother, Vinnie. Vinnie was a senior at Fordham.
Though only a couple of years older than Michael and me, Vinnie
seemed wizened. In his very cool apartment, there was plenty of
beer and pot, and psychedelic art on the walls and a black light
to enhance the experience. I remember hearing for the first time
The Great Mandela by Peter, Paul and Mary. Being with Vinnie
and his friends in that apartment in the Bronx felt like being in
a new world. And indeed, that was true. Leaving New York City,
and Michael's home on Long Island, we detoured to visit family
in Connecticut. There, I introduced Michael to my cousin Jane
Nordli. Soon they were a couple. Things moved fast in 1968.

But now, two years later, I was returning to New York, once
again to Fordham, the Jesuit bastion of a university, where my
friend and mentor Tom Shanahan was working on a doctorate
in theology. Tom, a Jesuit priest, had taught me as a freshman
at Prep eight years earlier, and he had become a central figure
for me for much of my young life. I had spent the summer of

1968 in summer school at Creighton, having dropped out the previous semester—thereby jeopardizing my student draft deferment—to work for the McCarthy antiwar campaign. Senator McCarthy's loss in the Nebraska primary was a great blow to me, and so I was still wobbly as I started the summer session. Tom was teaching on campus and was at the heart of a small intentional community that met most late afternoons for Mass in Kiewit Hall, often followed by dinner together in Becker, the dorm's dining hall. I became part of this small community and felt belonging within its embracing arms.

Eighteen months later, during the winter of 1970, I returned to New York to talk with Tom about my nascent vocation to the Jesuits. I had contemplated a vocation to the priesthood for many years, the seeds planted early, and reinforced in myriad ways by the encompassing Roman Catholic culture in which I had been raised.

In eighth grade, my essay on "Why I Want to Be a Catholic Priest" won the Serra Club award at my elementary school, St. Margaret Mary's. Serra was a Catholic businessmen's club—think Rotary—that fostered religious vocations, and my father was a proud member. I went to the fancy lunch at the Omaha Athletic Club honoring awardees and received the simple accolades such a lunch provides. I had thought of entering the minor (read: high school) seminary in the Omaha Archdiocese and even sat the entrance exam. I was accepted but deferred my decision. My dad's priest friend, Fr. Aloysius McMahon, had given me a relic of St. Pius X, the patron of priestly vocations, for that extra little boost, but I decided to go to Creighton Prep instead.

Toward the end of my four years at Prep, I had an overwhelmingly enriching experience at St. Bonifacius, the Jesuit novitiate in rural Minnesota, where I attended an Advent retreat. On the bus ride home from Minneapolis to Omaha, I engaged in a conversation with my friend Bill Laird that lasted the length of the ride. Soon afterward, I decided to become a Jesuit.

My academic career at Prep had not been stellar. Though I was tracked into Latin, the academic path for those thought worthy of studying the classics, after one year, due primarily to abysmal grades in Algebra, I was dropped down to Academic, for us slower boys. Once so classified, there was no climbing out. And in Academic, Latin was not offered; I would need it if I were to enter the Jesuit novitiate. Though I handily recovered my grades during my last two years of high school, my lack of four years of Latin was an impediment. To provide an assist, my freshman Latin teacher, the very old and very kind Fr. Charlie Kanne, a precise man, agreed to tutor me, which would hopefully qualify me to apply to enter the Society of Jesus.

But I didn't apply. I sensed I was not ready, if ever I would be. While many friends, including Bill, entered the Society, I decided to attend Creighton University, where I, along with my secrets, would spend the next four years. I turned around from my less-than-stellar academic career at Prep and made Dean's List by my senior year of college. I was very active in college politics and social justice issues, and grew close to Bob Shanahan, my professor and Tom's older brother, the rector of the politically and culturally divided Jesuit community.

I loved college life—*the all of it.*

As my years at college came to an end, I again felt the tug of a religious vocation growing in me, and perhaps subtly pressuring me, for entertaining this notion was complicated. To resolve my dilemma, I made the flight to New York to speak with Tom about my questions and doubts around my vocation. At dinner one evening, Tom asked me if I could be happily married, if a vocation to the priesthood was not an option for me. It didn't feel like this was a trick question. A standard deal-breaking question for all potential Jesuits, I surmised. I said, "Yes." Truthfully, I had never given marriage any real consideration, but, in any event, I certainly aspired to normalcy.

While in New York, I met several other Jesuits, one whom I will refer to as Adam, a *nom de guerre* of sorts. Like Tom, Adam was also in advanced studies, writing his doctoral dissertation.

Adam was particularly attentive to me. Though perhaps seventeen or eighteen years older than me, his focus on me was intense and flattering. I felt drawn to his powerful personality and honored, if somewhat baffled, by his attention.

My concurrent conversations with Tom helped me to decide to trust my interior inclination to affirm my vocation, even though doubts lingered. And so, in the spring semester, I applied to become a novice in the Wisconsin Province of the Society of Jesus and went through the requisite interviews and reference checks. My dear friends Art and Jo Moore wrote one of my *informaciones* (recommendations). Jo let the Jesuits know what a fine man they would be getting, though skeptical about my decision to serve the Church formally, critical as she was about the Church's relationship with its nearly half billion women members. I had my friend Nene Field, a contemporary of my mother's, write one, too. A devout Episcopalian, I thought that choosing Nene was rather ecumenical—and cheeky—of me.

I was accepted into the Jesuit novitiate that fall in St. Paul, Minnesota.

In spring, I also found myself in a long-distance phone relationship with Adam. I was enthralled by our conversations and looked forward to the calls with great anticipation. While not fully understanding his interest in me, I never questioned its appropriateness. He was a priest, and that fact made him utterly trustworthy. I simultaneously knew these calls would not be understood by anyone in my life, and the intimacies exchanged, while aboveboard, had a quality of secrecy.

One night late that spring, while talking casually, he made an explicit—and out-of-the-blue—sexual overture, articulating his desire to have explicit intimate contact with me. I was stunned, visibly shaken, and afraid. I had no response. Instead, I hung up the phone.

Although I was twenty-one, I had not had any sexual experiences—of any kind—with anyone. I had dated many delightful girls in high school and college but had usually broken up with them around the time that some relatively simple physical expression of desire was expected. Even kissing girls was a major challenge. While I had no desire for a physical relationship with them, I would often have a deep tenderness for the girls whom I dated. My ongoing lack of erotic desire for females continued to confound me. And I did not clearly understand my intense attraction to other males, which I had assumed was simply a desire to be close to them. There was no affirming social context in which I could understand my feelings.

I had been aware since my freshmen year at Prep of my strong attraction toward some boys my age, and later, to guys at the university. I had imagined—vaguely and imprecisely—about being physically close with some of them. I came to understand through the Church's and the broader culture's biases that these desires were wrong and, in fact, sinful. I slowly began to see myself as somehow deformed because of my desires, and I also knew, intuitively, they were to be kept a secret—from everyone.

In college, my dilemma intensified. One day, feeling an intense desire for another student, I thought I was going mad. I made my way to St. John's, the collegiate church, sat in a pew in the back, and wept. Inconsolably. But I could tell no one. And I believed God was having none of it.

Outwardly, I appeared to be bright, focused, and accomplished, and seemingly extroverted, warm, and quick-witted, but my inner life was a miasma of chaos. I would later come to understand this as *The Best Little Boy in the World* syndrome, one that afflicts so many gay boys everywhere—shiny on the outside; near despair within.

When Adam, this older, so accomplished, and very sophisticated Jesuit priest expressed exactly what his desires were, I was totally thrown off guard and felt defenseless. They compounded the deep confusion—at times, paralysis—of my inner life. I waited for some days and then called him back. I sheepishly apologized for hanging up on him, told me him how taken aback I had been by his overture, and that I was not in this for that. His response was to chastise me, he told me *to grow up* and never to hang up on him again. I was not fully aware of what this berating meant, nor foretold, though I indeed felt chastened. Yet I still desired to keep alive this seemingly vital connection.

What I so deeply wanted was his love—and his approval—both of which I thought he was offering me. I could not square love with sex and had no experience doing so. The thought both terrified and reduced me. I found myself very engaged by a priest considerably older than me, who desired me, or desired a part of me. But I desired him, too, though I had not eroticized that desire. After hanging up on Adam, and my later callback of apology, all mention of sex left our conversations. We continued our calls apace. And some weeks later, he asked me to come and visit him in New York the coming summer. I was eager to do so, wanting to be with him, having banished the sexual overture and its implications to a compartment deep in my psyche.

On this, my third flight to New York, Adam met me at JFK and drove me to Fordham University in the Bronx. Instead of walking me to one of the men's dorms, where he had suggested there would be a student room left vacant for the summer where I would stay, he let me know that he had arranged for me to stay in the Jesuit residence, Murray-Weigel Hall. This was an honor, particularly with my entrance into the Society of Jesus near at hand. While seemingly taking me to my own quarters at Murray-Weigel, he opened a door, and bade me enter. It was his room. He said we would be sharing his room. And this clearly meant we would be sharing the one visible twin bed, his bed.

Though I had naively believed that his sexual interest in me had been extinguished, upon entering his room I felt fear and excitement, and momentarily paralyzed, all at once. I knew this was an extremely unusual—taboo—arrangement. After closing the door, he came close to me and took me into his arms, encasing me in his compelling, larger body. He assured me everything would be all right. His personal magnetism as well as his position of priestly authority made it seem that perhaps, somehow, after all, this moment I had never really imagined with this man, nor consciously sought (being the recipient of his sexual overtures) was now somehow—God knows—okay. That he wanted my body, that he would touch me...well, no one to my knowledge had ever wanted my body nor really touched me. I do not remember the exact circumstance of what happened when, but he assured me that our loving each other physically—sexually—was good. Though confused, still in the adrenaline rush the moment produced, I received his overtures. For several days, I lived in a state of suspension from my whole lived life, having this intense encounter with this man who found me of interest, this man whom I believed loved me, and to whom I was powerfully drawn. I confused his desire for my body with a desire for me, which, over time I came to understand it in no way was. But this truth I could not then see, so deep was my desire to be worthy of his love. And so hungry—previously unbeknownst to me—for this touch. The exacting repression of the past eight years erupted, for I loved him. The possibility that he might, in fact, not love me did not enter my mind.

Of course, I was keenly aware that I was entering the Jesuits in a few short weeks and that he knew this too.

At the end of our week in New York, he said that he would like to come visit me and my family at my home in Omaha, knowing that I lived with my parents and several sibs. I said he would be welcome, and so, two weeks later, he arrived. On the first night, after cocktails and dinner with my family—and their valuing this honored guest—we retired to my childhood bedroom, which had twin beds. A few minutes after turning in and turning out the light and saying good night, he got up from his bed and came into mine, continuing this complicated and powerful and utterly transgressive secret over a long weekend.

My parents found Adam charming and were immensely entertained by his stories. Having a priest in the house was a blessing, and they clearly basked in his apparent affection for me. After his departure, they made only gracious comments about his visit. Some form of compartmentalization, the power of the adrenaline, and an emerging shame and attendant self-loathing concocted a potent brew that I sipped in preparation for my departure for the Jesuit novitiate that was now just days away.

In late August, after learning how to water ski at Art and Jo's family cabin in northern Minnesota, they dropped me off at

30 South Finn Street in St. Paul, the new Jesuit novitiate. I found my entrance amazing, meeting so many splendid fellows—Pat Gillick, John Melcher, and others who would become my lifelong friends—all of us drawn in some way to a life of service as Jesuit priests, to a life of intimacy with God. I found the routines and rituals of Jesuit life engaging, and in many ways familiar, having spent the previous eight years in their presence. Thoughts of my summer experience with Adam were both ever present and seemingly far away. How I thought I would manage those *in pectore*—those unspoken secrets—and for how long, I did not reckon with.

A few weeks after entering the Society, a highly regarded retreat director, J. J. O'Leary, came to the Finn Street novitiate to talk to the new novices. He suggested that there were, perhaps, some of us young Jesuits in the room who harbored secrets of which we were ashamed, and the only way to alleviate that shame was to share the experience with the novice master. I felt he was looking at me the whole time. (I later found out, of course, each of us novices pretty much thought the same!)

I decided that night that I needed to drop the masquerade—as if I was an innocent young man—and talk to Jim Hoff, the novice master. Jim was a complex combination of wise, stern, and gentle, both intellectual and emotive. I had known him while he was teaching at Creighton the previous year, and we had a comfortable familiarity with each other, as he had with my family. Though I was somewhat leery of him and clearly recognized his authority, I also intuited that he was trustworthy. In telling him my secret, I believed I would be asked to leave the Society, a decision that I was willing to accept. At this stage, I welcomed anything to alleviate the increasing self-lacerating feelings of guilt and shame that had developed ever since the day I parted company with the man whose intense interest in me I was slowly realizing was not love.

With trepidation, I entered Jim's office. He gestured for me to sit. I blurted out the whole story. As I finished, the room then grew silent. I felt, among other things, a great relief. I could not discern Jim's mood from looking at his face.

He then spoke. Perhaps he asked me what the experience I had had the past summer had meant to me. He certainly asked me some particulars about Adam and if I felt coerced. Maybe he asked me if my vowed life as a Jesuit was in jeopardy. He might well have asked me many other questions, too. I answered his questions honestly, relieved to have it out. So great was the fulcrum of sexuality in the Roman Church that no other burden could have been so imbalanced and debilitating. And I mean my homosexuality, of which the events of the past summer were but a brief, lived slice. My homosexuality was no longer a theoretical probability but had been made manifest in the Bronx. I knew that it would not go away, regardless of the vast amounts of time I had spent and would spend on my knees begging God to deliver me from this curse.

What did happen with Jim was that he received me generously—that is, humanely—that day. I did not sense any judgment from him. He did not shame me. He did not chastise me. He did not lecture me. He did not blame me. And he did not ask me to leave the Society. He did ask me if this Jesuit priest had contacted me since my entrance, and I said he had not since our last encounter some weeks earlier. And he asked me if I was okay.

Later that year, during the January long retreat, a thirty-day introduction to the spirituality of St. Ignatius that first year novices undertake, a postcard arrived from New York, with two lines of text. Adam wrote that he hoped my entrance into the Society had been unexceptional and that I was doing well. Nothing more. In the days and months and years ahead, only silence.

Over the years, I would share parts of my "Adam" experience with confessors, as if some residual stain was still darkening my soul. I did not reconcile the experience within myself, as I could not reconcile the incontrovertible fact of my sexuality with that of my spiritual aspirations. They remained at war for the next nine years.

Years later, after I left the Society, I would speak of my encounter with Adam in therapy, but subsequently did not focus on it. Like some discordant song hook, it was always in the background. I felt responsible for the encounter, so had not spent much time reflecting on—let alone much less blaming—Adam. I blamed myself, believing that I had led him on by my excitement to talk with him and my desire to be near him. I had caused this. That trope lasted for the next decade.

But patterns developed in my life—both while in the Society and later—that I eventually, at least in part, traced back to that encounter and its aftermath. Those patterns were to be durable, destructive, and eerily deepening of those already set in motion when I was a child. Later, they would slowly merge and reverberate within me in traumatic ways. My encounter with Adam foreshadowed an inner split between my sexuality and vulnerability, reinforced by centuries of an anti-body, narrowly defined, sex-negative theology and grossly misapplied ethical standards. As if designed to do so, these led me to distrust my desires, my instincts, and the veracity of my loves. It reinforced shame and its twin, secrecy, in matters sexual that spilled over into an enduring view of myself as damaged, perhaps irreparably. The sexual engagements I eventually enjoined were, from the get-go, ridden with an invisible veil of shame. I held no one other than myself responsible for my trials. I had given Adam and the Church a pass.

That was the status quo of my life for the next fifty years.

In writing this book, I asked a friend, a Jesuit and a clinical psychologist, Sonny Manuel, whose wisdom and trustworthiness I valued, to read an early version of this chapter, including some reflections on this long-ago relationship with Adam.

After his initial read, Sonny called and asked if we could talk about the chapter. For whatever reason, I didn't think that he would focus on my experience with Adam. That was all neatly packaged and had been for a half century! As our conversation commenced, this clinically trained man began to inquire about the spoken and unspoken outlines of my story. With his keen psychological insight, he asked me—in short order—to consider how I had characterized my encounter with Adam. After I finished a cursory account, Sonny offered a perspective that was explicit: in engaging with me, Adam had violated my sacred trust. My naïve and relative youth had been manipulated by someone who knew in very fundamental ways that he ought not engage me sexually. Rather, he had been grooming me from that first dinner in the Bronx and through those many early phone calls. A Jesuit priest had introduced me to sex, never withdrawing it nor acknowledging or inquiring about the emotional disturbance his seduction had caused me. He continued his pursuit, inviting me to visit him fundamentally to satisfy his own needs and, without asking me or telling me, brought me into his bedroom and initiated a sexual relationship with me, a young man about to enter the Jesuits. He then suggested visiting my family home—to which I concurred—where he continued his pursuits.

My compromised consent—an apt term the psychological profession has culled from the accreted wisdom of the significant research about sexual abuse that subsequent decades has provided—was no free consent at all. The pleasure I experienced was thrilling and powerful and yet in some vital way a betrayal of my psyche, for I had no experience in matters sexual, and no experience and awareness of my own potential agency in this imbalanced relationship, no notion of my ability to exercise any personal power. Sonny continued, "It was in violation of your personal integrity—however unformed—and you were not allowed the thought that you could say no, or even a full-throated yes." Sonny labeled this sexual abuse, a term I had never applied to my experience, and a term I found difficult to accept. I wanted to keep my own agency intact—though in fact it had been abrogated—so that I could in some sense control the outcomes—social, psychological, moral, and spiritual—and not be a victim, a status I despised. Taking full responsibility for the encounter gave me a false sense of control, one that I hoped—if unconsciously—would keep me from having such an experience again.

This conversation with my friend Sonny was confounding, upsetting, and, after fifty years of self-blame, weirdly, starkly clarifying. He continued—knowing the answers—as he asked, "Have you counseled any victims of sexual abuse in your years as a psychotherapist."

I said, "Yes, of course, many."

"Have you observed this pattern from your life, witnessed it, and worked to assuage the wounds from it, in those with whom you worked, in their lives?"

I found this question disarming and yet hesitantly replied, "Yes."

"And do you not see how subtle and nefarious these patterns are, that you, who have helped others heal, could not quite see the wounding that occurred to you? Could not see the grooming that had occurred to you, the violation of trust that had happened to you, the charming manipulation that had happened to you, and the confusion between love and his sexualization and objectification of you that was imprinted on you? Could not see the invited intrusion into your family home an arrogant and dangerous extension of his appetites, the price for which was to be paid by you? That after he used you, he tossed you aside, with no concern for your welfare, for your confusion about this relationship, for your emotional health—just as you were about to commit your life to the Society of Jesus? The baldness of it, the arrogance of it, the pathology inherent in it...and what, you merited a postcard!"

I finally asked him to stop.

I found my eyes welling up.

I had never allowed myself to think of or feel about my first sexual experience in these ways. Because I was not a child nor a teenager, but instead a college senior, I would not let myself acknowledge any of this. So blindingly potent had been my judgment of myself that I had blamed myself, saw myself as both responsible and sinful. But never—oddly—had I really questioned myself about Adam, his motives, his behavior, his not seeking after my welfare after I entered the Society. I could not even identify the compartment I had placed Adam in, so deeply had I imbedded him in my psyche.

Sonny wisely stopped, and we refocused our conversation. A strange peace settled over me, one marked by a clarity that had eluded me—in some important ways—my whole adult life.

Some years ago, I read Martin Moran's stunningly painful and finally agency-claiming memoir, *The Tricky Part*, which was later adapted into a one-man play about his molestation by a trusted adult, a parish leader, and the aftereffects on the rest of his life. He confronts the man who abused him, the denouement which grips the reader as it did Marty. I thought of Adam throughout my recent reading of this gripping account—though Moran's experience was profoundly more complicated than mine. Initially, I believed that, because I was a college senior when I encountered Adam, no real abuse had taken place—my subsequent deeply painful splitting notwithstanding.

Sonny powerfully disabused me of this notion. Several weeks after my conversation with Sonny, Scott and I were watching a favorite television family drama, the splendid *This Is Us*. In this episode, Kate, the middle triplet in the multigenerational family, now an adult, married and a parent, confessed to her husband that she had had a traumatic sexual experience when she was on the cusp of adulthood. With her husband Toby's encouragement, she decided to look up her former partner, the man who had cavalierly abused her. She discovered where he worked and drove to his place of employment. As she exited her car, she saw him standing outside his place of work, smoking. After some twenty years, he did not recognize her, though she and we, the audience, did him. He was utterly blasé about Kate's experience as she tentatively relayed it to him. Now, finally, recognizing his trivializing of her early experience, she grew furious, and she let out a brief broadside in which she said all that had been built up—and not dealt with—over the past two decades of her life. The damage, the trauma, the self-blame and fury poured out, succinctly and with curative passion.

That evening I knew I, too, had to finally—fifty years after the encounter in the Bronx—contact Adam.

I went into my study and Googled him, knowing he had spent his career at a distinguished university in the East. Immediately, he popped up, with several entries under his full name. The very first entry was startling—a quite recent obituary. I read with great interest. Adam had died—a man nearing ninety—of the coronavirus, just six weeks earlier. Accompanying his obit was a photo taken several decades before, Adam exactly as I remembered him: brilliant, handsome, charming, erudite, remote, a complex and perhaps wounded man whose Roman collar caught the intensity of the flashbulb. He had a storied career, had received numerous plaudits, extensively published, and held a named chair at the renowned university where he had spent his career. As I read and sensed my regret that contacting him was no longer possible, I had a feeling something like pity—one I am shy to acknowledge. Unlike Kate, I could muster no fury.

I knew, nonetheless, I had to write him a letter.

Working as a psychotherapist with many victims of sexual abuse, I have had insight into and some knowledge of how healing might work. That I had not allowed myself to be the subject of my own awareness in this realm light-bulbed me into a new understanding—one deep and personal—of how trauma can invade the psyche and the body, dictate so many of the terms under which we live, and require that we remain unconscious of its machinations as we work to create a life.

We often normalize trauma to manage it, to not assume the victim role so we can feel agency when agency had been denied us. Reading the powerful expository text *The Body Keeps the Score* by the Harvard psychologist Bessel van der Kolk, I understood more acutely the hardwiring that trauma inflicts on the psyche. I recommend this book—a perennial *New York Times* best seller—to anyone who has suffered trauma, or loves another who has, and wants to gain insight into and knowledge of how healing might be facilitated.

When I had departed the novice master's office, I felt an awareness that, contrary to my fears, I was accepted by him and that he endorsed my pursuing my vocation. Jim never referenced our conversation again, as no master of novices would have, given the confidential nature of my disclosures. More importantly, Jim always treated me utterly humanely. In my second year in the novitiate, he asked me to give the panegyric—a Latin word to describe a public speech given in praise of an individual—on St. Stanislaus Kostka, the patron saint of novices, on his feast day. When it came time to recommend me in taking vows, he gave me his approval, without qualification.

I chose as my vow name—a semiprivate appellation a novice chooses and announces during the vow ceremony, usually a saint who models certain characteristics one would like to mirror, and often the name of a celebrated Jesuit like Francis Xavier or Ignatius Loyola—the double name John Magdalene, for the apostle Jesus loved, and for the woman scripture suggests was closest to Jesus.

Jim went on to become the university president at Xavier in Cincinnati, and for many years our paths did not cross. Some twenty years later, I ran into Jim at Eppley Field, Omaha's airport, when Scott and I were there to spend time with my extended family. Of course, he was aware that I had left the Society, and he knew of my work in clinical psychology. Our encounter was sweet, and afterward I wrote him at his office at the university to tell him how much it meant to me to see him and to be able to introduce him to Scott. He wrote back a keeper of a letter, telling me how much he had admired me as a Jesuit novice so many years before, remarking on what he observed then as the integrity of my spiritual path.

As I neared completion of this volume, I rented a cabin in a remote section of the Nevada desert, a landscape I am drawn to. At the base of White Mountain, a fourteen-thousand-plus foot peak—containing the oldest life forms on earth, the bristlecone pines, and still retaining patches of snow as the drought encroached on it—I sat each day in silence on the porch, taking in a sweeping view of those immense mountains that form the border between California and Nevada. On the morning of the fourth day of my planned eight days of retreat, and after a psychic storm of lament, I could write Adam my half century-overdue missive. The storm had passed.

At first, I could muster little more than an abiding sadness for what might have been different in my life, sadness for that young man who did not have the tools to navigate his own sexual self, with a received (and since rejected) personal moral code that condemned me before I began. In the process, I became keenly aware that Adam, in his childhood and within the American church of the 1930s and 1940s, had been similarly condemned. I was also aware as I wrote, that, so great was my seeking of approval and love, earlier traumatic events as a child—noted elsewhere in this book—had laid the groundwork for my encounter with Adam.

But in time, anger came, and came at one point as a flood, and this writer was now not the seventy-two-year-old man but once again twenty-one, forlorn, confused, his shame unabated, and his sheer hatred of his sexuality penetrating full bore into his psyche.

How had this—*the all of it*—come to be?

As I wrote to you, Adam, I asked you explicitly: Who did you think you were that you had the right or the privilege or even the wherewithal to initiate me into the world of my sexuality? Who were you to use me? And, why me? Did you see your grooming calculations over time achieve their ends with me? Did you see me as some vulnerable creature so desirous of attention and love that you could parlay that into whatever you wanted and knew well how to secure? Did you even reflect on how this might affect me...as I entered the Society? Did you know that I loved you? That I was trying to love you? Did you know that I was a person?

With that last question, the anger abated.

I was a person, however unformed, and was worthy of dignity in every situation. That realization flooded me with a sense of calm.

I sensed Adam, too, had been trapped in a system of unacknowledged, secreted sexuality, in which his own homosexuality—a generation older than me and mine—was without hope, light, and acceptance.

What language I have used in the past or have come to understand, whether it be affair, abuse, exploitation, trauma, or tragedy, these two men, one barely a man, were caught in a trap set a millennia before and reenforced in every way imaginable by both the religious and secular cultures.

At the end of that day, in that scorching, beautiful desert, I finally prayed for Adam and offered him what forgiveness I might, bearing him no ill will, knowing we were two human beings caught in something way beyond our making. I was not a child, not quite yet a man, but I was a person who was trying hard to come to know what that might mean—to be a person—in a world offering few markers for all the murkiness inside.

The price paid for male clericalism—the progenitor of so much abuse—and all its nefarious effects is ultimately paid by all—women, men, girls, and boys. Of course, it will not be remedied until the many strands of the Church's sexual shadow are unraveled; the dark, musty veil pulled back; and all on both sides of the altar are finally seen as worthy of inclusion—until all hands are called to bless, all persons regarded as imaging the One.

Over decades of reflecting on this nefarious homophobia, I have come to understand that it is merely the forlorn stepchild of misogyny, the explicit and implicit control of women by men, and as the feminine is refracted in male love, men choosing to love men, men loving men, too, must be controlled and exorcised.

My wise and liberating teacher Robert J. Egan, SJ, once wrote, "The tragedy of contemporary American Catholicism is that so little is remembered of the ways to holiness, so little is said of silence and solitude, the existential ground of compassion, the mystery of time, the exaltation of the spirit, or the ambiguous unimaginable glory of the human vocation and mission."

So much needless loss and anguish. So much waste.

That the 1986 dictum issued by Ratzinger declares queer persons as having a "tendency ordered toward an intrinsic moral evil" still stands and is the Roman Catholic Church's official position, wreaking havoc on literally millions of emerging and already formed gay persons, is the real abomination. And I have an abiding admixture of sadness and anger—fury, really—that so many have been so wounded and cast into the Church's enormous and destructive sexual shadow, including those very priests who have preyed on others. I have a perhaps confounding but nonetheless real concern for these men, for I can imagine their confusion and self-hatred back when they were young and hoping that by offering their lives to God in the celibate priesthood, all might be well.

I look back at the young man I was—hungry for love—projecting onto this charming, handsome priest some regard for me and a capacity for loving me that may not have existed. Yet now I have an abiding gratitude for the exact contours of my life that have led me to be the person I am, no longer young, not despite but because of the exact experiences I have had.

And deep gratitude for Scott, whose love and acceptance of me—as I am—has been the most penetrating balm in my life.

I remained in the airtight closet for the next nine years of my life in the Society of Jesus, constantly praying—among other things—to have this defect—my homosexuality—removed from my life. The dynamics that were realized and inculcated in my brief experience with Adam drilled down into my psyche and became a template for how I would understand myself as a sexual—and really, human—being. The full effects of that experience would take many years to surface and be worked through, and honestly, I am still working through them. I expect that work to continue.

In June 2021, the Vatican officially added clergy abuse of adults to those persons harmed by priest-abusers. The reports highlighted the great number of young adult seminarians who had psychological harm inflicted on them by those who used their priestly charism of authority to sexually abuse them.

As Julian of Norwich intuitively said seven hundred years ago, "Though sin is necessary, all will be well, and all will be well, and every which manner of thing will be well." Impossible, but for grace.

6

THE EMERGENT SHADOW

California was almost entirely a dream, a dream vague
but deep in the minds of a westering people.

—Bernard DeVoto

I ARRIVED IN San Francisco in my seventh year of formation as a Jesuit. I had selected the Jesuit School of Theology (JST) Berkeley, as the place to study theology, over theologates in Boston and Toronto. Upon arrival, friends met me at the San Francisco International Airport (SFO), and we immediately proceeded to the rotating circular bar atop the Hyatt Regency on the Embarcadero. This was my introduction to the Bay Area! Wrong on so many levels!

I had recently left teaching at Marquette University High School (MUHS) in Milwaukee and was missing my midwestern friends and the many students and families with whom I had bonded during my years there. Teaching was really my first professional experience and one of deep delight and affirmation. The classroom was a comfortable and engaging milieu for me, a place where my students might benefit from my love of literature and my commitments to social justice, where my love for language and religion could be shared. As had been my high school experience, I took the relatively affluent MUHS boys into the inner city each week to tutor and mentor youngsters in an impoverished neighborhood. We would then return to the class-room, read from Michael Harrington's seminal work, *The Other America*, and reflect on this experience and the gospel values. This opportunity was eye-opening for these young men, being formed, hopefully, as men for others.

The pace of life of a Jesuit scholastic teaching in a Jesuit prep school is hectic, and that suited me. I was involved in the school from early in the morning often into the evenings. Many nights I would meet with friends—Jesuit and lay—and as is the custom in Milwaukee, share a brew, or several, maybe even more. During this three-year hiatus from studies, I subsumed many of my haunting internal questions and deliberations into my work. I developed friends easily and found the rhythm of academic life invigorating.

My drinking had increased over many years, though in the cultures in which I moved, I was not an outlier. It provided me relief from the voracious demands of my super ego and kept in check the feelings of shame I felt over my no-longer-deniable-but-deeply-sublimated sexual orientation that did not disappear no matter how much I prayed.

My years at Marquette High had been among the happiest years of my young life. And the prospect of returning to more studying was daunting. As I made the transition back to gradu-ate school, I increasingly recognized that my reliance on alco-hol was negatively affecting my life. I was terrified to admit it and what that might mean. Alcohol provided an ample escape where my more challenging feelings and memories could rest under-addressed and out of sight. But moving to California in late summer 1977, the airtight closets I had constructed were slowly beginning to emit constrained psychic material in ever larger doses. My first months in Berkeley would be consequen-tial in this regard.

From Donner Pass westward, California blew me away. It was nothing like Wisconsin or Nebraska, really like no state I had ever imagined. The Bay Area flora was intense, and my first letter home was a compendium of all the types of trees and plants I was seeing each day, including the palms that lined Ridge Road in Berkeley, where Chardin House was located. Walking down to the little commercial village of North Side, the telephone poles were completely covered with flyers announcing every imaginable type of esoteric experience, with names redolent of exotic destinations: India, East Asia, Persia, Mexico, San Francisco, with metaphors for spiritual experiences suggested in many clever, startling, and vaguely discomfiting ways: Feldenkrais, Rolfing, the Sufis, A Course in Miracles, Carlos Castaneda, peyote, Palmistry, The I Ching, Channeling, the Tao, Tantric Sexuality, Jungian psychology, the Enneagram—all within walking distance of LaVal's, my newly discovered pizzeria and cheap beer garden. Now LaVal's I could relate to. But in subsequent years, some of these exotics—the Sufis, the Enneagram, Carl Jung—would become facets of both my intellectual and interior life.

I settled in Chardin House, named for one of my great unmet teachers, Pierre Teilhard de Chardin, the early twentieth-century Jesuit paleontologist and highly attenuated spiritual man whose multifarious writings were placed on the "Index of Forbidden Books" by the Vatican, a fitting symbol of what would transpire for me over the next two years. Chardin House was a former University of California Berkeley fraternity dwelling, as were many of the Jesuit residences on the north side of campus; they had become leftovers from the Greek exodus of the late 1960s, as different forms of community living emerged. The Jesuits, smart at real estate, snapped up several of these former frat houses that then became the locus of the Jesuit School of Theology.

I commenced my three-year course of study enthusiastically, and had several influential professors, prime among them was Joseph Powers—perhaps the brightest, and among the most tender of men I have known. He led a seminar on *Spiritual Autobiography* and introduced me—now pulled off the telephone pole and into the classroom—to Carl Gustav Jung, where we read, among other gems, *Memories, Dreams, and Reflections*, a perfect introduction to the master of intuition and synchronicity. With Jung, I finally had some intellectual grounding for the powerful intuitions I had been having since childhood, awarenesses that were not the result of cognition, exactly, nor reflection, nor synthesis, but bright moments of knowing that felt trustworthy and incontrovertible. I took to Jung eagerly and was grateful for Joseph's introducing us to this man whose work was just outside the boundary of religion, but whose spiritual insights were profound and vital.

During these two years, I would study dogmatic theology, Sacred Scripture, canon law, church history, feminist ethics, nonfeminist ethics, a brave course in bodily theology. I took courses from every woman professor—there weren't many—I could, knowing instinctively that I needed to round out my profoundly male intellectual influences. And, in my last semester, I enrolled in a *descent into hell* course in sexual morality, which marred my otherwise stellar academic record. In that class, my final grade was an "F" as a result of my refusal to take the morally bogus final exam. The visiting professor, a Jesuit on the spiritual guru speakers' circuit, had little time for my challenges to his lectures and his—in my estimate—wildly homophobic spouting. That was an *F* to be proud of, for I challenged the dogmatic and psychological assumptions he made about homosexuality, and homosexuals, while having several—albeit closeted—gay men in his classroom. A year earlier, I would have sat in his lectures and not said a word, lest I draw any attention to my own closeted *persona*.

Berkeley was the heart of an interreligious scholarly community known as the Graduate Theological Union (GTU), a center for academic and cultural endeavors where Protestant, Roman Catholic, and Jewish spiritual traditions were intermingled and studied. Later, these traditions would be joined by communities comprised of most of the world's religions. I took courses at several of the member schools and had the great fortune to study alongside women and men from around the world. It was a time of great ferment in Western religion, before the exodus of clergy and congregants was keenly felt, and hope and promise abounded, fueled by the regular awesome sunshine of the Bay Area. After my initial hesitancies, I became a sponge for *the all of it.*

Always in the corner of my consciousness was the presence of San Francisco, a short BART ride away. That meant many
things, but primarily, it meant the presence of the world's largest gay community, the vaunted Castro District. In my first nine
months in Berkeley, I ventured to the city only once, and on that
occasion, my destination was Chinatown. The Castro loomed
large and foreboding, and I feared any identification with it.

Shortly after my arrival, I joined a small support group with
three other Jesuits, in which we met weekly to talk about our
lives, the challenges we faced, and the hopes and dreams we
each held for ourselves and our life within the Society as soon-
to-be priests. I don't remember how we pulled together, but my
friend Richard Howard was among the group. Howie became my
close friend and a source of critical support in the years ahead.

One evening, when we were meeting in my room, I shared a
vision I had been having, in which the letters *BG* and *SJ* were illuminated in three dimensions, and I was trying to jam the *B* and
the *G*, my initials, into the *S* and the *J*, the Society of Jesus. I could
not make it work! One of my brothers suggested lining them
up—B-G-S-J—but somehow that too didn't seem quite right to
me, familiar though it was. My internal conflicts—which would
ultimately challenge my staying in the order—were beginning to
emerge, though I could yet not identify them clearly.

On my second day in Berkeley, I met a Jesuit, a man my age,
from another province, one who would become part of this four-
man support group. We were drawn to each other from our first
meeting, and quickly developed a delightful routine of spending
time together each day. On some days, we played tennis, and on
others, we would take drives into the hills above campus. While
we socialized with others, it became apparent to both of us soon
after meeting that we were something very special to each other,
and we spent what time we could with each other, often alone.
He, too, was Irish and quick-witted, kind and aware. And, to me,
he was beautiful. I wanted to spend whatever time I could with
him, and the desire was mutual. We often found ourselves holding each other in the evening, mostly in silence, delighted and, I
suspect, scared, for what we had found.

Around him, I greatly curtailed my drinking. Being with him was utterly filling, and whatever I had been drinking to numb was supplanted by my awareness of this shared love. I knew when I was with him I didn't need to drink. We did not use explicit love language with each other, and we were aware of the articulated seminary posture warning against *particular friendships*, though we both knew—at least at the time—that whatever transpired to bring us together could only be known as grace. And we said as much, often. We felt a presence not of our own making. We were also somewhat wary of the larger world observing our closeness.

He would leave small notes for me many days. They were thrilling to receive. I had never experienced these feelings before and did not quite know these feelings were possible, certainly not with the many lovely women I dated in college, nor with the few men whose long embraces had led to deep feelings of self-loathing. And unlike the feelings with Adam, there was no embarrassment, guilt, or shame. I finally felt fully alive! I was twenty-nine years old and, for the first time, *in love*.

As perhaps all persons in love, *the other* became both the focus and the object of desire and of the best of projections. And we did this in a highly circumscribed world. We did not speak with each other about being gay, nor did we say to each other we were a couple, nor lovers. Nothing of the kind. Such language would have been quite foreign to us in describing what we had. In truth, we did not engage in sexual relations, though our physical closeness was transporting. We had no external context in which to speak positively of what we shared, and we could only individually imagine—but never spoke to—a future for this. This awareness kept us deeply rooted in the moment, in this time and place. What hopes we had for each other went unspoken. And the ardor we each had for the other could not have been more powerful.

I lived these first few months in Berkeley in a bright cloud. I was delighted, excited, opened, hungry, hope-filled, and carried with me each day a way of knowing myself previously unimagined. Most mornings, I would rap on his door, and we would go to breakfast together, with the many other Jesuits in Chardin. In late November, on the morning before Thanksgiving, I went to his room, as was my custom, and lightly knocked on his door, a tapping he would surely recognize for its familiar rhythm. We had spent the prior early evening together and shared how we looked forward to the many joys of the holiday weekend ahead. We acknowledged all for which we were thankful. He departed around 10:00 p.m. to retire to his room.

My early morning knock drew no reply. I jiggled the handle and found his door unlocked. I opened the door and beheld a room vacated. All his belongings gone. His books, his art, his tchotchkes, his clothing, his vow crucifix, gone. The bed had been stripped. The room was bare and barren.

I was immediately struck with grief. What had happened? What possibly could have made him leave? Where had he gone? And forebodingly, why had he gone? Why had he not said goodbye? A darkness settled over me. Through the halls of Chardin House, in inquiring with others, I sought answers but got no replies. No one had seen anything. No one had heard anything. No one had a clue.

Of course, these ones were other Jesuit scholastics, students like him and me, most of whom were aware of our closeness. There were no Jesuit superiors in our house. There were several houses for those of us in studies, with the superior of all of them living in a nearby house of studies, a man who barely knew me, or so I thought. I was glad there was no authority present at Chardin, other than the authority with which we are each endowed. But I was not yet trusting my own.

We had all been aware of Jesuits leaving in the middle of the night. Another close friend had left this way several years earlier, never heard from again. But *this* man, he was *this man* I loved. He was this man with whom I shared a bond. He was this man of such kindness that leaving me without saying goodbye I would have thought not possible.

I went to my room and felt such a range of scattered emotions and thoughts that quickly went to: What had I done wrong? Was this love we shared a dark thing? I now but began for the first time to see this love, of course, as manifestation of the perverse homosexuality I had kept at bay and that now, for allowing myself to feel this love, I was being punished by the wrathful God for whom I had worked and to whom I had prayed for so many years. Was this my heartbreaking comeuppance for my very real—but not acted upon—desire for this beautiful man? I spent that day alone in a darkened room, sometimes weeping, fearing for my misdirected self. The sadness that was overcoming me would last some time, and that Thanksgiving weekend, I spent little time in gratitude. I knew none of what lay ahead.

I stayed in this emotional dungeon for several weeks, and, for the first time in the nine years I had been a Jesuit, demanded to be allowed to go home to Omaha for Christmas. Permission was granted, with the help of Peter Fleming, my spiritual director, endorsing this trip. I fled for the relative safety of my family in Omaha. I ensconced myself in the highly familiar rituals of a Glenn Christmas. I dreaded my January return to Berkeley, but return, nonetheless, I did. I ventured over to Claver House, wanting to see Peter and avoid contact with the superior, whose inquisitive eyes were more than I could have dealt with. I had immediately suspected the superior had had a role in this sudden removal and assumed that a middle-of-the-night departure would not have been initiated by my friend. I would never know, and older friends, including Peter, never knew either.

Every Jesuit is assigned, or more typically, chooses, a priest to talk with on a regular basis regarding matters of the Spirit, hence, a spiritual director. When I arrived in California in that fall of 1977, I quickly chose, on the recommendation of several friends, Peter Fleming, SJ, a man I had known from afar for the past fifteen years. Peter had taught me English at Creighton Prep in Omaha those many years earlier, though we had not been close. In the interim, he had spent time teaching in the Jesuit mission in Korea. Finishing his doctoral work, he was assigned by the Society to be available as a spiritual resource to young men preparing for the priesthood at JST.

Peter had a small room in Claver House, named for the Jesuit saint Peter Claver, who was the patron saint of the enslaved, for his exemplary work ministering to the physical and spiritual needs of enslaved Africans in Cartagena, Colombia. Peter Claver's feast day was my birthday, so I had had some devotion to him since childhood. Claver House was a stone's throw from Chardin House. Not long after my arrival in Berkeley, I called Peter and asked if he had space in his schedule for another directee, and if so, could I make an appointment with him? He said, "Of course," and I did.

Some days later, I approached Peter's small study, where we sat facing each other. Peter was very forthright and struck me as no-nonsense. He intimidated me a bit, but I was also drawn to him. His gruff exterior was merely that. He recalled our relationship at Prep, nearly eighteen years earlier, and he did his best to put me at ease. I blurted out—as I had with Jim Hoff almost ten years earlier—probably not too coherently—what I was carrying inside me as I began my years in theology.

As I had often done in the past with other spiritual directors, I confessed, not sacramentally, but existentially, that I was homosexual. I uttered that freighted word with trepidation and shame, as I had many times before with men such as Peter. Unlike in the past, however, this time there were tears. The shame of admitting this condition once again, my dark inner awareness of the past fifteen years, was pushing me to a breaking point, one that was yet unclear.

I could not look Peter in the eye, and I deflected his gaze whenever he asked me direct questions. It was an old, routinized posture: I would tell the wise priest of my shameful secret, hoping not to be banished, expecting pity, some pastoral concern, or compassion that separated the sinner from the sin. Since I had some experience of the sin already, or so I believed, I felt it necessary to share two or three events from previous years in which I had hugged exactly three fellow Jesuits beyond the acceptable time constraints of a typically friendly embrace. Yes, the hugging was mutual, and no, it was not sexual, but whatever. I was sure it was evidence of my cravenness. After relating my condition, Peter reached over and lifted my chin, so that he could see my eyes, which I had been withholding during my confession. He said slowly, simply:

"Billy, we get to approach all of our problems with dignity."

Nothing more. No identification of what exactly the problem was. I knew intuitively that he was not equating my sexuality with the problem, but that my problem was real: how I judged my state of being so harshly, hid within myself a penetrating shame, and prevented Divine Love from fully dwelling within. Peter got all of this.

How did I know? From the tone of Peter's voice, his clarity, and his refusal to judge me with the look of his eyes. Instead of disgust, always transferred by the eye, his eyes bore love. In that moment, he required of me to hold myself with dignity, possibly knowing more than I did of what lay ahead. He proffered an invitation to be present in a new way, one in which the Divine was not to be considered the Judge, but perhaps as the Beloved.

As the fall semester progressed, I found myself sharing with Peter the depth of my burgeoning intimate friendship, but I did not focus on it, and nor did Peter ask for anything more than what I offered. His sheltering of my heart was also an invitation to cease equating my affectional life as outside the milieu of the Spirit and to bring what had so far only been held in the shadow slowly into the light. I suspect Peter knew more resonantly than me that what I was experiencing was vital and transformative, and perhaps even holy. After my shattering experience the previous Thanksgiving, I began to talk with Peter more frequently. I did not easily move out of what I now know was a situational depression. Peter sat with me patiently and invited me to experience more fully these very uncomfortable feelings, but he refused to tolerate the recriminating comments I directed at myself.

On January 15, after a life with little athletic activity, and with my friend Howie's encouragement, I trod over to the soccer field in Berkeley, tennis shoes firmly tied, and ran the surrounding track. I was exhausted—and sweaty—at the end of the mile run, but surprisingly also elated. This appeared to me to be a remarkable feat. The next day, I returned and ran a little more than a mile. On the third day, perhaps I was up to a mile and a half. With this, I began a life of running, soon running regularly and eventually doing four to five miles every day. In California, that privilege was exercised year in and year out. Little did I know this new regimen, which would last into my late sixties when my knees one day refused a run, would impact me in considerable, life-altering ways.

By late February, Peter, who always embodied the Jesuit mantra, *a man for others*, suggested that I might speak with a therapist and recommended I see one he knew—who apparently also worked with many other Jesuits. I called Mario DePaoli, MD, and made an appointment to visit him in his office in San Francisco. On the day, I sat in his waiting room and noticed another client about my age. I turned away, not wanting to be seen as having to bring this mess, which I must have believed others could see, to a professional! What I thought the other young man was doing there I didn't speculate!

Mario called me at the appointed hour. As we entered his office, he pointed to a small sofa across from him where I might sit. I sat on the far end, as far away as possible from the easy chair in which he had ensconced himself (he was much too relaxed, or so I thought, for what I was about to say!)

But I could not speak, nor look at him. He waited. He must have waited for much of the hour, for I cannot imagine I had much to say, other than that I was ashamed to be there. After a while: "I'm here because I think I'm gay!" I said what I had never spoken clearly before. The word "gay," dripped with a mixture of dread, snarl, embarrassment, smarm, cynicism, snark, and shame. He took it all in. After the extended silence, the hour was almost over. Mario proposed—and I agreed—to come again the following week. I departed, my eyes again downcast, walking out through his exit door, so as not to encounter others in the waiting room.

At the beginning of the next session, Mario spoke first. He said he did not want me to use *that* word again in his presence. "What word?" I asked curiously, really having no idea of what he meant. "Gay," he responded. Aha, I thought. This man, a doctor no less, was judging this condition as I had been. In response,

I harrumphed. "No," he said, "I don't want you to use that word because when it came out of your mouth, it felt like you're clubbing yourself with it, and I don't want any of that in my office. So please don't use that word in here." There was the tiniest hint of irony in his voice.

Whoa.

Though I couldn't quite see him, I was not positive this man saw me, but I was pretty sure he did. I was embarking, unknowingly, on a journey that would unalterably change the direction of my life. In that moment, and subsequently over the next two years, that premise—*You get to live your life with dignity*—was the one on which I stood. It was the starting point, in its utter simplicity, for my becoming a human being, a man, a person. The problem had never been my sexuality, either for Peter or Mario, and perhaps for others who loved me, but it was for me and for the cultures that errantly had shaped me. I began to see that the problem was, in truth, the gift to live a true, authentic life and to become one's self. To become a person.

Challenges to that newfound dignity were soon to coalesce.

7

HERE I AM, LORD

For me to be a saint means to be myself. Therefore the problem of sanctity...is in fact the problem of finding out who I am and of discovering my true self.

—Thomas Merton

THE SUMMER AFTER my first—painful and demanding—year of theology, I went back to the Midwest, first to Omaha to visit my family and witness the ordination of a friend, and then on to Milwaukee, where I had previously taught and lived. I was to return to Berkeley that fall to begin the second year of study on my way to ordination as a priest.

While in Omaha, I stayed with my parents in their spacious ranch-style home west of the city. The night of my friend's first Mass in Council Bluffs, across the Missouri River in Iowa, having been drinking, I drove my dad's persimmon-colored Cadillac—his unmistakable ultimate symbol of success—off the freeway into a concrete abutment. Somehow, I ended up in a field nearby. How I maneuvered that automobile back home remains deep in the mists of the blackout. That I survived the accident is in its own way miraculous.

Nonetheless, against all logic—one of the confounding aspects of alcoholism—and despite what happened or what might have happened, I continued drinking. And my drinking was marked by a mood of increasing darkness. I knew I was in trouble, and I had known this for some time. I knew I could not continue to drink, and I knew I did not know how to stop or even if I really wanted to. But the main thing I felt was alone.

Back in Milwaukee to see friends and twelve weeks after my accident, I spent the Sunday evening before Labor Day at our favorite haunt, John Hawkes Pub, a jazz club on the city's East Side. We were sending off my friend John Shekleton to study theology in Boston—such a sane choice, I thought, after my tough year in Berkeley, somehow conflating the city with my pain. John would have none of the many temptations of the Bay Area, I thought. The next morning, I woke up, as usual, hung over. My body was racked. I had been hosting a nine-year hangover, one day at a time—until late in the afternoon, most days, at which time I would nurse the egregious condition by having a drink.

Later that Labor Day morning, I checked out a bicycle from the Jesuit community and headed to Lake Michigan. Milwaukee's lakefront is spectacularly beautiful and there is a gorgeous drive wending its way up the lake for several miles through a half dozen wealthy suburbs. About a mile up from the celebrated County Museum, near Bradford Beach, as I was pedaling north, I was caught short. I stopped my bicycle and heard the words: *You never have to drink again*—not "you can't drink again," or "you shouldn't drink again," or "you won't drink again," but, "you never have to...." I knew in that instant—with an intense clarity—it was over.

The decade of heavy drinking, begun with earnestness in college, increased exponentially each year. Years of hangovers, years of numbing the inner critic who made mincemeat of my psyche, years of habituated responses so as not to feel these most uncomfortable feelings, were over. I knew as clearly as I do at this moment, forty-three years later, that my alcohol drinking was over. I didn't have to drink any more.

My initial wonderment: I'll never be able to go to a party again! I liked parties. And people. And singing, especially in Irish pubs. And the camaraderie that came—or seemed to come—from the sauce. But I did not doubt that it was over. I sensed that whatever it meant would be revealed in time. The next night, my second day of sobriety, I was invited to a going-away party for some recent graduates of Marquette High. I went alone to the gathering, at the Ardmore Apartments across the street from the campus of Marquette University. I got there late, and the kegs, as they so often do in Milwaukee—Beer City—were flowing. But in the kegs and their contents, I was—incredibly—not interested. I got into a conversation with a recent grad named Dave Dries, with whom I could not recall having ever really spoken, though as a former teacher I was close to some of his friends. That night, we had a most engaging conversation; I found him delightful and present. (In a recent conversation, he reminded me that Little River Band singing *Reminiscing* was one of the background songs to our conversation.) Jung would appreciate that! Unbeknownst to Dave, he was my first sober conversation, and I have held him with gratitude ever since.

In engaging with Dave, the extent of this affliction became evident. A compulsion, yes. A disease, well, yes. Self-medication, yes, and very effective, I might add. Repression, certainly, and within the cultures I lived, appropriately so. Incompatible with running, with finally respecting my body, testing my physical limits? Yes, too, and of course. And a grace, too, a gift with which I would not willingly part, for it was the necessary beginning for me of the journey I find myself still on.

I soon returned to California to begin my second-year theology and to discover what it might mean for me to live more fully. Another Jesuit and I drove from Milwaukee across the Great Plains and into the West. Crossing into the Golden State from Nevada with the incredibly beautiful High Sierra vista suggested that there were more heights to climb though little did I know how many.

Something profound had shifted in me. I have come to understand becoming a daily runner was affecting me physically, of course, but also spiritually. It was not until I began this practice that my mind, heart, body, and soul worked as an integral whole.

The integration allowed me to attend more closely to my intuition, the inner voice. Was the unconscious finally bursting forth into consciousness? Was the will to live erupting? The scapegoated child finally in full exhilarating rebellion? Was it grace? Yes, and yes, and yes again to all these possibilities.

As I settled into the first semester of year two of theology, there was raging in California that autumn a campaign over a looming election in which a heinous proposition—it might appear that this is the only form of government we exercise here in California, and there would be some truth in that—would require all schools to terminate any homosexual teacher in schools, public or private, throughout California. Proposition 6, as written, said that when a teacher was discovered to be gay, or if already out, s/he would need to be dismissed summarily and immediately.

In September, the proposition was ahead in the polls, to the alarm of many, including me. Still doing my psyche's work with Mario, using my newfound freedom from addiction to large effect, I was still—nonetheless—not fully acknowledging my sexuality. No longer in denial, just not yet embracing.

In San Francisco, Harvey Milk was the newly elected City Supervisor from the Castro district, the first out-gay person to hold elective office in the nation's two-hundred-year history. He was a gregarious and winsome character and was a close colleague of San Francisco's affable and widely loved mayor, George Moscone. Milk's central belief—political and spiritual—was that the liberation of gay persons rested on one fulcrum: *coming out.* He believed that if all gay people came out, the intense homophobia of the dominant culture would end, for everyone would discover that they knew—and often loved—a gay person(s). And they might finally begin to fully love themselves.

During that first week of October, Milk called for a campaign rally of religious leaders in San Francisco's splendid Civic Center in front of City Hall. There would be speakers, Bishop Kilmer Meyers, the rascally Episcopal bishop of California, and Willie Brown, the voluble young state senator, and a charming elderly Roman Catholic nun, Sr. Eileen de Long, the highest-ranking

Roman Catholic willing to speak in public about this proposition (and synchronously, a woman I had met nine years before, when she and some of her Good Shepherd sisters had visited the Jesuit novitiate in St. Paul, and one whom I would subsequently hire as my secretary when I would become the principal of an inner city school in Oakland the following year).

After these other dignitaries spoke, Milk came to the dais. As you will remember, if you saw the fine Gus Van Sant movie, Milk gave what was a standard stump speech for him but which to me was *cri de coeur*. I was standing far back from the speakers' platform on a small patch of grass at the immense Civic Center. Just in front of me was a young couple, one man cradling another in his arms, both about my age. I was transfixed by their openly displayed affection as Milk spoke, and I paraphrase:

> We are not here today for ourselves, because we're already free. We're here for the little boy in Fresno and the little girl in Bakersfield, kids who will go to bed tonight afraid, believing they are alone in all the world, already aware of what would happen if anyone ever found out. We are here for them!

Tears started to roll down my cheeks. I had worn my Roman collar and black clergyman's shirt to the rally, so that I might be thought of as a straight religious friend of the gay community (in whose mind?). But the tears would not stop, and I pulled out the white tab from the clerical collar, so ashamed was I that I had hidden behind the demarcating religious garb.

Milk knew about love—love denied, thwarted, judged, condemned, perjured, slandered, attacked, and marginalized. For these kids, and for me, Milk held such compassion. At the rally's conclusion, fired up by Milk and all that tenderness and beauty, I rode BART back to West Oakland that night where I was living in a Jesuit enclave within a desolated Black community, a neighborhood beleaguered by poverty and neglect, with all the attendant challenges social inequity manifests. I was glad to be living there, conscious that I was, like my neighbors on Peralta

Street, an *other*, too. When I got home to my little community, I went into my room and put a piece of paper into my Selectric typewriter and typed: *I am a gay man.* Each word meaningful.

Such a simple thing to do, and yet, it was an astonishing act. A declaration. A moment I had been unconsciously waiting for since my first inclinations at Creighton Preparatory School seventeen years earlier, when I wanted so badly to be so close to that boy in my homeroom who appeared to be, for me, everything one would want to be close to.

I had never unqualifiedly, fiercely, proudly claimed these words before. I had known them since I was a boy, but they were always a curse, an impediment, a marker, a qualifier for scapegoating. And, most significantly, a permanent blot of sin. But no more. It was over. Like a month earlier with alcohol, it was over.

I pulled that piece of paper with its newly minted declaration out of that typewriter and pinned it onto my bulletin board where I would see it every day—as if I would ever again need to be reminded. Like sobriety, another, a second gift, a manifestation, a great grace, finally acknowledging being gay. The decades of hiding, of presenting a not-quite-true *persona*, a pretending, a donning of the masquerade of being straight, of denying myself, of the many complicated gyrations designed to please others at all costs—though more intricately woven into the porous material of my psyche than the presence of alcohol had been—those decades began, with a typed word—*gay*—to unravel.

The next day, I returned to my classes at the Jesuit School of Theology, notwithstanding my keen awareness of this potent declaration. This coming out did not alter my sense of vocation, my call. I had felt this call since a boy. For some Catholic boys, this was the path we had always been on. I was a Jesuit, and I had given over my life to these men and to the One who in my heart had always been the primary object of my desire. I had, as far back as I have memory, sensed the presence of Someone whose name I could not really know but whose finger, if you will, was pointing to something just over the horizon, almost imperceptibly touching my right shoulder, nudging me on. But who knows? I trusted what I knew.

As I returned to classes, I began, at first quietly, later, not so much, to share the news of my discovery broadly. I believed that within the Society, my home for all my adult life, I could find a place and a way of ministering as a self-identifying gay man and priest. In that time of ferment on campuses, my fellow theology students were encouraging, but as my spiritual director blessed me, he warned me, too.

The provincial, the man who headed my Jesuit province, Wisconsin, would soon be arriving in Berkeley, for his annual visitation. I made the perfunctory required appointment to see him. When I shared my good news with him, he grimaced and told me to never speak of this again. I had been similarly chastised a week earlier by one of my professors whose course in Spirit—no less—had been such a revelation for me. I thought the line—*never say this again*—might have been copyrighted, and I just hadn't been aware!

The provincial did not understand what I was saying, I surmised, because this was an essential part of my humanity, and saying this was similarly essential to ending its brutal hegemonic silence. But then a clue emerged. In leaving the meeting, he addressed me by my last name. Glenn. Just Glenn. I had never had that experience in the brotherhood before, unless in jest, by close friends. And never from a man thought to be my superior. In the unsubtle use of my family name, rather than my Christian one, a plate had shifted.

As I would come to know in subsequent decades, the process of coming out is complex, and never fully completed. There are always new moments when I am invited to be fully myself to others, especially to others who might not be welcoming. But the work that began that early September Sunday night— sobriety—and that continued this early October Sunday night on Peralta Street, would change almost every aspect of my life.

Proposition 6 was defeated in the fall election of 1978, a victory of epic proportions for the gay community and, in truth, for society in general. Two weeks later, Dan White, a boyishly handsome and entitled young city supervisor from San Francisco's large Irish American community, who had recently—surprisingly—resigned his seat, decided he wanted his former job back. But the mayor, appreciating the opportunity this vacancy afforded him to appoint a more like-minded supervisor, and knowing White to hold some retrograde political views in a more liberal San Francisco, declined to reappoint him. It was well known that Moscone and Milk had created a formidable alliance during the recent campaign to defeat Prop 6, much to the surprise of old City Hall hands.

A few days later, on a beautiful sunny November afternoon, White sneaked into City Hall through an unlocked basement window. A former cop, he carried a loaded weapon. He traversed the halls of that magnificent building until he came to Supervisor Milk's office suite. He entered, greeted Milk's secretary, proceeded into Milk's chamber, and fatally shot him. He then went across the hall, into the offices of the mayor, and similarly assassinated George Moscone.

A few minutes later—White having departed, unapprehended—then-Supervisor Dianne Feinstein, as the president of the San Francisco Board of Supervisors, announced this horrific news. Word spread lickety-split that a memorial march was being planned for the city for that night, beginning in the Castro, the gay neighborhood, downhill along Market Street, the city's main thoroughfare, to City Hall. I knew I had to be a part of this march. So did several tens of thousands of others, including the mayor's newly widowed wife.

That evening I had a class in feminist ethics. At the beginning of the class, I sought out the professor, Karen Lebacqz, and explained to her why I couldn't stay. What happened next startled me. She asked me to wait a moment. She then motioned to the class, still milling about (we had been meeting in the nave of the chapel of the Pacific School of Religion) to form a circle around me. The class, almost all women, quickly did so. Of course, everyone in the class knew of the tragic events of the day, and they mostly knew, too, of my recent coming out, for there weren't that many of us. The professor asked my fellow students to place their hands on me, and as they did so, she led us in prayer. She then missioned me to go to the city, bearing the love of this little momentary intentional community, to be a healing force for the now devastated Bay Area.

Thanking them all, and fortified for the painful evening ahead, I headed for BART. I was joined by a fellow Jesuit, and we took the train to Castro Street Station. With distributed small lit candles, we marched with tens of thousands of others the several miles to City Hall. Outside San Francisco City Hall, there sits a life-sized statue of Abraham Lincoln on a large stone pedestal. The dais for speakers—as had been the case just several weeks before for the "No on 6" rally—was set up on the steps nearby. Following the speeches of several grief-stricken politicians, including Supervisor Feinstein, the recently constituted Sisters of Perpetual Indulgence—not a Roman Catholic order, but men dressed in outlandish habits with deep spiritual intent— movingly led the mass gathering in prayer. By the night's end, the statue of Lincoln was covered head to shoe with candles glowing, left by the bereft marchers, as we faced the gloomy days ahead.

That was the first of so many candlelight marches down Market Street that commemorated so many events—tragic and otherwise—that were to mark the gay community's life for the next quarter century. Over the subsequent forty years, I have marched in near all of them.

Several days later, a public memorial service for Harvey Milk was organized at the stately Temple Emmanuel in the Richmond District of San Francisco. I planned to go and was among the hundreds of mourners that filled the cavernous synagogue. After several moving speeches, all marked by profound grief and disbelief, we were invited to walk past the casket placed on the bema to bless the slain supervisor in whatever fashion we might. The casket was overwhelmed by sprays of chrysanthemums, and as I passed, I pulled two small ones from one of the many bouquets. The remains of these auburn autumn flowers reside still in a little pottery jar that graces a shelf in my study, reminding me of those tempestuous times, for me, for the city, and for the nation.

The following month, December, I flew to Omaha to celebrate the holidays. But I really flew to Omaha to give my large Irish Catholic family an unusual Christmas gift. I planned to come out to them, who, along with their spouses, numbered thirteen at that time.

I had written a coming out paper in a pivotal class, *Theology of Social Justice*, taught by the brilliant young Jesuit theologian Robert Egan. Egan regularly instructed us that to do justice in the world, we first must go inside ourselves and do justice therein. What a concept! My friend Richard Howard and I again formed a study group, and Howie encouraged me to write that paper on what was becoming my truth, my doing justice within. That was the paper I wrote, which I have ever since regarded as my coming out statement.

As I departed the Bay Area, Howie drove me to SFO. As I was leaving his vehicle, he gave me a small tin heart-shaped box. I opened it on the plane and read the note it contained, in which he offered his encouragement and love for what he knew was soon to transpire. His friendship remains a vital one, as his note to me that December morning remains prescient.

I took that coming out declaration with me to Omaha as my entrée to this personal matter, and on my second night home, asked my brothers Brian and John, both still living with my parents, if I could have time alone to talk to Mother and Dad. As cocktail hour commenced, as it had for decades at 4:00 p.m. sharp, I sat with them in the living room, each in our regular places, me *sans* drink. I handed my parents copies of this coming out paper. I asked them to read it, and then we could talk about its contents. Ever the teacher!

I sat across from them as they read, a glass of cranberry juice in hand. I watched them carefully. Mother finished first, and she folded the paper, as well as her hands, in her lap. As she saw my father finishing reading, she waited and then, looking at me, said,

"I have known this since you were four."

Silence.

Woah. "What?"

More silence.

I asked her why she hadn't ever told me this. She said, with shaky composure, "What if I had been wrong? How much might I have hurt you...with what goes on in this culture?"

Again, silence.

Then, my father stirred, and haltingly, not acknowledging the paper's what-must-have-been-startling revelation, and unwittingly channeling the Jesuit provincial, quietly said, "Now we never have to talk about this again." My mother turned her head toward him, looked at him, and said, not missing a beat, "Oh, Bill (my dad's name too), we are just beginning this conversation. It's one I believe we'll never finish."

After that exchange, which seemed to clarify things sufficiently, they both had questions and concerns, and my mother shared more about her intuition over the course of my life. She recalled events from my younger life, of which I was unaware that she was even remotely aware, that confirmed her insight. I found the conversation both consoling and amazing. And they let me know, each in their own way and in no uncertain terms, that I was a part of this family.

Over the next few days, I spoke with every one of my siblings, and they were, if similarly startled, accepting. I told my youngest brother, John, a football-playing senior at Prep—the one who I thought would find this most daunting—over pepperoni at Fred's Pizzeria, after we had watched *Saturday Night Fever* together. His immediate response: "O.K. That's cool!" One sibling told my mother later that "Billy isn't really gay. He just identifies so much with the suffering of others." Mother offered assuring words:

"No, Billy is really gay."

Christmas for me was both complicated and joyful. What did this mean for me and for my family, and what did the future hold? Perhaps I thought coming out would be an earthquake, while my family members mostly took it in stride and resumed their daily lives. They could not know what this journey home meant for me, though they had gleanings. After Christmas, I flew to Minneapolis to come out to my dear friends Art and Jo Moore. They seemed unphased and absolutely welcoming. Then on to Milwaukee, to come out to friends there. I was on a tear, a mission, and I was not going to waste one more day of my life masquerading as if I was other than who I was. My first night in Beer City, I met with my friend Dan Taylor at our old hangout, John Hawkes Pub, on the City's swank East Side. Dan had been a student at Marquette High, though not one I had taught, and we had become friends. I was nervous, holding my club soda elixir. As I said I had something important to tell him, he interrupted and told me he had something important to tell me. He then blurted out, "I'm gay!" Well, I got un-nervous very quickly, and within minutes, our years of mutual masquerade ended. Our desire to be more human and more real entered a new phase. And the synchronous sharing of this mutually vital news was not lost on me, nor Dan, whose beautiful paintings grace our home as I write these words. As does Howie's little red tin heart box.

While teaching at Marquette High, I had been close friends with several fellow teachers and their spouses. I wanted to share this news with them, too, and so I called a particular couple and asked if I might stop over. When I arrived at their home, one that had welcomed me many times before, I was greeted warmly. My colleague was not yet home, and I was invited to follow my friend, his wife, into the kitchen as she prepared some appetizers. She soon sensed my anxiety and asked me what was going on. In short, I came out to her, telling her that I wanted to share this important part of my journey with such close friends.

Her jaw dropped, literally. Her eyes filled with some combination of fear and disgust. "Are you telling me you're gay?"

"Hmm, yes."

She reacted indignantly, withdrew her person to several feet away, and told me she could not accept this and if it were true, I was not welcome in their home. I didn't bother repeating its truth, and with great pain, I left.

Similar experiences happened with two other Milwaukee families with whom I had become close while teaching there. One father, with whose family I had spent the high holy days of life—Thanksgiving, Christmas, Easter, birthdays—during my several years teaching his sons, and with whose large family I had felt close, told me point blank, "Don't ever come again. You're not welcome here."

These rebuffs hurt and were unexpected. My internal response:

But this is me! This is Billy, whom you have loved, and who has loved you! We have broken bread together too many times to count! We have mattered to each other! I need you in my life! And I love you!

I could not have predicted those who would have been naturally accepting and loving, and those who would hereafter lock me out. But those who were accepting and loving increased their presence in my heart, even as I grieved, some for many years, the loss of people who had meant so much to me.

One of my former student's mothers, having heard through the very efficient grapevine of my painful experiences, called me before I could call her. Rita Coffey, whose son, Michael, I had taught and who had subsequently joined the Jesuits himself, asked me to come over. When I rang the bell of their suburban home, Rita came out onto the porch and embraced me, letting me know by this simple and profound human gesture that I was loved by her. She assured me, and later, Scott, that we always had a home—the Coffey residence—in Milwaukee. Over the subsequent years, our friendship deepened, and Rita has remained vital for me still many years after her death. I came to understand my experiences in Milwaukee would be mirrored in the many worlds in which I lived.

Returning to Berkeley as the second semester commenced, no longer quite so afraid to be seen, I continued to see Mario de Paoli for what became really liberation therapy, and for spiritual direction, Peter Fleming, who no longer had to lift up my head. He would be the last brother Jesuit whose embrace would send me into the world with grace enough.

He had listened the previous year as I acknowledged a love in me that was stirring and felt sacred; as I came to terms with alcohol and began a life of sobriety; as I challenged a virulently homophobic visiting professor; as I worked on campus to support the ordination of women in the Roman Church; as I went from an occasional walk to becoming a daily runner; as I volunteered in a roughneck neighborhood, the Tenderloin in San Francisco; as I wrote myself into coming out; as I marched down Market Street in San Francisco on the night Harvey Milk was assassinated—me again in my Roman collar but now wearing the prerequisite Levi 501s and sneakers—as I travelled to Omaha to share my glorious news with my family who had ultimately embraced me as brother and son; and as I prepared to seek ordination officially.

That spring, as young Jesuits in the second year of theological studies, we were invited to make formal application to the province so they might subsequently seek holy orders from Rome. One could not make such final application without the prior approval of one's many superiors, a necessary winnowing out process. I asked for permission and, without comment, was invited to apply to be ordained a priest in the Society of Jesus. I did not know quite what to expect after my experience with the provincial, but I knew I had many supporters in the ranks, and I felt at peace, if my request was deferred or denied.

I had been a Jesuit for nearly ten years and had been their student for eight years prior to joining. In fact, I had belonged to them for eighteen years. Their ways, language, theologies, intellectual erudition, cultural savvy, manners, illustrious saints, deep contemplative spirituality, vision, clarity of purpose, preferential option for the poor, situation ethics, focus on the *magis*, worldliness, equal appetites for the arts and sciences, being a man for others, and life-giving brotherhood were in my very marrow. This was the way I knew much of what I knew in the world, how I knew how to be in the world. This was how I knew myself. This way acknowledged the vagaries in my personality, blessed my gifts, worked with my deficiencies, and—in part—embraced my person.

With my second, more formal letter of request, the one that would go to Rome, due on Easter Monday, I preached my first public homily at the Maundy Thursday Eucharist in the chapel of the Pacific School of Religion where the Jesuits celebrated the liturgy, having no chapel of our own. Preaching that night, I felt deeply alive and very grateful. The memorial of the Last Supper, Jesus with his friends, is in some ways the most compelling Catholic ritual of the liturgical calendar, with Jesus's washing the feet of his friends being perhaps the truest sacrament. I went home after the liturgy to my small community to write my formal request, now that I had been permissioned to do so, to be ordained a Jesuit priest. I prayed for clarity that night, mostly to be myself and to do what I could discern was God's will. Finishing prayer, I once more put a piece of paper into my Selectric and began to type, but on this occasion, nothing.

No words escaped my fingers onto the page. That which I had spent much of my life preparing for, I found I could not request. The response to my lifelong desire to be ordained a Jesuit priest was silence.

As I sat at my desk, I felt peace and an acceptance of the previous nine or more years, of the previous eighteen, and of *the all of it*, my life of thirty years.

I knew that evening that both the what and the how I was to be a true man for others, a priest, if you will, was elsewise and elsewhere. I loved the Jesuits so much; they had been for me a gift of profound proportions, an ever-extended grace. My departure would be bittersweet.

I shared my news with my beloveds, with Howie and with Joseph Powers, my beloved professor; and Jimmy Murray, who had schooled me in self-acceptance; and several other fellow Jesuits, men I had loved for many years. Those conversations were difficult and warm, and ultimately peaceful. In a few weeks, on my last day in the Society of Jesus, I wrote my Jesuit brothers a love letter, one of affection and gratitude for all that they had been and given to me and for having invited me into their company, first as a boy and finally as a man. A harder letter I have not since written. But I was to be a Jesuit no longer.

Only later did I understand that I needed—perhaps unconsciously—to apply for ordination to challenge a lifelong disbelief as to my worthiness, not just for orders, but for life. In the Jesuits, by blessing my request to be ordained, which I was earnest in seeking, and perhaps only after being affirmed, could I know that the more final and, for me, real decision was to take the path least travelled, the one that meant a life deeply imbued with all the values and the wisdom that the Society of Jesus incarnated, but to be travelled and practiced outside the borders of the order, and perhaps—at times—the Church.

Peter was one of the hardest with whom I would share this news. He had encouraged so many other young Jesuits like me to hold our heads up, to live with dignity and integrity, and to apologize to no man for our being ourselves. But, of course, he at some level already knew. I made an appointment to meet in his tiny study, just like I had two years earlier, and told him of my impending departure. He treated me with the same affection and keen respect as he had at our first encounter.

The deep joy I received from community life in the Society of Jesus was captured in the convulsive tears I shed as I read my letter of leaving in Mario's office the following day. The text of the letter acknowledged my love for my companions and the necessary pain of leave-taking that I, and they, were undergoing. I acknowledged so much about the Society of Jesus that I loved so dearly. But my life was meant to be lived in a manner still unfolding.

Years later, Peter, who had gone back to Korea to teach, returned to the Bay Area for a visit and he called. Scott and I had him over to dinner at our apartment on Oakland Avenue, after which he took us to the Ringling Brothers Circus in the Oakland Arena. He loved the circus, perhaps because he lived so much of it metaphorically. He loved that whole evening and took obvious delight in the love I had found in the person of Scott Hafner.

Later that week, Peter and I dined alone at the French/Vietnamese bistro in the Fillmore in San Francisco. We reminisced about our pasts and our fortuitous coming together. Loving food as he did, he offered me my first taste of Vietnamese cooking, as he had years before offered me my first taste of real dignity.

I never saw Peter after that night. He died a relatively young man of an undiagnosed heart condition. Without his intervening presence in my life, I could not now be writing these words some forty years later.

Gifts are given where and when they will. We are only to be present and disponible. The events that visited me throughout 1978 and into 1979 altered the outward direction of my life, while shedding more light on the ongoing interior work. Sometimes, the visitations we receive are sweet; other times, not. Afterward, and always, the work of becoming a human being remains, really only each day, one day leading into the next.

Not so long ago, Scott and I were invited to the home of my longtime friend Dan Schutte, who had been the designated *angel* on the day I entered the Society of Jesus fifty years ago. The *angel* is tasked with keeping watch over the new novice and making the person feel welcome. Dan did his job ably that year. Now, too, a former Jesuit, Dan and his loving husband, Mike Gale, were hosting a dinner party to which we were honored to be among the guests. We were there to celebrate Dan having recently been awarded an honorary doctorate by the University of San Francisco for his renowned and celebrated career as a liturgical composer. Present were several current Jesuits, including my old friend Sonny Manuel and the president of the university, Steve Privett, and several former Jesuits and their spouses.

It was a most expansive evening, and glittering, too, the candles glancing off the stemware, illuminating the faces of all present. Each guest was undoubtedly aware of the paradox and complexity of life, each in his and her own way, too, aware of the presence of Love at that table. As I reflected on the beauty of this gathering, I imagined us as a graced tableau in our desire to be but ourselves and to remain open to the voice that invites us to that seat of wisdom within, that *still small voice*, the one the world cannot know, but that—in the din of material desperation, and in the loneliness and vacuity of much of contemporary life—hopes against hope that we each listen to and discern.

Some years ago, while retreating on the desolate Achill Island off the coast of County Mayo in Ireland, I entered a rustic Catholic chapel one morning to attend Mass. My companions that day were several older women and an elderly priest. As he began the Eucharist, he started to lead us in the entrance song—no booklets instructing us—and we joined him in singing Dan Schutte's evocative "Here I Am, Lord." We all knew it by heart, of course.

The intense beauty of that meal remains with me, a tactile reminder of the breadth and depth of what my eighteen years in the Society had wrought in me in the subsequent years.

8

WHAT COULD POSSIBLY GO WRONG?

> If you bring into being that which is within you, that
>   which you have will save you.
> If you do not have it within you, that which you do not
>   have within you will kill you.
>
> —The apocryphal Gospel of Thomas

IN JUNE 1979, after leaving the Jesuits, I quickly established myself. I had the five hundred dollars I had been given upon my departure from the Jesuits, my books, and my bicycle. I entered the *adult* world, taking responsibility for *the all of it*, at the late age of thirty. I had no money, no abode, no job, no local friends. What could possibly go wrong? And yes, having no history of credit meant I could get no credit! So, I began the second phase of my adult life.

I soon found an apartment and anther community as I began worshipping at Dignity, a way station for gay Catholics, where I met many others and began to cultivate budding friendships. I missed my Jesuit companions, but I was excited to explore this new life.

I was hired to be the principal of a Catholic elementary school in Oaklands's inner city, a school with no staff since all the former teachers had quit, a pastor who drank, and no separate school budget. The parish secretary—who did not cotton to me—ran the whole parish compound. Again, what could possibly go wrong? I set about hiring teachers in early June, from what pickings were left, for an August opening. I assembled a good crew, with some exceptions that would become evident over the next several months.

On the weekends, I ventured into the Castro district, and often settled in at Alfie's, a dance bar, *my* dance bar. I loved to dance and dance I did. I dated guys I had met at both Alfie's and Dignity. Dignity was still *tolerated* by the Church, but over time, it would be banned from most dioceses, including San Francisco's, as the Church formed its intolerant attitude about gay peoples, as distinct from homosexuals: gays would be out and self-affirming; homosexuals still pliable and obedient. Obviously, I was with *the gays*.

Halfway into the school year, the pastor, inebriated, fired all the teachers at the parish retreat. The following Monday, I rehired them. The superintendent of schools, Sr. Rosemary, knew how bleak it was at my school, and when I told her I would not be signing a contract for another year, she asked if I would lead another inner-city school. I knew these problems were systemic in parishes, in which no real authority was given to the principal but always reserved for *Father*. I declined her warm offer.

Through my friend Mary True, I landed at Mercy in San Francisco, a large girls' high school. During my interview, I was asked if I was married. I said no, in fact, I was gay—and *out*. The principal, Sr. Lois, did not blanch and offered me a contract. I was to stay for the next eight years, in various capacities, being invited into administration in my second year where I functioned as *acting* principal while five principals came and went. I had initially left after one year, seeing no future for myself in Catholic schools, but when a new principal called and asked me to return—at the request of students—I reluctantly agreed.

At Mercy, I taught religion, created the counseling/campus ministry team, and served as vice principal for student services. I loved the students—constantly telling one Peggy Farrell that her gold lame shoes were *out of uniform*, but I grew increasingly uneasy in the employ of the Church, every year more retrograde.

I kept a corkboard in my office at Mercy with the quote from the apocryphal Gospel of Thomas that prefaces this chapter. I would read it every morning, wondering when I would fully act on it. Gay people were not *really* welcome in this Church. Of course, this was something of which I had now been long aware. One had to wade through the verbal jujitsu about sin/sinner, but in the end, the same reality. Working in Catholic schools was what I knew how to do and what I loved doing. But I began to contemplate a new career, and in the evenings, I earned a master's in clinical psychology at the University of San Francisco. I began accruing the necessary hours of counseling to qualify for the State of California licensing exam to become a psychotherapist. When Mercy's board of trustees terminated the fifth principal during my near decade of service there, I told the board chair—a Sister of Mercy—with whom I had a close working relationship, that I had more than qualified myself to be the school's principal. She replied, sincerely but awkwardly, "Oh, Bill dear, we know, yes, but the Archdiocese would never allow that!" And that I already knew. I announced my departure in 1988, and, luckily for me, kept my friendships with Mary and Peggy and Shirley Kaiser.

In late 1979, while home for the winter holidays at the *only* gay bar in Omaha, I met Randy. We soon fell in long-distance love. He had recently left a marriage and had as little experience with men as I. We were filled with the best of intentions, desirous to be together, our hormones raging. What to do? Randy moved to California to live with me, but soon, the challenges set in—cramped living quarters, our unexamined masculine character traits, and our own internalized homophobia—all worked together perversely to prevent a successful coupling. We didn't know how to make it work. We knew how to love each other but not much more. A relationship was just beyond our grasp. I told Randy, after several weeks, this was not working, which of course he knew. He shortly returned to the Midwest. And I sat on the stoop and wept.

The following year, while home for Christmas, I met Philip at the same *only* gay bar in Omaha. The next summer, at my request, he also ventured to California. This budding relationship again turned out to be a *nonstarter*, hopeful as we were but naïve, as it turned out, as to what a relationship entailed. After several weeks, Philip found another place to stay. Later that evening, I called my mother while sitting on the same stoop at my flat and wept. I did not know what had gone wrong. How could two loves that were so strong dissipate so quickly?

Philip Justin Smith stayed in the Bay Area, became an actor, met a wonderful man, and eventually moved with his partner, David, to Los Angeles. Like so many sweet and wonderful men in my life, Philip eventually died of AIDS. We had stayed friends and spoke on the phone shortly before his death; his sweetness and fragility still evident. At his funeral at his hometown Catholic church in northeastern Nebraska—which my sister Joyce attended as a favor to me—no mention was made of the cause of Philip's death, nor any reference to the fact that he was a partnered *out* gay man, let alone any mention of his next of kin, his partner, David, also a man living with AIDS.

After these two wrenching experiences, I wondered if I would ever have a partner, a spouse, a companion with whom to share life. I wondered what was wrong with me. I had been given these two very fine men and could not make either relationship work. In the calculus of religious guilt—an ever-present barometer—I despaired that I would have another chance.

On top of my failure to thrive in these two relationships, I had earlier stepped down—after just one year—from my teaching position at Mercy. During that initial year there, the celebrated San Francisco Gay Men's Chorus had been invited to give a concert at St. Ignatius, the college church at the Jesuit-affiliated University of San Francisco. Right-wing Catholics, learning of the concert, created quite a stir and the beleaguered archbishop forced the university to cancel the concert. This felt like a body slam to me. When it came time for me to renew my annual contract at Mercy, I declined, writing to the principal who had previously welcomed me to say I could no longer work for the Church which treated *my* people with such disdain. During my last week of the school year, to solidify my position internally and to tell my truth—for those few who did not already know—I told my many students that I was gay. The sexual orientation of my straight colleagues, their lives, their spouses and children, pictures of their family life, of the woes of married life in the faculty lounge, without, of course, having to use such clumsy nomenclature as the word *straight*, never had to come out. *Straight*? No. Just natural, in no need of identification. I was continuing in my challenging commitment not to place myself in any position in which my *person*, my essential *person*, was denied.

The following autumn, I did manual labor—with the flexible hours that would allow me to return again to graduate school and develop a profession for which my life had unwittingly prepared me. I enrolled at San Francisco State University to take some necessary prerequisites to apply.

That same fall, after Philip moved from my tiny apartment, I got sick and then grew very sick, bewildered and having no idea what was happening to me. I had no doctor and, after two years in the *civilian* world, was underemployed and without health insurance. My therapist Mario referred me to a physician in the very upscale Pacific Heights neighborhood of San Francisco. At my appointment, he had his assistant draw blood for panels. Later, he called to say I had acquired Hepatitis B, a potentially life-threatening liver infection transmitted by an exchange of bodily fluids. Apparently, there had been a mini epidemic of Hep B in San Francisco that year. His next question: "Just how promiscuous are you?" I took affront at the doctor's questions and determined not to see him again. After a decade of celibacy, I was thrilled to be among *my own* and dated several men over my first two years of *eligibility*. As with Philip and Randy, the men I dated were lovely, generous guys, many of whom were fellow refugees from the Church, as was I. As to who had this virus, and from whom among these sweet guys I had received it, there was no telling.

I was forced to bed by the powerful fatigue and nausea that soon took over my body and spirit. Having no choice but to leave my meager employment and having by necessity dropped out of the university, I found myself alone and scared. Since Hep B can survive for seven days outside the body, quarantine was recommended. I had never been alone like this before and, with the attendant emotional effects of this virus, hard days were heavily upon me.

But I was, in truth, not alone. Mario, who had seen me through my early vital work of reclaiming my life, began to drop off bags of groceries at my front door, particular attention being paid to high butterfat content chocolate for, as he said on the phone, "You need to get some fat on that body," as *wasting* was not an uncommon side effect, with a lack of appetite being the daily phenomenon. My friends at Dignity, led by the indomitable Sr. Eileen de Long, who had been my secretary at the elementary school I principled two years prior, took a collection at Dignity's Mass and paid my rent so that I would not be evicted. And Dennis, a gay doc, also a member of Dignity, began making no-fee house calls. I experienced the humanity of the gay community in this most generous and beautiful fashion. My mother regularly checked in by phone and would surreptitiously send me small checks from time to time. My father did not call.

By mid-November, I had improved markedly and could venture on my own to my doctor's office out in Concord, an eastern suburb of San Francisco. He confirmed that what I was feeling was real progress, but he recommended I still take it slowly to avoid a relapse.

I had been a daily four-mile runner since moving to California in 1977, I and missed the invigorating exercise and the endorphin high that this regimen provided. I regarded running as concomitant with sobriety and did it as faithfully as I had previously consumed alcohol. To much better results! I pleaded with Dennis for permission to run. Perhaps seeing the anticipation in my own face, he said I could do a brief run, but no more than a mile.

The next day, I put on my New Balance running shoes and drove up the canyon of the University of California's campus, parked my car, and traversed the path I had run so many times, my beloved fire trail on the top of the Berkeley Hills. I ran most likely two miles, thrilled to be back and not so tired as to quit before I had accomplished the task. At the end of my run, I returned to the parking lot, doffed my shirt, and began toweling off.

Across the parking lot, I noticed a couple stretching, about to launch their own run. The man, a very attractive guy, instead of focusing on his stretch, was focusing his gaze at me.

9

A SHARED LIFE

Love him...love him and let him love you. Do you really think anything else under heaven really matters?

—James Baldwin, *Giovanni's Room*

THE MAN STARING at me in the parking lot at Lawrence Berkeley Lab that late afternoon in November 1981 jaunted over and asked, "Run here often?" I said, "Every day at 4:00." He said, simply, "I'll see you tomorrow." The following day at 3:45, I was there, waiting. He was cute, tall, blond, iridescent blue eyes, wide smile, broad shoulders...what more need I say? At 3:58, a beige VW pulled up, and this handsome man, whose name I did not yet know, got out of his car, dressed in running clothes, ready for what was to come. Or so I hoped. We shook hands, introduced ourselves, and quickly began our run on the fire trail that overlooked UCB's campus, widening to take in the shimmering bay, through the Golden Gate and beyond.

We got about fifteen minutes into the run, and our attempts to converse and run simultaneously ended our jog. We walked and talked our way back to our cars. As we approached the cars, I asked Scott if he wanted to come over to my place. He said yes. We met up at my tiny apartment in the Berkeley flatlands and introduced ourselves properly. I had previously made plans to celebrate my friend Mary True's birthday in the city. Trusting him utterly, I asked Scott if we could meet afterward and suggested that he could stay at my place if he wanted to. He said, "Sure," and I went to San Francisco and returned with a plate of enchiladas for him. He spent the night, and as fate would have it, we have been together since that day.

We have had a complex, loving, challenging, easy, and on occasion, difficult, stretching, grace-filled life together splashed with heaping dollops of humor. After that first encounter, we never ran together again. It had accomplished its purpose, though I continued my running career for many decades.

The night of our first *real* date, I invited Scott to Mass at Dignity at St. John of God in the city. I had been scheduled to preach a homily that I titled, "Mary as an Outlaw," for that first Sunday of Advent. Afterward, we returned to Berkeley and shared moussaka, the first meal I ever cooked for him. Prior to eating, we took each other's hands and prayed a blessing, adding our concerns for the various plights of others, known and not. That became a nightly tradition we share, and I don't think an evening has gone by these forty plus years where we have not prayed together. When I got to know Scott, I observed what I would call a natural spirituality, a posture not freighted by the inculcation of formal religion's many layers of dogmatic accretion, though he was happily raised in the Congregational Church. He expresses his interior life simply and clearly and appears to have an innate trust in the wisdom of Divine Providence. I learn from him acceptance, trust, and joy, a most remarkable trait.

Several weeks after we met, he arranged a cocktail party at his parents' home in the Uplands neighborhood of Berkeley, followed by a gaggle of Hafners and friends—and me—trekking to the city to see the San Francisco Ballet's *Nutcracker* at the Opera House. When I arrived at the Hafner house, dressed to impress, Scott's mother, Mary, answered the door. She had in her hand a tray of half-dollar-sized hamburger appetizers. She introduced herself, as did I, and asked if I would like one? Those delicious little sliders became symbolic of my welcome to Scott's family. Scott's brother, Parke, and his new bride, Sarah, were there, and as I love recalling, Parke's first question, knowing that I was doing some *domestic work* while going to grad school, was if I could recommend a brand of vacuum cleaner. Scott's sister, Julie, and her boyfriend, now husband, Jack, were on the East Coast that Christmas, as was Scott's younger sister, Betsy, studying the law on her way to a stellar legal career.

Scott's parents must have had some significant questions about me and us. They noted the age difference of nearly ten years, and Scott had told them I had been *a Jesuit.* They were thoughtful but relatively inactive Protestants. I came from a large Irish Catholic family in the Midwest, a region from which Scott's dad, Richard, also hailed, but place-names many of his family members only knew from flying over—the latter of which would be difficult to change. My extensive education had been exclusively in Jesuit schools, theirs at the liberal University of California and *good* private schools in the East. I was sober three years; they, budding winemakers. I was deeply underemployed doing *manual labor*, but thankfully for me, Scott was also under-employed, by a local delicatessen creating Christmas baskets. They treated me graciously, and slowly came to know this man whom Scott had brought home.

We spent the next year hanging out, slowly getting to know each other. Early on, aware that my two previous relationships had not lasted, with the best of intentions on both sides, and already feeling fear creep in on this one, I sought out a fellow teacher, Monica Olsen, who had been married for decades and whom I regarded as wise. I asked if she could give me insight on what sustains a relationship, hoping that she would say some idealized version of love. She thought for a minute, and then she said, "Work and courage."

"Well, what else," I asked.

"Nothing," came the reply. "Work and courage every day."

I have never forgotten her instruction that has been borne out daily.

Scott often stayed in my small apartment on Hopkins in Berkeley, as he lived at home with his folks, prior to getting an apartment in the Berkeley Hills. On Sunday mornings, Scott would often get up first and go over to Brothers Bagels on Gilman and get hot poppy-seeded ones, and we would sit in bed, and nosh and read the *New York Times*. We spent some weekends travelling to some of Northern California's many sites of natural beauty—Carmel, Mendocino, and Sea Ranch. I had a television the size of a toaster, but on Sunday nights that winter we were transfixed by *Brideshead Revisited*, with its subtle theme of gay love, and became acquainted with each other's many friends. Miles, Scott's best friend since childhood, and Debbie, now wife of many decades, became our regular companions, along with Michael Foley, David Smith Fox, and Larry Tozzeo, among others.

To be *perfectly* honest, Scott had been a "hottie" at Connecticut College, his *alma mater*, on whose board of trustees he would later sit. When we first met, he spent a lot of time—I observed—sending postcards to his female besties, some of whom were decidedly not clear on the concept that he was, in fact, a gay man. Over the years, I have met them all, and they are all fine women—but there was a period of adjustment on the distaff side as they were introduced to Scott's boyfriend.

At the end of our first year together, we flew to Omaha so that Scott could meet my family. We arrived the night before Christmas Eve, just in time for my brother Doc's annual Christmas party. We went from Eppley Field directly to Doc's apartment, where several Glenns were waiting in the vestibule to greet me and meet my *boyfriend*. My family outdid themselves in welcoming Scott. We ventured up the stairs to the third-floor landing, and out of the front door strode my father. That he had not been comfortable with my being gay was clear to me, but my mother had told him earlier in that year, "You'd better welcome Billy—and whomever he brings into our home—or I can assure you, you won't see him again. We need him more than he needs us." Of course, at the time I didn't know this. And here I was, venturing with this eager twenty-four-year-old into the heart of my family's midwestern Irish Catholic Christmas. My father took one look at Scott and the first thing he said was, "Wow! You're better looking than you are in photographs!" My collective family happily breathed out. Many of them greeted him with a hug. My dad treated Scott warmly ever after, and as a tribute to both of them, my mother chose Scott to be a pallbearer at my dad's funeral seven years later.

Early the next month, Scott and I went strolling on the Embarcadero in San Francisco. We stopped at one of the empty piers and began a conversation. I proposed, not for the first time, that we move in together. Scott hesitated, finally giving a noncommittal answer, something like, "We will someday." I said I wanted to move in together *now*. I somehow communicated it in a voice that echoed through the vast and empty space. Perhaps veins were popping out, I don't really recall. But Scott knew so clearly my desire was to live together. He responded confidently that he agreed and that he, too, wanted to live together. And so, after a brief search for a suitable place, we did indeed move in together. We rented a place in Oakland and began our domestic life.

Scott manifests so many of the fine attributes one observes in an Eagle Scout, of which he is one, but attributes as found in a scout who has matured into a generous and thoughtful man and citizen. He is involved in the community—currently the chair of the board of the local health-care foundation in northern Sonoma County, the past chair of the board at the Pacific School of Religion, and active in land conservation in our beautiful rural county. He is a most faithful friend, a source of optimism and humor and hope. He has been a dutiful and loving son for his parents as they aged, his mother now deceased, and a beloved son-in-law to my long-departed parents.

During COVID, Scott has taken his ninety-six-year-old dad to do driveway visits with his old friends, and each such companion is given a large tin soup can filled with zinnias from our garden, planted in memory of his mother. And, like her, he regularly creates delectable, beautiful meals for our friends. At our annual Friends Christmas dinner, he puts on a repast that is received with the oohs and ahhs of our beloved community.

Written about elsewhere, early on, AIDS became the dominant concern of our lives, and our life together, for the next fifteen years. We progressed from relative youth to middle age under the shadow of suffering and death, as did *all* our friends in the San Francisco Bay Area. Scott began his work by caring for men dying of AIDS, being a volunteer *buddy*—support person—for several afflicted with HIV disease. As his many gifts were recognized, he eventually chaired the board of the AIDS agency in the suburban county where we resided.

In 1983, Scott went to work at the family business, Hafner Vineyard, and along with Parke, his brother, the winemaker, they have been the managing partners for this winery for many years, creating an enviable family enterprise known for their fine vintages, their generosity to the needs of the community, and for the care with which they treat their employees.

We have lived in five charming homes in four Northern California counties over the past forty years, the physical upkeep on each Scott's ongoing task. We have loved three Airedales, adored our nieces and nephews, buried friends and parents, evacuated our home several times in the face of advancing fires, and been lucky to have travelled and to have had remarkably good health.

For the first nearly thirty years of our life together, during the decades in which the benefits of legal marriage were denied to us—and all queer couples—we nonetheless created a rewarding life. Community service—considering the gravity and demands of the epidemic—occupied much of our time during the first two decades of our life together, a pattern of civic involvement we maintain to this day.

Marriage equality—and *all* LGBTQ rights—have been the subject of ugly and dispiriting political attacks and legal skirmishes over the years. Combined with the wrenching politics (e.g., internment camps, as proposed by some right-wing congressmen) of the AIDS epidemic, there has been no rest in securing, merely, our right to a dignified—and legally secure—life together. The political right has used queer people as their scapegoat for decades, *pace* Anita Bryant forty-five years ago. Trans folx are currently the right's bête noir. You'd be hard pressed to find a more heroic soul than a *trans person* who is living their life freely, with integrity.

In the absence of the right to marriage equality, Scott and I called each other many appropriate names. Sometimes *spouse*, hardly ever the ubiquitous *partner*, which sounds more like two guys who own a hardware store, but it was the title with which straight people seemed most comfortable introducing us. Mostly, I called Scott *Lover*, and he called me *Honeybee*.

We were married—finally—in the narrow window the State Supreme Court carved out in 2008 for gay marriage, following one lawsuit and prior to another state ballot proposition that coming November, in which the citizens of California would once again deny us this right to legal dignity, responsibility, and commensurate benefits. We called Scott's parents the morning of August 8 and asked them to come over to our home in rural Sonoma County at noon. Our friend, Matt Lawrence, the pastor of an Episcopal church blessed our marriage, along with a friend, Kathi, and Scott's parents. These four were the only ones present to witness our vows.

I recalled that day, preparing for this simple rite, that my mother was married similarly in a four-witness ceremony—one uncle and aunt present—when she and her first love, Lt. James T. Hogan, were married at McClellan Air Force Base in Sacramento, in early 1943, during WWII. After their marriage, Lt. Hogan was shipped off to the South Pacific and dispatched as a flight navigator and, like so many young men, was never to return home. That hot August day, Matt ratified our twenty-eight-year engagement, and we cut a small lemon cake. Mary, Scott's mother and for all of ten minutes, my *mother-in-law*, asked what she was to now call us, and the elegant word *husband* rolled off my tongue as if I had been saying it since the very beginning. Looking just a tad flustered, she readily complied. Not having another Glenn present made for a bittersweet overlay upon an otherwise joyful and satisfying day.

This was not the Hafner's first *gay marriage* rodeo. In 2004, Mary and Dick had risen at 4:00 a.m. one February morning to meet us at the Beaux Arts-designed City Hall in San Francisco after the then mayor Gavin Newsom declared it a *marriage equality* city. We stood in line with the Hafners and our friend Mark Cloutier for several hours, alongside many other soon-to-be-married couples. At one point, Mary strode off and found a Peets, and returned with a tray of hot coffees and sweet breakfast treats. She shared them with a very young Lesbian couple in front of us, two young women with no apparent family to support them. We were finally ushered into the City Supervisors' chambers, where *out-gay* Supervisor Bevin Dufty officiated at our *first* marriage ceremony. Afterward, exhausted, we travelled north to our home in Marin County, stopping on the way at an In-N-Out Burger to share our wedding meal of burgers and fries, and chocolate shakes to complete the august occasion appropriately.

It proved to be a short-lived marriage, as the Supreme Court of the United States soon declared all these historic and hope-filled marriages *null and void*. We were not surprised. We had been dealing with this homophobic culture all our lives. But they were nonetheless deeply felt. Despite, and in no small part, *because of*, the cultural milieu in which we have lived, we long ago carved out a most gratifying *marriage*, decades before the rite became accessible. But we learned to do this, and the learning was not so simple. Scott has been a patient and resilient partner, and a husband of great warmth and love. He brings to our marriage, sweetness, humor, and optimism. Each day he emerges from our bedroom upbeat and welcoming the new day. On some days, it astounds me! Our routines, refined over a long time together, are comforting and necessary, as all couples know.

Two men, perhaps like all couples, but with significant differences, have to figure out *how* to make a viable, loving, and resilient couple. Gay men do so in a world that is at best mildly supportive, typically ambivalent, and at its worst, hostile. But that hostility and ambivalence have been shadowed gifts, for we were clear coming into this, that we—not supportive institutions nor religious blessings nor legal ratifications nor even always family—would provide the level ground and the foundation for our life together. Neither of our mothers ever got a phone call telling them what a miserable partner we had. Having to trust each other strengthened us in ways we could not have imagined that remarkable November day in 1981.

Throughout our marriage, Scott and I have had to sustain a big bucket of re-learnings, of virtues we thought we already had, patience and humility strong among them. Forgiveness had to become the daily coin of the realm. One of the many gifts Scott has given me—from the very beginning—is the art and practice of forgiveness. Whenever we would have a painful encounter, with regrettable words exchanged, he would say, before the end of the day, "I am sorry for my part in our difficulties." I had never experienced such a thing with a man, perhaps with anyone. Two healthy—or unhealthy—male egos must contend with their counterpart, whom they might call *Lover* or *Honeybee*, or on a different day, something a bit less elegant and kind. There are no textbooks, I can assure you, that suggest how to make it through these thickets. Anger needs to be tolerated and negotiated; vulnerability acknowledged and cherished; regression allowed; and space has to be made.

Resistant family members have to be acknowledged and negotiated with, or, as often the case, around. The shadow of the culture, encountered in ways large and small, on most days, had to be identified so as not to poison the marriage and the home. Age differences and the different stages of maturational development that accompanied them had to be acknowledged but not canonized.

The often unspoken but deeply imbedded traits of shame the culture implants in gay children remain as gay boys grow up. Scott and I had not escaped this shaming. We suffered it differently; we came from different home lives, were raised in different religious cultures, and had differing relations with our respective families. But negotiating the effects of shame has been, from my perspective, the single most challenging aspect of the formation of our healthy and loving marriage. The defenses we build to survive are the very ones that limit the flourishing of love. They need to be recognized, often living in the shadow of our lives, then teased out, their nefarious effects forgiven, their repeated return tolerated over and over, forgiven again and again, over the lifetime a couple is invited to share. Shame needs to be identified and acknowledged and its horrific claims on the soul recognized by daily living through it in the presence of another, in our case, each other.

So, being seen together in public places—as we are quite often—can render a look of disgust from homophobic individuals.

The many words that slur gay men can be uttered in an instant, even under one's breath, and instantly trigger this shame. Inviting a repairman into our home—how often does this happen?— always raises the possibility that something untoward might happen when the workman eyes an indication that the couple whose home he is in are two...what, men? Really, ad nauseum. But nonetheless, and partially because of *the all of it*, what we have is a life, a married life, a unique-to-us life, and a graced and contented life. Scott will often say, out of the blue or so it seems to me, in a moment of otherwise shared silence, "We have a pretty good life together, don't we?" Not a question, really, an affirmation. And I respond, because thankfully it is true, "Yes, we do."

We have been at this for four decades, and we are still learning, making mistakes, delighting in each other and in our life together, apologizing and forgiving, bearing each other's wounds and moods, and holding each other in tenderness. And when sorrow invades our lives, as it often does, we make space for that, too. Our gratitude for each other is bedrock—lucky, blessed, fortunate, and graced beyond measure. As for humor, it has been the sine qua non without which none of this careful navigating would have taken hold.

For our tenth anniversary, thirty years ago, I wanted to get Scott a special gift to mark the occasion. Jewelry was out of the question! He doesn't even wear a watch. I decided to ask him what he'd like, thinking I would get him a deluxe version of whatever his request might be.

So, I asked. He listened to my request, thought for a minute, looked me in the eye, and said, "Would you please never again say, after we've had an argument, that you're *pretty sure we don't have a real relationship.*"

Hmm. Not something I could get at Gump's, and costing me a little more than I bargained for. *Deluxe* was not quite the appropriate word. But I never said that offensive and condescending thing, or its many facsimiles, again. But of course, we have said other things. Among them, with regularity, *I love you.*

10

AIDS, MEDICINE, AND MIRACLES

Believe in miracles and cures and healing wells.

—Seamus Heaney

SOME TIME AGO, I was asked to give a keynote at an assembly entitled "AIDS, Medicine, and Miracles." The paradoxical title was created by my friend Gregg Cassin, the convener, while sitting at Café Flor in the Castro, where he has served as the district's unofficial mayor for years. He is ensconced there with his laptop propped open, though I've never seen him touch the keys. He holds court, and we, his faithful subjects, come to bid his blessing or to dish as we go about our days.

I've known Gregg, a Boston College grad, since 1980. We are still here, forty years later. Back then we were talking about everything, but two years into our conversation, it changed. We started talking about a word we would have never chosen to know: *AIDS.*

Now, I do not have AIDS nor do I have HIV, but I am, in some manner, a longtime survivor. While the virus has not breached my body, it breached my soul long ago. I have no opportunistic infections, but somehow, I became *infected*, not by the virus, but by this epidemic.

When I speak to groups concerned with the epidemic, I begin by saying,

> I stand before you as one of you in every way that matters but one. I am your brother. I am your witness. I am your scribe. I am your counselor. I am your friend. At least to some of you. And to some of you who are not here. Some of you gone thirty years. To some of you who will easily outlive me. But it is not about our eventual dying that we are concerned. It is about our living. It is about finding out just who we are in light of, in spite of, because of, and over against this epidemic that has done much to define the lives of each of us and to the many who will read these remarks.

This epidemic also relates to our anniversary. As I write, we approach the AIDS epidemic's notorious fortieth anniversary. The traditional gift associated with this anniversary is the ruby. And we know about rubies, do we not, as we learned from Dorothy in *The Wizard of Oz*. Those Wicked Witch-besotted ruby slippers were the key to her getting back to those who loved her, away from the madness—and wisdom—of her journey, not so unlike our work these forty years.

In February 1982, I was sitting in my studio apartment in Berkeley reading the *Advocate*, the national newspaper that was about all things gay. At the bottom of the front page there was a short article about a doctor in Los Angeles who had seen several people, five as I remember, all gay men. They had each developed a rare cancer seen primarily in old men in the Mediterranean. The article said little more. I shared it with Scott that night. We thought little of it. But in the weeks and months to follow, physicians in San Francisco, Los Angeles, and New York noticed this deadly cancer, Kaposi sarcoma. Within a year, they named the disease *GRID—Gay-Related Immunodeficiency Disorder*—having identified several symptoms in addition to this cancer: a rare pneumonia called pneumocystis; toxoplasmosis, usually associated with cats; and wasting, for which there was no specific clinical term, though in Africa this disease became known as the slim disease.

The week I read that article, Scott and I had been together just two months. He was young, a year out of college and I was three years out of a Roman Catholic seminary. What did we know? Very little, it turned out. But soon we learned much more. Not just about what would be called AIDS, and medicine, but about the miraculous, too.

Through the lens of this mysterious, voracious, and instructive virus, we would come to know about ourselves and much about the world in which we live.

Those who lived in the Bay Area or other large metropolises will remember how scary those early years of the epidemic were. No one knew how AIDS was transmitted or who had contracted it, how dormant the symptoms might be or how they were spread. Was it poppers? Was it kissing? Was it sex? If so, what kind of sex? Some thought sharing needles was the culprit. Was it blood borne? My God, the nation's blood supply! You can only imagine....

Gay people were just starting to *come out* in numbers. Stonewall was in the recent past. Decades of fear, pain, hiding, and lies were being turned aside. Folks were flocking to big cities like San Francisco for some measure of safety, community, and love, and then: Wham! Right in the face. Wham! At the groin. Wham! In the heart.

Sex, this throbbing life force and elemental, instinctual connector of human beings, this root of delight, sensation, and love-spreading energy suddenly, with no warning, out of nowhere meant death, disease, or plague—about the worst anyone could have imagined. This small beleaguered and fragile community of boys and girls, young men and young women, and some older queens (I say with deep reverence, as they watched over us) shuddered as this tidal wave of scourge hit our cities.

The men—and they overwhelmingly were men—who were infected early on were young, not long out of the closet, and were filled with *a significant amount of self-loathing*, raised as they had been to mirror the social mores of the culture in which each of us had been, to see ourselves as the worst imaginable and most maligned of human beings. Just a few years earlier, I had believed that I—and people like me—were sick, repulsive, disgusting, shameful. Maybe you used these words yourself? Maybe on your worst days you still do?

To add insult, the churches added other words: the dark twins *immoral* and *evil*; the state provided *illegal*; medical science offered *abnormal* or *perverted*; and families added *ashamed*. Not a few kids were kicked out, as some still are, and some took their own lives, as some still do. *The all of it* led and leads to a deeply degraded self-image that is most profoundly damaged and wounded. You couldn't write fiction like this.

In 1982, it was these young men just coming into their own, into some measure of self-respect and into the light after so many years in the dark. That's a miracle, no? This miracle was quickly turned on its head.

Many of Scott's and my friends became very sick, bad and quickly. Our friend Randy Harvey started to lose weight. A good-looking man and charming, and not wanting to appear ill, he hid his weight loss with extra layers of clothing and a little blush. With no noticeable symptoms. Michael Foley, who was like a *queen mother* to me when I came out, returned to his native Manhattan to await the inevitable. My friend, Steven Swanson, the wrestling coach at a Catholic boys' high school, who was as cuddly and kind a person as can be, got sick. Even as he deteriorated, he told no one, not wanting to jeopardize his job and his insurance. Another Steven, after having gotten clean and sober and with tools to deal with the emotional onslaught after receiving his diagnosis, eventually found it too much and returned to his drug. He was found dead in his garden. He was thirty-nine.

The body of Ken, an ex-boyfriend of mine, became ravaged with the afflictions of AIDS. His legs became bloated and were covered with the lesions of Kaposi sarcoma, encrusted with scaly pus. Getting out of bed became difficult and painful. He lived in a cocoon of fear and was near inconsolable. But his main symptom was shame. His parents had jettisoned him when he had broken through the closet doors several years before. He died bereft of familial love. I preached his memorial service at Most Holy Redeemer in the Castro. Although he was from a large Catholic family—one of six children, with parents still living—we were his family that day.

These friends were often émigrés from other states with no real resources, living alone or in pairs in small apartments throughout the city, and whose health-care system was totally unprepared for an epidemic within a resistant society feasting on its bigotry. We all have similar stories: friends healthy, then sick, then dying, and a culture of silence. There was the stench of fetid limbs and broken hearts and constant death in the air. Where was the curative medicine? Where were the miracles? What were we to do?

One day in the *BAR*, the gay rag that was published in San Francisco every Thursday (*purple* day, *pansy* day, *queer* day), I read an ad for volunteer counselors to give AIDS test results to men who had been participating in a longitudinal hepatitis-tracking study. This cohort of young gay men had given blood in the late 1970s, and when a test for HIV antibodies was developed, it was possible to test their now frozen blood for this newly named human immunodeficiency virus. This was the first HIV antibody testing program in the nation. I volunteered to be a counselor for these men and trained to deliver this sacred information—sacred in the darkest sense because, in 1984, a positive result was tantamount to a sentence of death. It was ominously named the San Francisco Gay Men's Health Study, but health it did not foretell.

There were no drugs, prophylactics, or *cocktails*, no course of treatment or vaccine, nothing but palliative care from the day of diagnosis and a relatively swift path to the end. Everyone knew this. It was a wonder anyone would want to know their results. We counselors worked on Tuesday evenings, and one by one these young men—my age—would come and be told by the likes of me, a total stranger, whether he was positive or not. The ones who were negative were hugely relieved. The ones whose blood had tested positive responded in a variety of ways: from the stoic to the furious to the sobbing to the utterly blasé. I could offer little comfort or solace. There was no real help in sight. There were no miracles to record. The men I shared results with were mostly in their early thirties, had donated their blood in their mid to late twenties. They were the émigrés, fit and full of life. I remember one man crying so hard and finally saying, "I am all alone."

What were we to do?

As the numbers mounted, and they did so weekly, small clusters of women and men, mostly from the gay community, but others as well, began supporting the burgeoning number of people with AIDS (PWA). Organizations were founded to provide care and relief and to assist those infected with the exigencies of living and the *work* of dying. I called the largest of these, the San Francisco AIDS Foundation (SFAF), to volunteer. In 1984, I was invited to go on their board. Calling the foundation was my response to our friend Randy's diagnosis. I remember a moment earlier that year when a friend told me that I should no longer kiss any gay man. I had waited thirty years to kiss men! I thought to myself: *If I risk getting the virus from kissing, so be it.* The next time I saw Randy, I planted a big wet one on his lips. I had waited *too long* to be a man-kissing man and never looked back.

I knew that *everyone* was needed in the AIDS epidemic, and that the only way to emotionally survive this was to be as near to the epidemic's heart as possible. Psychology has long identified the human response to danger, *flight or fight*, and the epidemic poised that threat like nothing else. We had friends move away, friends who said, in response to yet more deaths, "I don't do funerals." I had a friend say to me one afternoon, while taking each other's leave, "Well, I'll let you get back to *your* epidemic." My epidemic! Well, it was, but it was his, too, though he didn't want it to be. It was all of ours, and still is, in all its complicated manifestations.

Most of our friends jumped in. Scott and my mother-in-law, Mary, became emotional support volunteers and both graduated to become board members—Scott in our home county,

Contra Costa, and Mary, who joined me at the SFAF, as did my friends Deary Duffie and Jude Sharp. A former Junior League president, Mary got into the AIDS trenches and never blinked. My in-laws, Parke and Sarah, raised a victory garden for the local AIDS food pantry, and then raised money to build that pantry a home. Women and men began making and delivering hot meals to the homebound, taking care of the pets of the infirm, offering accommodations to visiting relatives, legal counsel to the sick, collecting pennies for service organizations, providing transportation to and from medical appointments, offering hospice care to the fragile, staffing the be-sainted facilities at San Francisco General Hospital and other institutes of healing, serving on boards, going into the homes of gravely ill strangers to assist with bodily functions, to hold hands, to cheer hearts, to relieve souls, to swab decaying limbs, and to close the eyelids of the *now in this moment* newly deceased.

In Omaha, my family annually hosted a large dinner as part of the Nebraska AIDS Project's *A Night of a Thousand Stars* gala, putting card tables in every room, while my sibs and their spouses created a festive meal. My mother—compromised by *poliomyelitis*—regally presided over the whole affair from her chair in the family room.

These were the everyday tasks performed by thousands of citizens, neighbors, brothers and sisters, angels, human beings doing the only thing possible for those in need: providing love. And this was soon happening everywhere there were PWAs. This was AIDS. This was the only medicine; this was the emerging miracle.

The furious pace of the epidemic became that of Scott's and my life, as well. AIDS defined our external world and worked its way inevitably into our internal lives. We were keenly aware that we had not contracted the disease, grateful for this, of course, as we prayed nightly for those we loved, and over time, mostly lost. A certain pall hung over us, though it was plentifully marked by the campy and wise humor that is a salvific aspect of gay life. Illness and death are sobering. Constant illness and death are debilitating.

Ronald Reagan, the faux-cheery landslide president, could not say the word *AIDS* for the first several years of the epidemic. It was well into his second term before he could utter this monosyllable, after tens of thousands of citizens had died, and then, only because his friend Rock Hudson had acquired the virus and, with his gaunt self, went public. As the full force of the epidemic became the wary concern of local public health officials in the United States, the national government was silent. At the SFAF, we compensated for the government's tragic malaise. We raised money any way we could. We had walks and runs and dances and dinners and garage sales and booths at street fairs and phone-a-thons and endless direct-mail campaigns. We did whatever was imaginable to scrounge the necessary dollars to sustain the work. And every other AIDS organization—local and national—did the same.

Castro Street was increasingly marked by emaciated young men walking with canes, skinny bodies dwarfed in well-worn 501s. Angry young men and women founded ACT UP to do whatever it took to address government inaction and to draw attention to this tsunami of an epidemic. At the Foundation, we organized needle exchanges in the Tenderloin to teach junkies to clean their *works* and to slow the infection rate. We worked with *working girls* of all genders to demand the use condoms. This was AIDS. This was the only medicine available. And let me assure you, there were miracles.

When I joined the board at the AIDS Foundation, I was vice principal at Mercy High School. Our counseling team organized the first on-site student forum on AIDS in any San Francisco school, public or private. We required the whole student body to attend. That day, on the stage of the school auditorium, my friend Pat Christen, then an AIDS educator, later a national leader in the epidemic, went to the podium and warmly greeted our girls. Then, without ceremony, she pulled a banana out of her large bag, she took out a package of condoms, and after opening the cellophane, she began to demonstrate the effective way to place a condom *on a banana*, so as—*via* the grounded metaphor—to teach our students how to prevent the transmission of the virus.

Several of the Sisters of Mercy, whose school it was, were in the auditorium that afternoon. Unlike some other *seemingly* responsible adults, they knew their primary job in this early stage of the epidemic, and at this early stage of development of their charges, was to keep our students alive. They took Pat's instruction on how to *condom* the banana in stride. They knew they were doing the good Lord's work that day. For this, too, was AIDS; this, too, was good public health medicine. The courage of these religious women was a miracle.

The next year, I transitioned from my decade of work providing leadership in Catholic schools to what was becoming apparent was the deeper work to which I was being called. I had returned to the University of San Francisco the same year I went on the board at the SFAF and completed my graduate degree in clinical psychology. I began a private practice in psychotherapy, working primarily with men who discovered that they had this dreaded and deadly virus. It was confounding work and I had had no training *for this*. Young people are supposed to grow up, to thrive, have dreams, and fall in love. They are not supposed to die, not in such great numbers. And most certainly, not in such dreadful ways.

Most discouragingly, many of my clients regarded AIDS, with deep pathos, as a punishment, as a consignment of their lives to the death chamber, some affront to the Divine, some insult to humanity. It confirmed for them that being gay was deserving of disdain. It was a violation of some immutable natural law. And of course, the forces of darkness in the world, who mistakenly believed they were forces of light, swept in with their condemnations and assaulted the dying, who too often believed this indeed was the result of their heinous crime, their piteous lives.

During the burgeoning days of politically agitated homophobia, a strategy effectively utilized for decades, I remember that the former beauty queen Anita Bryant, then a spokesperson for

Florida orange juice and an antigay fomenter, was quoted in *Newsweek*, calling gay persons *human garbage*. The men in my office, now afflicted with this disease with so many cultural components, had been young when Bryant began her reign of terror, supported by her dark minions. They had, as had I, been infected by this other most virulent virus, the precursor of the biological one that would ultimately take their lives. The great freedom that *coming out* and coming to San Francisco had provided now seemed to be a surreptitious comeuppance, the dooming lie beneath the prospect of a life openly lived.

However, to be present with a human being near death, one struggling to make sense of a life held in contempt by others, at times including one's own family, was a humbling grace.

Ken, for example, had used his charm combined with his good looks to win over many men and women. As his disease progressed, this just recently compelling body had become a visible wasteland. Toward the end, he could not leave his bed, but he would put moisturizer on his once-beautiful face and proclaim, "One has to keep up appearances!" while we tended the ravages on his body. One afternoon shortly before this death, he asked if I would get up on the bed and hold him. I said "Of course." As I snuggled next to him and pulled his ravaged body in to mine, he trembled with the accumulated fear he held inside. And he sobbed, as did I. This was not how he, nor any of us, could have imagined our fate. He was thirty-five years old.

The enormous courage and self-effacing honesty of these women and men put to shame all those who trod so falsely—and hypocritically—on their good names. This was the emotional reality of this disease. This was AIDS, the medicine yet scarce, but their abiding humanity was the miracle.

The real offense that unleashed this hatred, applicable whether we are gay, lesbian, bisexual, transsexual, queer, questioning, or not knowing but hopeful, was and is the shattering proclamation that any two human beings might love one another, over against all the forces in the world committed to isolation, greed, numbing, control, and fear, and over against all who shout *No!* This earth-shattering and authority-defying *No!* This was, is now, and will always be, the miracle.

I served on the board at the San Francisco AIDS Foundation for six years until late 1991, the last three as president. To climax that work, Pat, the then executive director, and I went to Washington, D.C., for a confab with the leaders of the largest national AIDS organizations: New York's Gay Men's Health Crisis, AIDSAction Boston, AID Atlanta, AIDS Project Los Angeles, AIDS Foundation Chicago. Others sent representatives. The board presidents and executive directors had committed to civil disobedience in front of the White House, protesting the Bush (41) administration failures to adequately address the epidemic. We began our day at the New York Avenue Presbyterian Church, and as we assembled for our instructions, I scurried to find Abraham Lincoln's name-plated pew. I placed my butt where his might have been and took my inspiration from his wise and valiant leadership. Several score of us were arrested on that World AIDS Day, December 1, 1990. We squatted down on Pennsylvania Avenue and did not get up when the constabulary so advised. We were then handcuffed and led onto large buses for transport to a police facility for arraignment. Placed into a cell with several other male AIDS leaders, we chatted about the unforeseen place our work had brought us, and to the now eight-year dark reign of this epidemic. A cellmate that day, a San Francisco gadfly working in another more "street" AIDS organization, took the opportunity to let me know the SFAF wasn't doing enough either! That, too, was the epidemic.

I found the experience of sitting with my respected peers, among them Tim Sweeney, then head of GMHC and a friend, both moving and humbling. They ultimately dropped charges against us. But significantly, after my many years of being involved, it had come to this: our asses on the pavement of this street to motivate government into action so that our friends would stop dying in such great numbers. After eight years, we were still waiting for sufficient federal assistance.

For the next several years, I primarily saw gay men in my private practice with HIV; Scott had risen to become the chair of the board of the AIDS Project in Contra Costa County, the key service provider where we now lived; Parke had become chair of the board of Food for Thought, a conveyer of life-giving resources for people with AIDS in Sonoma County; and Mary, having moved north from Berkeley to Healdsburg with my father-in-law, Richard, volunteered to provide emotional support for a young man living with AIDS. She called one evening with the question, "What is crystal meth?" The answer and its implications for her work were not simple. Nevertheless, she stayed with that young man, *in loco parentis*, until his death some months later.

The winter following my departure from the board of the SFAF, I was asked to provide *interim* leadership for a hands-on health-care agency aptly named Continuum, in the heart of the Tenderloin, what I often call San Francisco's *soft underbelly*. Walking on the slickened brick sidewalk in a downpour in the historic United Nations Plaza that first morning, I pulled open the front doors of No. 10 and had the powerful intuition that I had *come home*—I stayed for the next seven years. Each year, the center of the epidemic moved slowly down Market Street from the Castro, a few blocks at a time, and now its truest home lay in the Tenderloin. At Continuum, we welcomed those with triple diagnoses: HIV disease, substance abuse, and mental illness. Not all we served were afflicted by all three and some also had a fourth or fifth diagnosis. We formed a community—a medical, a social, a recovering, and a spiritual community. We had scores of *members*, as we called each other, members of this caring community as the epidemic raged so fiercely outside our doors. But as was the virus's want, it seeped in, and we lost on average one member a week, every week, for each of those many years. We served gay men and, mirroring the increasing infection rate among people of color, many Black women and men, and trans folx, denizens of those mean streets. We provided the only apparent shelter for numerous street people and the many who lived in the area's bleak Single Resident Occupancy (SRO) dive hotels who came to regard Continuum as their real home.

We provided medical care, mental health support, three meals, physical therapy, a robust art program, substance abuse services, a daily morning community meeting with a spiritual focus, and a beautiful facility that our supportive community built. This was the bleak time, post-AZT but pre-protease inhibitors, pre-cocktail. But hope we nonetheless had, and joy, as well as pain, and suffering, and order, and chaos, and, like a big Irish Catholic family, or an African American extended family, or smaller Jewish family, or two-lesbians-with-their-three-kids family, like most families, there was plenty of dysfunction but plenty of underlying love. At the end of the day, it was a community whose sole undergirding was love. It kept us alive or helped some of us die with dignity, and it allowed some of us to be buried with grace, never alone. Furthermore, should death occur while with Continuum, no one would be forgotten or die unloved. This was a miracle, and a miracle in the bowels of the Tenderloin.

By the mid to late 1990s, when prophylactic medicines finally arrived, like the delayed cavalry, there had been a dozen years of plague, and people were exhausted, beyond tired. Multitudes were dead. Some hoped the epidemic would be declared over, and all wanted the suffering to end. Lives that were previously called out were now given a shot at time. Organizations morphed to focus on the new realities that living with and managing HIV meant. Agencies combined, changed, and some appropriately closed. Hospitals adjusted and many PWA's grew much healthier. Gaunt people began gaining much-needed weight. Opportunistic infections could now be managed and jobs were reclaimed. So much had finally changed that demonstrated the many profound miracles in this. But the epidemic did not end.

I met David Smith Fox at a supper following the Jesuit School of Theology Maundy Thursday service, at which I had been asked—as a scholastic—to preach. Later that weekend, I would make my decision not to seek ordination, and leave the Society of Jesus. Some months later, David and I went on a date, one of my first. At the end of the evening, he said to me, "We could date for a while and then break up, you know, like people do, or we could become friends that would last a long time." David was prescient.

David had been the faithful longtime companion to his partner, Bill Kenkellen, both of whom had lived with HIV for many years. One evening in early 1992, we gathered around Bill's sick bed in their apartment on 15th Street. We gathered to assist Bill in his transition from life to death and what may lie beyond. A cradle Catholic, his Irish mother and a sister had come from Philadelphia to provide their son and brother comfort. Several of us, friends of David and Bill, were also present in the room. Bill's sister had brought blue Day-Glo rosaries for everyone, and David asked if I would lead the prayers.

These vigils, regular but never routine, combined the holiness of the sacrament of the sick with the sometimes irreverent warmth of a gay Irish wake. Here we were, a small group of kin—family and friends—in this elegant city apartment, kneeling around the bed of a man who was *too young to die*. The room was bathed in candlelight. We proceeded to pray the Rosary, a repetitive medieval chant, for this man we loved. At David's request, I began with the ancient creed and the quickly formed congregation responded with the string of well-remembered prayers. We prayed through the five *mysteries* as they are called, and mysteries they were, as was this whole saga of AIDS.

After prayers, and with Bill still breathing that very labored breath of the near dead, we took turns reading from the poetry of William Butler Yeats, the Irish revolutionary bard whom Bill, a self-styled rebel himself, loved. He took his last breath hearing the words of the poet, the candles flickering, this makeshift community of love silently present, some softly weeping, others carefully drawing his eyelids down over his eyes, and reverently placing the sheet, out of the deep respect for human life and death, over his face. Bill died, steeped in David's love, and the love of a beleaguered community of friends, another of the unheralded stories of gallant love that the epidemic silently recorded.

David had been the consummate caregiver. He had left his employment as an attorney in San Francisco to tend to Bill's needs. Bill was a cranky sort, fastidious and very private, but he let David, *Mr. Gregarious himself,* care for him for the many months it took for his spirit to leave his body. After Bill's death, David was lost. He could not return to work. He, too, had HIV and was a spent man. He descended into the dark edges of the community where numbing agents and self-loathing intermingle. He withdrew, lowered his shades over his windows, and stopped communicating with those of us who loved him. His caring sister, Catherine, and I made a pact to look in on him periodically to ensure, if nothing else, that he was alive. He took on Bill's cantankerousness and his penchant for privacy but forgot to claim the fastidiousness and rebelliousness that Bill had been. This went on for several years. David seemed lost to the living.

David experienced the ravages of this cursed and blessed epidemic. With his charming and impish personality and his extraordinary caregiving self, he nonetheless could not sustain himself. The church of his youth, to which he once aspired to be a priest, had made itself—in essence—unavailable to provide any honest spiritual succor. The community he loved, LGBT people in the Castro, was dying or tired and often increasingly finding those same numbing chemicals that David found, no-brainer antidotes to years of plague and bigotry and piled-up death.

I was angry at David, and I missed him terribly. I felt hopeless and powerless to make a difference with him, or even for me—for anyone. David felt dead to me. And he was not the only one. Many who had survived the poisoned grip of the virus succumbed to subtler and more onerous *diseases*: addictions of many kinds, isolation, the durable effects of trauma, the additive nature of accumulated grief, and the loss of hope. And like AIDS, these diseases expanded silently and multiplied exponentially in this rare seedbed of self-loathing and disregard that has always been the true epidemic in this growing queer community. These were adults convinced that they are damaged goods. These were adults—once children—convinced, listening to their parents or the preachers tell them that they were sick, responsible for their own *lesions*. They grew convinced that their future—if at all—was murky, far away, and fundamentally and ultimately to be lived alone.

But this even more insidious epidemic was not to claim David. His *elan vital*, his humility and the grace that enveloped his life eventually won out. One day, in early 2001, David emerged from his years in that darkened cocoon. He found the 12-step program, immersed himself in its wisdom and fellowship, and became, honestly and movingly, *light*: a transformed being, a beacon, a truth teller, a bodhisattva, a force of love. Everyone who encountered him knew it, and, as it says in scripture, *were sore amazed*. He was alive—finally, fully, and forcefully. He made Spirit Group his spiritual home and became the emotional center of that blessed group of women and men. He was by now fifty years old, but he was newborn. Like Lazarus, he had come back from the precincts of death to the land of the living. We easily regained our friendship, and Café Flor, the social center of the Castro, again found us sitting on its ample patio, chatting, hoping, and sometimes crying. Like Gregg, David knew everyone, so our table became a reception desk, folks stopping by, many to marvel at David's renaissance.

David celebrated Thanksgiving in 2002, eighteen months into his new and hard-won life, with friends. We had spoken earlier that day and were looking forward to spending Christmas in each other's warm company. He went home early from that Thanksgiving table, not feeling well. He called me the next morning to say that he felt bad and was going to see his doctor. That night, he was hospitalized at Davies, a few blocks north from his home on 15th Street. He never returned home.

I visited him several times in the next couple of weeks. While his spirit remained light, his body was clearly failing him. At one point, he took off the Claddagh ring that he, a true Irishman, had worn, and gave it to me as a sign of our long friendship and our graced love for each other. It now resides on my right ring finger. The end was to come in a matter of days.

On the Feast of Our Lady of Guadalupe, his sister, Catherine, who had been present when we fingered our rosary beads at

Bill's bedside many years earlier, called and suggested we get to the hospital. David's remaining time appeared to be short. Scott and I called Mark Cloutier, Guy Vandenberg, and a few other close friends and met at Davies Hospital on Castro Street. We proceeded to his room, yet another bathed in candlelight. We gathered around him as the combination of years of virus and other body invaders took its toll. Nonetheless, David, though now in a coma, remained a witness to something light, large, and true. Present in the room when we entered were some of his siblings—and our friends—Catherine, Greg, and Anita, and various nieces and nephews, and friends of theirs. This was a worn group of men and women, worn down by death, by exhaustion, and as they say in Ireland, by *the all of it.*

At Catherine's request, I had brought some chrism, holy oil our rituals of death had blessed, oil used to anoint other men's bodies over the past sixteen years, including that of his beloved Bill. We anointed David's body, each person thumbing the holy nard and making a blessing on his beautiful person, as we each prayed for him. He breathed those deep and labored breaths. After our anointings, we each took moments alone with him to say our farewell.

Taking my place at the end of the line, I wanted to postpone this for as long as possible. As others departed, I went back into his room and held this dear man in my arms and thanked him for being my friend, my longest California friendship that began in the spring of 1978. I kissed him, cried softly, combed his thin hair with my hand, and finally left his side. He waited till after we had all departed Davies that evening, in a manner the dying so often do, to breathe his last.

Some days earlier, he had asked me to help organize his funeral, as he anticipated what I could not comprehend, and to deliver the eulogy. He gave me only one instruction: "Billy, tell the truth." The truth is complicated, and it is simple. The truth is that there are dark forces within and without that always need to be contended with, for they can take us down. They do their dirty work not only on our bodies but on our souls, but they do not have final power, and they do not have the final say. There are even deeper truths at work. The revealed truth is that the miracles are everywhere.

We gathered at the glorious St. Ignatius Church on the campus of the University of San Francisco, the Jesuits graciously giving it over for a memorial service. The gathering was large—for as mentioned, David had known *everyone*. True to my promise to my friend, after family members had offered tender prayers for David's soul, and for us, his beloveds, for our needs for comfort and solace, I approached the pulpit. I *preached* as David had asked, speaking of both the darkness he suffered and the tremendous light that once and again radiated from his face, his heart, his presence.

During my remarks, I noticed a woman enter the side chapel and take her place among the mourners. Immediately after I left the altar, as the service ended, I went over to her and we embraced. With no makeup, not wearing any of her stunning red and cantaloupe-colored outfits, her head shrouded with a dark scarf, Nancy Pelosi, who like so many others had admired David, had come to bury her friend. I told her how honored David would be that she would be here. She said, "Bill, there is nowhere else for me to be today but here with you all. I love David, too."

I have spent considerable time reflecting on the effects of AIDS on our beloved community and, while reading *The Body Keeps the Score: Brain, Mind and Body in the Healing of Trauma* by the Harvard psychiatrist Bessel van der Kolk—as fine a book on trauma as you are likely to find—I identified so much with the wisdom van der Kolk's experience holds for those of us— in the millions—who were and are part of this mass dying. The effects of trauma last, often for a lifetime, but their amelioration often comes amid the presence of a loving community. In my work as a clinician, the aftereffects—the incidents of post-traumatic stress disorder (PTSD) in our community—were and are evident in what individuals present and work on in therapy. Those effects are often subtle and have become so normalized in the gay male community that they are often not regarded as aberrant. But the effects are large and still mark the community in all the ways that trauma manifests itself.

David's life and death symbolized the deepest of truths. Like David, we are all deserving of complicated and rich lives. Like David, we are each a reflection of the Divine. But we only really see this once we have emerged from our dark cocoons, once we have stripped from ourselves all the illusions that we are anything else.

My years of working in the epidemic taught me this: We are given each other, but only if we are willing to break out of the alluring prisons that keep us apart. The most complicated and simple truth is that we are made for love. But to receive this terrible knowledge, we are required to let go of the lie that keeps us wedded to some false and puny facsimile of our divinely wrought selves, to be vulnerable enough to avail ourselves of this vivifying love, the only force that transcends every other force we know.

There is AIDS in each of us, but also the gifts of real medicine and efficacious miracles. We are given these gifts so that we can offer them to others. It always redounds to us. The Hindus call it karma. We might call it grace. This is the enduring truth of our lives. This work is assured and blessed and is what brings us out of these cocoons into the light we first witnessed that day we emerged from our mother's womb.

The truth of AIDS, the truth of any medicine that heals, and the truth of the only miracles that matter is that love heals, love opens us up, love releases us from our prisons, love makes us human, and love connects us to one another and to that *presence* in the universe we know most intimately in the silence of our hearts, that scent of the divine irresistible in its draw, and defiant in its demand to claim us for its own.

So, while we have marked this distinctive anniversary, our work of loving one another yet and always awaits.

11

THE MAN WITH AN EARRING

It is not fitting, when one is in God's service, to have a
gloomy face or a chilling look.

—St. Francis of Assisi

HE WAS SO fragile that Scott, with his broad back, would need
to pick him up out of bed and deliver him to a dinette chair at
the breakfast table, where Larry and I would commence *the dish*.
Scott would fix dinner, which meant, at least on Monday nights,
Larry Tozzeo would dine on *cuisine*.

Monday was *our* night. As the ravages of HIV took their
toll, Larry grew increasingly frail, his body the unwitting host
to various opportunistic infections that would eventually take
his life. In the meantime, his close friends divvied up the days of
the week. Each evening of the week saw a different set of friend-
caregivers descending upon the little row house on Godeus
Street at the bottom of Potrero Hill in San Francisco. Its front
door opened onto the sidewalk like all the others in that pre-
earthquake neighborhood.

I had met Larry ten years earlier at a Roman Catholic Mass
celebrated for Dignity. Larry was *out* in a manner that none
of the closeted gay priests who celebrated Mass dared to be.

Like them, when I first attended—still a Jesuit—I was nervous, overdressed, formal. Larry was the celebrant that evening, and he preached with a gold lamé fan in one hand and the radical demands of Jesus of the Beatitudes of Matthew 5:3–12 in the other. As I received communion, in addition to saying the sacred formulaic "*the Body of Christ*," Larry offered an additional verbal snippet: "*...and welcome home, handsome.*"

We became fast friends, though seemingly opposites. Although we were the same age, our backgrounds diverged greatly. He grew up in the crowded, tough Hell's Kitchen neighborhood in New York, and I in the leafy confines of Happy Hollow, a distinctly upscale neighborhood in Omaha. He was Italian raised in an Irish neighborhood; I was Irish raised among non-Catholics. He joined the Franciscans after high school; I entered the Jesuits after college. He was gregarious to a fault and lived each day with an enviable dramatic flair; I, though plenty outgoing, had no gold lamé fan, nor probably ever would.

Larry modelled *outlaw* qualities I admired and hoped to acquire. He was an inveterate flirt, a trickster, deeply committed to social justice and to the absolute inclusion of gay persons in the life of the Church—*without conditions*. He wore a small hoop earring, eyes ever twinkling, was an insightful and most present listener, loved to cavort with friends, told outrageous stories, and embodied what many must have thought were the salient characteristics of the saint of Assisi himself. And he was an extraordinary preacher.

Larry invited me to let go, unclench the fist, slack the jaw, loosen the body, abandon the perfect, love myself, laugh at my many obsessions, love the divine within, especially as that divine was expressed as joy, play, and eros. Larry came to embody for me what I knew of Jesus. Over time, Larry and I became a team at Dignity, offering an annual retreat for women and men, inviting us to take our interior lives with a seriousness the established Church denied us—in its scapegoating of gay people with all its sexual projections. Larry and I both knew the extensive wounds gay people suffer, and how doubly wounded were those who had grown up in religious households, having the wrath and disgust of the Divine laid on top of them like a binding blanket, a judgment both damning and inescapable. Larry was patient with our inner critics, understanding how the profound homophobia of the culture got hardwired into each of us, and how it, in turn, became identified with the voice of God.

On one retreat, we had used the word *precious* to describe how tenderly we believed God regarded all of us, gay people included, maybe even in particular. One of the retreatants rose and said that he knew that God could never embrace *us*, we besotted homosexuals, *with tenderness*. We were marked for judgment, not *tenderness*! Scornfully, he muttered *Precious, indeed!* Such were the straightjackets many found themselves in, and still do.

Larry lived as a self-supporting extern outside the Franciscan community, though he remained a friar in good standing. He had taught religion, or *his* version of religion, for several years at an exclusive San Francisco girls' school. At some point, his contract was not renewed, perhaps because of the earring he wore, and all that it meant, or perhaps because his health was failing.

At the time, I was vice principal at the *nonexclusive* Mercy and offered Larry a contract to come and teach religion and become a member of our diverse counseling team. He quickly became a fixture in the school, a sought-after counselor for the girls, and a confidant to many of the faculty. Over the relatively brief time Larry was at Mercy, he grew more ill, and the deprecation and ravages of the virus became more pronounced. Larry would sit in his little office—across the hall from my friend Shirley Kaiser, whose husband Florian would die of AIDS—scarved and sweatered to keep what warmth he could in his emaciated body, while a constant stream of girls came, ostensibly for counseling, but more often to express their care for him and to just be in his presence. What usually emanated from his office was soft laughter.

I was *out* at the school, and Scott was one of the favored faculty spouses. The girls took it in stride, as young people usually do, though some parents found my leadership role confounding.

But over my eight years at Mercy, no parent raised a public voice in protest, and no child was withdrawn from the school.

There was considerable turnover in the top position at Mercy, and I would often function as the effective school leader for months at a time, along with another senior administrator, as the board searched for a new head. One of the many principals for whom I worked over those nine years called me in to his office a few months after his arrival and asked if I knew that Fr. Larry wore an earring? "Yes," I answered. "Of course. Everyone here knows that." He thought it highly improper, asking, "Why? What kind of person would wear an earring?" As I began telling him that almost everyone at Mercy wore earrings, he reached into a drawer of his desk and pulled out a bottle of Dewar's and a pair of Waterford highball glasses. He poured himself a stiff one, and then offered one to me. I politely declined. While sipping his scotch-on-no-rocks, he continued to question my rationale for employing an earring-wearing priest. I offered no defense except to suggest that the near-universal love and respect that Larry engendered among the students, and the faculty, qualified him for his continued employment. That principal did not last the year, though Larry did, even as he grew frailer.

After dinner, on those Monday nights through the last year of Larry's life, Scott would carry Larry back to bed, and we would join him atop the bedspread, me sitting crossed legged, Scott, with his long legs stretched out. With his now slight frame, we tucked Larry in so that he was comfortable. Our pooch, Phoebe, a rascally Airedale, would hop up too and snuggle with Larry. I would read a psalm, spend a few minutes in silence, and end with the three of us offering some apropos prayers. On what would be the last night we were with Larry, at the end of our time together on the bed, Larry asked Scott if he and I could have some time alone. Scott, of course, easily agreed. He kissed Larry good night, and he and Phoebe went out into the parlor after shutting the bedroom door.

Larry, sensing the end was near, asked me to go over to his chest of drawers. As instructed, I opened the bottom drawer. As I did, I saw Larry's stole, the vestment a priest wears when hearing confessions or doing other sacramental works. Larry was wearing this stole ten years earlier when I first went to a Dignity Mass. It was a pale yellow and brown blotched affair that he had most likely gifted from friends back in the tie-dye heyday. No watermarked black silk for him! He asked me to bring the stole over to him. I got back onto the lumpy bed and handed it to him. He took it, kissed it, as a priest always does, and then asked me to lean over and then placed the stole around my neck. His face was now devoid of the premature aging AIDS inflicted upon these young men, the ever-present twinkle in his eyes softened into a glow, and a look of expectancy framed his countenance.

He then said, "I want you to hear my final confession."

His face was beatific, eyes recessing and lips in a faint smile. He was hunched over, propped up by pillows, a wasting away version of his earlier self.

I balked, and said I couldn't, that "you know I'm not a priest." He said, again, "But I want *you* to hear my *final* confession." In repeating his request, the words *you* and *final* riveted me, and the gravity of the moment shook me. He knew something about the proximity of *Sister Death*, as *il Poverrelo* had called her.

I allowed Larry to rest the stole on my shoulders. I loved Larry deeply and knew him to be an avatar of the divine who touched many lives, including mine. I knew, too, that he was serious. With heightened, complicated emotion, I bowed my head and said, "Yes, of course I will." We held the silence, and then, with great humility, he proceeded to share what he regarded as his failings. Here was this man, my dear friend, my colleague, my peer, frail and emaciated, dying at the age of thirty-nine, the age we shared, making his last confession with a man *unsanctioned*, one who had left the ordination path to be true to an unmarked spiritual path, a path that had then and has subsequently found me working to see that the divine presence is made manifest in frail and wounded lives, like my own.

As Larry finished his recitations, he asked me to give him absolution. I placed my hands on his balding head and pronounced the words of the sacrament—*for your sins are forgiven you*—and signed a cross on his forehead, and then we embraced—in silence.

As I raised my head to take off the stole and return it to him, Larry said, "Keep it on. This stole is yours now. You must embrace the priest that you are, and you must be the priest for those for whom others won't be." I began to weep, as I do now, knowing that objecting would merely be another valiant attempt on the part of my resilient ego to continue to oversee the universe.

Our *sacramental* time came to its end, as if it could, and I beckoned Scott to rejoin us. After a few words of parting, we hugged and kissed Larry goodbye, all three of us now understanding, somehow, that we would not be together again. We drove away from that tiny house on Godeus, grateful and very sad. We were aware that we were living in a time we could not fully comprehend. By late 1988, we had buried many friends, grieved their losses deeply, and remained within a culture of dying, the full effects of which we could not clearly ascertain. It seemed that it was all that there was.

I wore the stole home.

Larry died one week later.

At his funeral Mass the following week, at St. Paul of the Shipwreck in San Francisco's Black neighborhood of Hunter's Point, I was invited to read an *Exsultet* that Larry had composed years before:

> Hearing our names, we would know in some hidden place, known only to a few even now, that we were the seed of light and carried in our flesh that same blossom that sprang from your heart—"Promise." We rejoice...because in holding this flower out to you, the second greatest moment of creation is completed, and we finish the story you began so long ago. With heart and voice, we—the flesh of your flesh and the bone of your bone—say to you: *Come, our God, come and be our Lover...*

The inner sorrow Larry's death created in me has never quite vanished. I speak to him frequently, mostly telling him how much I miss him, thanking him for what he taught me and for what he demanded of me, and how glad I am for his continued presence in my life.

As most of my cohort of friends died, often wrenching deaths, I found myself in many ways alone, having left the beloved community of the Jesuit brotherhood, and the beloved community that was the young gay world I had similarly entered that had welcomed me, embraced me, invited me, and encouraged me. I lost my peers, men largely my age, as we went through developmental stages together, understanding our common experiences as previously nascent gay boys in the 1950s and 60s, our coming of age in a seemingly liberated Roman Catholic Church, only to experience the slamming of the door with the advent of John Paul II as the pope in 1978.

As I turned forty, and as I began my private practice that fall, I entered a workplace for the first time in which a crucifix was not on the wall. A slight detail perhaps, but a significant one. Moving fully into my self-authored life, with the abiding questions of authority slowly being answered, or perhaps more correctly, revealed. And with a heart that would be seared for the rest of my life by the waste and the grace of the epidemic.

12

SAN QUENTIN

Light the candles wherever you can, you who have
them. They are a real symbol of what must happen...if
we want to live.

—Alfred Delp, SJ, Tegel Prison, Berlin, December 1944

AS THE EXECUTIVE director of Continuum, I spent a great deal
of my time raising money—some days, it felt that was all I did—
essential though it was to its survival. One evening, as I finished
my pitch at a fundraising event, a stranger approached me to
thank me for what I had just shared. He then said, "I think you
should come and work with me in prison." That was my first
encounter with Jacques Verduin, a Dutch émigré and one bold
hombre. Yikes! What in God's name led him to think that? Let
alone ask? He added, "I work with lifers, and that's where I think
you'd be good."

His boldness intrigued me, and I had an intuition we would
meet again.

Two years later, I retired from Continuum and resumed my
full-time work as a psychotherapist, a career I had interrupted to
lead that beloved agency. Within days of my departure, Jacques
called and asked, "Are you ready?"

In a timely issue of the *New York Review of Books*, Darryl Pinckney, the insightful and incisive Black writer, in an article entitled "In Ferguson," wrote,

> After the Civil War, thousands of black men were on the roads, looking for new starts but mostly looking for loved ones sold away. Vagrancy laws were passed that said if you couldn't say where you lived or worked, you could be picked up and put on the chain gang. America has always felt the necessity of keeping its black male population under control.

Of relevance to me, as a former Jesuit, was the Jesuits' illustrious history in the United States, specifically at their prestigious Georgetown University, where they had held slaves. In America, even in the churches, there is a long and complicated history that leaves a sordid legacy of enslavement with which, as we know, we will either grapple, or ignore at our peril. In his haunting book *The Life of a Klansman*, Edward Ball, the chronicler of his New Orleans ancestors of the 1860s, calculates that 50 percent of all Americans are descended from slave owners. So, keep reading and bear with me. Here are some stats to concentrate one's attention:

> Between 1980 and 2016, the number of persons incarcerated in America quadrupled, from five hundred thousand to 2.3 million.
> The United States contains 5 percent of the world's population and 25 percent of the world's prisoners.
> Black Americans make up 9 percent of our population, but now constitute one million of the 2.3 million incarcerated Americans—that's 43 percent of incarcerated Americans; add in Hispanics and other men of color, these groups comprise more than 60 percent of men in our prisons.

One in three Black boys can expect to be incarcerated
in his lifetime, a larger probability than his
chances of attaining a college degree.

Black men, and women, are the victims of police
violence in untold numbers, as witnessed by
millions in the horrific and merciless death of
George Floyd.

Black men are incarcerated at nearly five times the
rate of white men.

In raw numbers, there are five times as many whites
using illegal drugs as are Blacks, yet the latter
are sent to prison for drug offenses at ten times
the rate of whites.

In any given year, I suspect that a significant percentage of
students at suburban high schools use an illegal substance, and
yet few of these students end up in the criminal justice system.
For example, in my eight years as dean at a large, urban Catholic
girls' high school in San Francisco, no student was jailed for any
offense, though I encountered students and their similarly situated boyfriends illegally using alcohol and/or drugs routinely.
Most of those students came from upwardly mobile families. No,
I did not narc on them.

Back to Jacques. I intuitively agreed to his invitation, despite
my trepidation, and one day twenty-two years ago, I found myself
going through multiple security barriers to enter the central yard
of San Quentin State Penitentiary, ironically named for a Catholic
saint and patron of locksmiths. When I cleared that last security
hurdle and entered the yard, I felt a sense of freedom!

This was an interior freedom, a gift that has never left me in
the many years since I first entered SQ's gates. At first, I worked
with determinate-sentenced men—those serving terms of one to
five, two to ten years, whatever. Mostly drug offenders, they were
difficult to work with because they knew they would be getting
out soon, and so they unwittingly kept the ties on both the inside
and the outside that bonded them to the "locked-in" behavior

that would return them to prison for graver crimes. There were exceptions, but those men rarely see any horizon other than the bleak one created for them, often at birth. The generational social pathologies that lead men to prison often begin in the womb. Many incarcerated men are born to very young women, girls really, without prospects, many themselves generationally involved in self-destructive behaviors, often without effective social structures of support, and most often without a mate—not unlike the conditions of chattel slavery.

If I could cite any singular significant standout in the experiences of prisoners it would be that most often grew up without any male figure, no father, no male boundary setters, no loving man in their lives. Let me repeat, *no loving man in their lives.*

And again, not unlike the conditions of chattel slavery, where families—mostly fathers, sometimes mothers—were being sold and children were being raised by aunties or whatever extended family remained.

And now recall Darryl Pinckney's words: "mostly looking for loved ones sold away."

Soon, Jacques asked if I would assist in leading a group in the maximum-security section, a selective program that invited men who had been in prison for many years, for capital crimes, to meet weekly—three hours at a stretch—to work through the internal issues that landed them in prison and kept them, crucially, imprisoned within themselves. Our work was a combination of insight-oriented group psychotherapy, tough love group dynamics, and spiritual practice (we taught and practiced a Buddhist technique—Vipassana, or Insight Meditation). Many men also took yoga in a sister program. Really, it was all soul reclamation work. Our goal was to help men get out of prison, the prisons that were self-imposed, while still incarcerated.

The environment in which these men live is one of twenty-four-hour continuous ambient noise—radios, yelling, bodily noises, pitched howling, laughing—constant stress, verbal intimidation, physical crowding, stifling heat, boredom, anxiety, stench, a sterile and deeply regimented hopelessness. In this group, there would be no excuses, no blaming, a full releasing of resentments, a withdrawing of projections, fully coming to terms with their crime—for most, murder, accomplices to, or for a few, manslaughter—and dealing with the spirit-shattering guilt, shame, regret, grief, and loss that marked, in no uncertain terms, their internal, and therefore, external lives. Perhaps the most painful work the men faced was that they could never express to their victim, nor to their victim's family, their deep sorrow for the heinous deed they had done. They are shackled for life with that reality.

What Jacques and I and other facilitators did, primarily, was listen. Heidegger said that true listening is worship, and don't we intuitively know that truth in our own lives?

Listening and the discreet interventions of traditional psychotherapy guided the group for many years. Over time, an annualized curriculum was developed: GRIP (Guiding Rage Into Power). More groups formed but the waiting list was long. The programs of Insight Prison Project and its progeny, Insight Out, and its most recent iteration GRIP, all Jacques's babies, grew. GRIP is now in several California prisons, and Jacques has taught the curriculum to penal reformers in countries throughout Europe, as well as spreading this gospel stateside.

The men in the group began working with the restorative justice program—using the principles for helping both criminals and victims' families effectively deal with their mutually unbearable—for profoundly different reasons—burdens, and many men have met with the loved ones of someone else's victims, a sine qua non of restorative justice.

The principles of restorative justice mirror the congruent underpinnings of both psychology and human spirituality, and forgiveness, and for me, the sine qua non of an interior life is at the heart of this transformative work. At SQ, the men prepare for many months to meet with family members of a crime victim, often the beloved ones of a person murdered (not the victim of their crime, nor the family's perpetrator). The goal is to produce outcomes for the participants that will free them each from the terrible burdens they face each day, the shame and guilt of the perpetrators, the terrible anger and resentment and victimization of the family members.

Both parties are brave, and resolute, and honest. "I" statements are the rule. Emotional claiming and clarity are demanded. An openness to listen to the other and be present to them is the encounter's palpable heart. Humility is the common denominator that leads to the enormous healing that results from this intricate and potent work. For a man who has borne the guilt and shame of his crime for three decades or more to be able to express his profound sorrow to someone who has lost a daughter to murder is as *raw* and *human* and *healing* as it gets. For a family member to sit with a murderer and tell the man what she has experienced daily for the past ten years, maybe twelve, and then to offer him forgiveness for his grave sin is as raw and human and healing as one can imagine. There is no papering over, no glib recitation of formulaic statements, no false hope that scars will not remain. No formulaic absolution, but it is healing of the highest order.

Early in my work, I told Jacques that I wanted and needed to come out to the group, honoring our principle of radical honesty, a criterion for any growth, as we each know. Among most prisoners, the reality of gay sexuality was totally denied but simultaneously, there was, in prison, a lived-out dark underworld of hierarchical, shame-inducing, male-on-male rape. Jacques and I agreed it was important, even necessary, for me to do this. On a given Tuesday, I asked for group time, and I shared with this group of incarcerated men these taboo words: "I am a gay man." In prison, no one easily, or rarely, says, *I am a gay man*.

The room fell silent. Many eyes held my gaze. The eyes were both sympathetic and perhaps confused. Soon, Miguel broke the silence. He had been in prison for close to thirty years, a former gangbanger from Los Angeles who had killed a man in his youth, now a real leader among men in the prison, and a macho, born-again Christian—of recent conversion. Since I began my work with the group, I sensed he had been drawn to me, as I was to him. I also knew some of the subcultures in which he had lived, all of which might have made my announcement foreboding for him. And I was aware that his response to my revelation would hold enormous sway among the other men assembled that day.

After a while, Miguel rose from his folding chair and approached me. He said, "Guillermo" (William in Spanish), which many native speakers, and therefore others, called me, "I obviously have a lot to learn. You always bring your full self to us, and from you I have learned more about how to be me. So, even if I don't fully understand yet, you are welcome here." He came closer and stood next to me, and I rose to receive him. He placed the palm of his hand on my heart, and said, "Guillermo, there's a fire inside of you." We then hugged—both another prison cultural taboo and against regulations. The men slowly put their hands together and began applauding both Miguel's words and my decision to be, as we ask of each other, fully honest in each other's presence. We know that is for all of us the balm that heals.

As they came to know more of my story, the men were soon asking to meet my husband. Scott eventually came into the prison. The men, as most folks do, loved him. And then my in-laws, Scott's parents—Mary in her late seventies and Dick in his eighties—were invited in. The men were fascinated and told them how courageous they were to come. Mary and Dick were nonplussed and expressed their gratitude for being there. Recently, my preternaturally wise niece, Kate, who had first wanted to come to SQ when she was fifteen, now in her thirties, joined me for an afternoon with the men in GRIP at San Quentin State Penitentiary, and soon, my vivacious cousin, Leslie, and her inquisitive son, Jack, also joined us. The group had grown accustomed to Guillermo's people coming to prison.

One year, with the enlightened female warden, we were given permission to bring in a Thanksgiving meal for the men in the group. Prison food is at best unremarkable and mostly worse. Our volunteer crew brought in everything you might associate with that resplendent meal, including plenty of collard greens—a favorite of the men—seldom on the prison menu. We obtained the use of a large room and set up a connected square table, dressed it with linens and plasticware, placed around it thirty chairs, eighteen for the men, and twelve for those of us who worked with them or who visited the group regularly. The men, as they entered, were slack jawed, for it was a sight that many of them thought they would never again behold.

One of us, Kat, a natural-born entertainer, began the meal with an a cappella version of "Tis A Gift to Be Simple." Prior to digging into this savory feast, Jacques asked if I would lead the group in prayer. We held hands, some hands that had not been held by another's in decades, and I expressed thanks for all that we had with each other on this solemn occasion. I asked that each of us might say a word or two of thanks. We went around the table. Our collective prayer lasted perhaps fifteen minutes, so copious were the thanks offered by these incarcerated human beings. The penultimate man to speak was just to my left, Israel, a Black man in his mid-forties who had been in the system since he was seventeen. He held the room in silent presence and then said, "I am grateful for Now. No, no, for Now. NO, for NOW. For Now. I am grateful for Now."

Around this table, these so-called hardened criminals and their fortunate guests had tears streaming down their faces, perhaps having believed they would never again partake of such a feast, nor perhaps, that they would be part of such a loving community as those of us gathered to give thanks. I concluded with a prayer that acknowledged how much we had to be grateful for, mostly by just being together.

One Tuesday soon after, my friend Robin, a Native American, who had been imprisoned at nineteen and was now in his sixties, and was recognized as a bodhisattva at SQ, including by the correctional officers, said to me in a moment of silence in the group, "Guillermo, I have something for Mary." I was not quite sure what he meant. He said that Jacques had shared the news of my mother-in-law's difficult cancer diagnosis and had asked the men to pray for her. Having gone through the proper clearance process for giving such a handmade gift, Robin handed me a bright, beaded necklace with a medicine pouch, into which he

phrase, "the preferential option for the poor." Our magnetic and most human pope, Francis, expounds on this with regularity, appropriately considering that he, himself, is first a Jesuit. That person, that one for whom we would exercise a preferential option, is everywhere, and he is in prison, where we have put him so that our social order will appear to be free of all that his presence calls out, both historically and in this moment. This is scapegoating on a grand and cruel level.

I am reminded of the Beatitudes, and of Jesus's compelling story of the man observing the splinter in his neighbor's eye. These and so many other stories call us to withdraw our projections onto the other and to see ourselves in the other—the homeless panhandler we'll see on the street; the prostitute flipping sex for drugs downtown is us; the transgendered kid who is scared to death of the social milieu in their high school is your neighbor; and the homeless and underemployed person whom we pray not to be.

In serving the poor, which includes the poor in us, however, and to whomever that service is rendered, the grace redounds to others and to ourselves. We change. We stop. We see. We listen. We act. We are the great beneficiaries. The other changes, too, and thank God so does, hopefully, some aspect of their arduous conditions. But Jesus was no mere social worker, nor was he a psychological slouch. His care was always ultimately for the spiritual deepening of the one whom he met. And it is for our spiritual deepening, so hard in this world of pervasive material distraction, that our service is ultimately rendered.

Working at SQ has changed me. It is gratifying and sustaining work. Over time, the positive transformation of derelict human lives—mine among them—by the simple acts of emotional honesty—or Love, as my cloistered friend Grace writes—is breathtaking. Yes, our prisons house, appropriately, society's criminal psychopaths, but they are also full of bodhisattvas—men and women whose presence is helping to keep the world aright. If you find yourself hankering, against your better judgment, to work inside, follow that intuition. It is one that will reshape how you encounter the Divine, yourself, and every other human being. These men, Israel, Miguel, Robin, Red, Bernard, Rafael, and my friend and teacher, Jacques, along with so many others, have qualified me to be a human being. For this, and for them, as I was at that Thanksgiving feast, I remain most grateful.

13

HEALING ENERGY

All is gift, all is gift. Give it away.

—Daniel Berrigan

ONE OF MY prevailing senses, an intuitive metaphor, if you will, is that over us all, over the entire universe, is a membrane that extends to the endless edges of creation. Its composition is gossamer—we sense without ever seeing its evident matter. We see only its not-quite-visible-yet-dense expression that is manifest in love, particularly through healing. For healing is the most immediate effect and proof of the energy of love. The wisdom of the Jews offers us the compelling notion of *Tikkun Olam*, acts of kindness done to repair of the world. Thomas Moore says that Jesus had a dual mission: to teach and to heal. The Gospels are littered with abandoned crutches of various kinds, physical, emotional, spiritual.

Pierre Teilhard de Chardin, the Jesuit paleontologist and cosmologist, understood that the very stuff of creation—the mud and rock and stardust and human flesh we see—is the *very stuff* of the divine. From the Big Bang—the moment of the singularity of creation's ultimate expansion—emanated all the material that is, in its splendiferous magnificence and intricacy and complexity and simplicity—at once—for Teilhard, love: love as energy; love as effect; love as agency; love as relational; love as connection; love as silence; love as touch; love as awareness; love as presence; and love as healing.

Martin Buber said that *all real living is meeting*. And, to me, *all real meeting* ultimately heals us. When we come into the presence of one who is fully present to us, we leave them more whole, more integral, than before. Healing is needed, in every part of us and in every person we meet. For brokenness is evident everywhere, in each of us—in our minds, hearts, and souls—in the other, in the providential planetary mother who sustains us.

For many years, I have had an awareness that I have been called to be in the world in certain ways. I suspect you do, as well. One of those ways is to be a source of healing. And somehow, sometimes, I have sensed this call was to be manifest physically. I have found the notion confounding and have resisted exploring its implications in my life. Maybe, in truth, we all do. What does it mean? I have felt the beneficial healing presence of others— teachers, spiritual directors, therapists, friends, and on occasion, even strangers. But to be a healer explicitly?

When I was a Jesuit, I never mentioned this nascent sense of being called to be a healer. But as I began my subsequent life in the world, as I pondered this, I sought the wisdom of others. In 1992, in a conversation with my Jesuit spiritual director, Richard Smith, he suggested I meet a woman, Laura Gans, whose deep intuitive gifts served many Jesuits. He sensed that she might speak to this query of mine. I was skeptical but also *intuitively* drawn to meet this woman.

An *intuitive* person is, according to Carl Jung, who gave spiritual precedence to intuition as a gift from the Divine, a person with a heightened sense of awareness, one who can apprehend reality with clarity, one who cultivates and learns to trust their *knowing* as an internal guide. I understand intuition as a spiritual gift available to us all, often unrecognized, or untrusted. Or perhaps it is. I have been working with my intuition since I was a boy, paying attention, learning to trust it as an *infallible* internal guide. When I have *not* trusted my intuition—out of fear or for ego gratification—the results have been correspondingly negative, and on occasion, disastrous.

I made an appointment to meet Laura at her office in San Rafael, the northern suburb of San Francisco where we lived. After greeting me, she began by asking what I had come for. I wasn't quite sure how to answer her. I had some perplexing intimations that perhaps she could see more clearly than me, conundrums that my internal work had not addressed, and I had intuitions, for which I was looking for confirmation. When she noticed my hesitancy, she suggested that we both close our eyes, be still, and that she would share what had come to her during the silence. I felt self-conscious but willingly closed my eyes as did she. Perhaps six or seven minutes passed; then again, it might have been only two. Then Laura spoke. She shared the images—always images—that came to her. I found them of interest but wasn't sure of their relevance for our work that day. Nonetheless, I got the hang of what might transpire.

When I had moved to California in the late 1970s, it seemed to be the center of alternative modes of being, of knowing, of medicine, of spirituality, and of what one might call various cosmologies. Some sounded downright kooky, some scary, and others had appeal. To some, I felt intuitively drawn. Berkeley was at the heart of this alternative landscape. Posters for every type of neo-spiritual practice papered all available telephone pole space. Something was at work here, but what, I was not sure.

Prior to my arrival in California, I had never had any bodywork done and I kind of shuddered at the thought. I had not yet discovered Carl Jung, but soon did, thanks to my teacher Joseph Powers, SJ. The Enneagram, to which I have devoted considerable study, and which I have been teaching the past thirty-five years, was just slowly emerging—thanks to spiritually forward thinkers. My liturgy teacher, Jake Empereur, SJ, got Rolfed—it sounded excruciatingly painful—and where was the wisdom in that? Meditation sounded vaguely Eastern and there were calls for the ordination of women priests. Men's groups were sitting overnight in sweat lodges, and not until I got to San Quentin years later, where my friend Robin, the Native American holy man, was incarcerated, did I come to appreciate their profound function.

Acupuncture...putting several needles into your *dermis*—to what effect? But it was not until many years later when I encountered David Russell, who had trained in Beijing, that I experienced the near miraculous healing of my annual bouts of asthma. I am often in the prone position come winter with two score needles protruding from my flesh, all to good effect.

I had experienced none of this before California.

Now with Laura, if you walked past her on the street, nothing would necessarily draw your attention. She would appear as another woman going about her business. But inside this rather ordinary appearing woman, was a brilliant gem: her active and finely honed intuition. That day, I shared with her some of my quandaries—places I felt stuck, couldn't see my way through, and where I was confounded. My *knots*. She listened intently; her eyes closed when I was speaking. And then, eyes wide open, she addressed me. Her insights were striking, clear, nuanced, and *intuitively* spot on. Each quandary I presented she spoke to and connected them to comments I had made earlier and to some of the images she had processed at the hour's beginning. The hour we shared passed quickly. I went away curious and grateful. Thus, we initiated annual visits that were to last for nearly three decades.

On a subsequent visit, I told her of this intuition I had that I was being *called*—that word again—to use my hands in a healing fashion. Laura was still. When she spoke, she said she knew that I had this gift and had known it since first we met. I was startled. I asked why she had not shared that with me. She responded that she didn't think I was ready to hear it. And she was right. She sensed in me ambivalence about this gift, and that if it were to be developed, I would have to be in a place to bring it forward. She often used the phrase *bring it forward*, though I was not quite sure what that meant.

Or again, perhaps I did. She suggested I make an appointment to meet with a man who had a practice in *the healing arts*. So very Marin County, I thought. But I agreed, with some ambivalence. I scheduled an appointment with Greg, who, like Laura, had an office in San Rafael. I entered a crowded waiting room, filled with other people who seemed *ordinary*—men, women, and children, old and young. What had I expected? Was this a counterculture of which I had known nothing, one to which I was being invited? I was led back to a room with an examining table and was told that Greg would be with me shortly, and he, too, looked quite ordinary. What I had been expecting?

I told Greg pretty much what I had told Laura earlier. He invited me to hop up on the table and to lie on my back. In a fashion not unlike Reiki, an ancient Japanese technique of energy healing in which a *universal energy* moves through the outstretched palms of the practitioner to effect physical or emotional healing—shifting, clearing, freeing—in the client, Greg slowly swept over my body, not touching me, paying particular attention to my belly—my gut center—and my chest, where of course the heart resides. He then asked me to flip over, and he performed the same slow sweeping movement. I had come to appreciate the flow of energy between persons over many years and how we harness and utilize energy in our everyday lives. Greg, this respectful practitioner, had recognized his own healing gift and found a way to make it of service to others. By the looks of the crowd in the waiting room, many people had experienced his healing presence. Greg asked me to sit up, he startled me with his words: "I've never met anyone with this gift more resistant than you. But this is your work! You won't be able to help others until you remove the internal blocks that keep you so stuck!"

I have regarded my clinical work as a psychotherapist as healing work, in which the presence I brought to the room was met by the presence—or at times resistance—of the client. The interaction of my being present—an active and disciplined posture and gaze and ear—invited the client, over time, to be present too, and in that mode, the material that had been so wounding and confounding found a way for some of its effects to be expressed and released. I had been invited—from an early age—to be present in specific ways. I sensed some others intuited this quality in me—consciously but perhaps more often not.

Greg acknowledged that my clinical work was indeed healing work, and he invited me to be open to *all* the additional ways
I might be invited to be a healer. He said little more. He offered to
do additional *energy* work with me, for which I expressed gratitude.

I left his office instinctively knowing I was up against the
residual strictures placed on me decades earlier, ones that
advised me not to trust myself and not to self-validate what gifts
I may have been given.

This dynamic had played itself out in many areas of my life
after I left the Jesuits. Soon after departing the Society, individuals initiated intimate and self-revealing conversations with me,
asked me to share my writing, by praying with them, to accompany them to their deaths, to preach their funerals, and to bless
their illicit but genuine marriages. I felt this to be my true call,
one I understood only vaguely when I left the Society of Jesus.
I was willing, and much of my work over the next few decades
was embracing these gifts. But exercising what I regarded as this
other gift—as *healer*—was another, very complicated matter.

After visiting Laura and Greg, I became more aware of how
I used my hands. I would be intentional when placing them on
others, not haphazardly embracing or gesturing or touching. I
worked to be conscious of reverencing these encounters. Sometimes I found myself pulling back from a gesture of simple touch,
knowing somehow that the contact would be startling to the
other. During the dark days of the AIDS epidemic—days that
lasted years—touch was the clearest gift one might give to a
dying man, holding his hand or placing hands on his forehead or
rubbing his feet to lessen the pain of the neuropathy he suffered.
My dear friend Ken, just days from death, asked if I would hold
him. Of course, I said *yes*. As I cradled his body in mine, his sul-
phureous legs distended, he wept. No miracles, only the density
of the immediacy of love. I came to understand this was what
healing meant, loving with presence and focus. Being attentive.
Being *here—being here now*.

I ventured to bring up this question of healing in therapy.
Gordon Murray was bright, about my age, and was studying at

the Jung Institute on his path to become a Jungian analyst. My lifelong admiration for Jung was complemented by the way Gordon and I did this work together. He knew I was intuitive, affirming this on many occasions, always acknowledging these were to be trusted. He also required of me that I house and express my power—a difficult word for me—and to use it to full effect.

The Jungian Helen Luke remarks wisely that a true healer "is always an intercessor, not a remover of symptoms, which then simply go from one part of the psyche to another...(rather), interceding by his own experience of suffering, he carries for the other." This seems apt, for those who have been healers in my life have all—by my lights—integrated their suffering. As a therapist, I would often sense when a client was withholding, or when a wound was not quite conscious, and would work to allow that material to rise to the surface. In my work at San Quentin, where so much shame, guilt, repressed anger, and fear permeated the room in which we gathered, Jacques, my partner, would often ask me, when the group seemed stuck, to share what intuition I was having so that the blockage in the group could be removed. I always responded to his request. And the blockage was often removed.

I often know beforehand when I will be called on in groups, and what I will be asked to address, and by whom. I am often aware when another is lying or hiding, and simultaneously aware that the other knows I am aware, too. This has caused me a not insignificant number of challenges over the years, and sometimes leads to the other departing my life.

During lunch with a friend several years ago, he told me—out of the blue—that he did not want to meet for lunch anymore because he could not handle the discomfort caused by my seeing him so clearly. I found his subsequent withdrawal painful. That has happened, in variations, on several occasions over the course of my life. I hold secrets for many individuals who confess their transgressions before I clearly understand what is transpiring. Often, after the *confession*, the person who shared the intimate details of their behavior is no longer comfortable in my presence, and I have come to know that their distance is an

152

unconscious move on their part to no longer be identified with the corrosive material that I was often left holding. Laura told me years ago that people see me as a vast concrete basin with an unlimited capacity to hold their *shit*.

I am convinced that we all have this capacity, and with attention, we can access these complicated—and necessary—gifts. I shared with Gordon that I thought I was called to use my hands for healing. I felt bold and vulnerable in sharing this. He was momentarily silent, per usual, and then, like Laura had, simply said, "I know." Gordon often asked me the meaning of various words that I had used in our work, terms from my background in religion and spirituality. When he said *I know*, I was silent but quickly asked him, "How?" We had a simple ritual of embracing each other at the end of our sessions, a gesture that acknowledged the intricacy and intimacy—and really, the humanity—of the work. And, as gay men, it was a no-brainer. He told me that one day he felt a surge come from my hands—resting on the back of his shoulders—that reverberated throughout his whole body, an effect that was calming, assuring, and powerful. I asked him why he had not told me this, and, again, like Laura, and Greg, he said that he was not sure I wanted to receive this affirmation. He was waiting for me to speak about this, if ever I would. Again, all at once, I felt startled, a bit confused, but also confirmed.

In time, while leading Spirit Group, the intentional spiritual community I led that gathered twice monthly for many years, I offered to stay after our prayerful gathering had concluded and sit with anyone to pray for healing, if they so desired. Over the years, various members asked this of me. We would both begin in silence, and I would then ask them to mention what was present in their minds and hearts. Again, we would return to silence. Then, at their invitation, I would place my hands over their head or, if invited, place my palm on their heart, gestures that were both sacred and seemingly mundane. I would pray for them and for their concerns and invite the Spirit to be present to us. What healing took place was interiorly directed, and I came to understand that the work, the healing work, was nothing if not subtle and was heart and memory focused. We would end acknowledging our gratitude for the presence of the divine and our gratitude for this time together.

We are all conduits for grace—another word, perhaps, for the uncontrollable presence of the divine, and grace works its way as it will, using us as vehicles, if we are but open. Nothing miraculous in this but the presence of *Love*. We all have this experience, we have all been touched by grace working in those who love us, in the variety of ways they do. It shifts us; changes us or frees us. It is all healing work. And it is so often mysterious.

Another beloved unmet teacher of mine, Alfred Delp, an extraordinary young Jesuit priest, while awaiting his execution in Tegel Prison in Berlin in late 1944 for his part in a conspiracy to end the Third Reich, cramped into his four-by-six-foot cell, hands bound together, managed to write on scraps of paper, later secreted out of the prison:

> We are to be announcing messengers ourselves. So much courage needs strengthening; so much despair needs comforting; so much hardship needs a gentle hand and an illuminating interpretation; so much loneliness cries out for a liberating word; so much loss and pain seek a spiritual meaning.

Given all our technological advances, not so much has changed. Our work remains.

One night in 2012, I had a stirring dream that woke me. In the dream, my old high school friend Chris Vacanti came to me and asked me to heal her by placing my hands on her lower right side, which I obliged. Nothing more was said, though the dream—experienced as taking place at night—was suffused with light. The larger environment of the dream fell away as I awoke, but the heart of the dream stayed with me vividly. It required some response. Jung, and so many others, including the writers of the New Testament, have understood dreams as carriers of import, of wisdom, and when understood, designed to affect our lives. The flight into Egypt with the divine Child was the result of his dad's attentiveness to *his* significant dream.

I had only seen Chris once since her wedding to my friend Joe in Omaha over the summer that we graduated college in 1970—but certainly not in decades. Neither did I have much current consciousness of her, though my memories of her—and of them—were sweet. The dream ran in current time, as we are both older adults. No other people inhabited this dreamscape. The next day, the dream still alive in my memory, I called another old friend in Omaha, Bill Laird, who had earlier told me that he and his wife, Susie, were in a prayer group with Chris and Joe. I asked him for Chris's contact information, which he graciously gave me.

So as not to startle her, as I suspected a phone call out of the blue might, I sent an email. I wrote that I had recently experienced a dream about her and wondered if we might talk. I would be happy to share the content of the dream with her. She emailed back immediately and agreed. I called Chris the next day, and we had a delightful time catching up on time that had passed since we had last been in each other's lives. Our comfort level in the call was high. Then she asked about the dream. I shared the contents of the dream with her, verbatim.

The first question she asked: "When did you have this dream?" I told her, and she emphatically said the dream "wasn't about me, it was about my oldest grandson, Paul," a vital but very ill ten-year-old. On the day following my dream, Paul had surgery to remove cancer from his kidneys, near where Chris had asked me to touch her in the dream the night before. Paul had come through the surgery, and while there were no results yet, they were optimistic.

We were both dumbstruck and momentarily silent. I didn't know what to say. She said that she was sure this is what the dream had manifest. She thanked me for the dream and for my willingness to reach out to her. We chatted some more and made a commitment to stay in touch. The reconnection we made that day on the phone strengthened an invincible—and for decades, invisible—bond between us. In our reconnection, I suspect, the deeper healing occurred.

That Christmas, when Scott and I were in Omaha for a family holiday, we planned to meet Chris and Joe, with our mutual friends Bill and Susie, at Mark's, a charming restaurant nestled in Dundee, the village neighborhood in which I had grown up.

Scott and I arranged the seating, to me always an important task. Chris and Joe walked in, and immediately, it felt like we were back at Creighton Prep, circa 1965. But more than we could have so long ago experienced. Chris and I embraced and started to laugh out loud. We did not know exactly what had transpired, and we knew it was beyond our comprehension—but a new source of life for both of us. At dinner, with our dear friends Bill and Susie, who already treasured Scott, Chris and Joe fell in love with him also, as everyone does, and the six of us had a reunion of immense graced memories, and requisite *dish*. Over dessert, Chris reminded us that I had introduced her to Joe while we were in high school. Such reconnections marked the evening.

That was over a decade ago. As a result of this potent dream, I am bonded to Chris in an irrevocable way. In our phone conversations, there is no distance, neither time nor, seemingly, space. She will sometimes mention Paul, that the surgery was successful, and they hope, of course, for a life of remission. And, of course, gratitude for this connection we have been given, a source of much mutual delight and amazement—and healing for each of us.

Therein lies the deeper truth of healing. Most healing does not involve the use of hands. As a therapist, I came to understand real healing occurred in the hour with my clients, over time, almost imperceptibly. I did not use my hands, nor did they, except to gesticulate a feeling. The healing occurred in the interaction—really, *the presence*—that the work invited, even required. I was present as they sat, faithfully, telling their story, which contained the seeds of healing. Presence, like fertile soil, opens the story to reveal the healing truth therein.

My friend Kathy Hurley, at a dinner celebrating a significant anniversary of my oldest friends, Art and Jo, said, "I take none of this for granted." Her comment moved me to tears that night, as it does now writing these words. We take none of it for granted. We are healed by *the all of it.*

My reconnection with Chris and Joe suggests that there are unforeseen forces—grace—that keep us connected to one another, the membrane of love surrounding us and the whole world, available to us with clarity at moments, including in our dreams, always leading us on the integral path, if we are willing. I am reminded of Dan Berrigan, another of my beloved Jesuit teachers, who wrote many years ago, *All is gift, all is gift. Give it away.*

14

ROSSERK FRIARY

"Whom shall I send, and who will go for us?" And I said, "Here am I; send me!"

—Isaiah 6:8

THE RUINS OF the fourteenth-century Rosserk Friary are nestled on the banks of Killala Bay near the market town Ballina in County Sligo, just east of County Mayo, on the northwest coast of Ireland. The exterior walls and the adjacent inner ones demarcating monks' cells and community rooms are intact, as if the buildings had been erected recently and were awaiting windowpanes, a roof, and suitable flooring. On my second visit, I came with intention. This sacred site, still faintly reeking of the consecrated place it had once been, struck me as providentially suited for what I felt drawn to do.

The friary was compact, a home to perhaps some twenty monks, if not fewer. Friaries are the domiciles of Franciscan brothers and priests, *friars*, who, in a short span after St. Francis founded the order in 1209, rapidly spread throughout Christian Europe. They came upon this remote spot in this equally remote corner of *Irlandia* in 1440, as other *beggars* planted additional friaries nearby. In fourteenth-century Ireland, there were hundreds of monastic communities: Benedictines, Trappists, Franciscans, Norbertines, Augustinians, and others indigenous to the island that St. Patrick had been instrumental in converting to Christianity in the fifth century.

Like many Irish Americans, which Ancestry.com includes all Celtic language peoples—Welsh, Scots, and Breton—I have been drawn to primitive Ireland, expressed in the Celtic underpinnings that are still so evident in everyday life, in story, art, and the cleaving to the land. If you have not seen the marvelous film *Dancing at Lughnasa*, I heartily recommend it. Jack, the brother of the sisters—the family at the heart of the movie—is a priest returned from the missions in Africa, a changed man, and not in a good way in the eyes of his puritanical sister—played at her best by Meryl Streep—nor in the eyes of the local bishop. But Jack is fully enlivened by his experience of something closer to the earth, an old man newly pulsing with life, transformed by his years away. The movie is pure Irish.

The contemporary writer, Esther de Waal, suggests that the Celts "made no distinction between the secular and the sacred. They were unable to discern boundaries of where religion began and ended and thus found it natural to assume that God was lovingly concerned in everything they did. They felt totally at home with God." The Celtic Church thrived for centuries before they were *conformed* to Rome, with Rome's remove from the wilds of the natural world. It is a community to which I aspire!

Among my regular reading companions is *The Celtic Year*, a compendium gathered by Shirley Toulson, with stories of the Celtic Church, and its hundreds of founders, all of whom were building monastic dwellings and then leaving them for others to inhabit, as they traversed the Celtic world of Ireland, Scotland, Wales, across the wide western mouth of the English Channel from Cornwall, to the expanse of Brittany, even beyond, to Galicia, in the distant Iberian Peninsula. Many of these Irish establishments were to fall during the English Reformation. Rosserk, this ancient friary, was to meet this fate. The calamitous religious persecutions of Henry VIII's revolution led the Anglo-Irish military governor of Connacht, an appointee of Elizabeth I, to assault this spiritual center and burn it to the ground, a feat he nearly accomplished. Many monks were killed. The acrid odor of that slaughter still permeates the landscape.

Ireland is soaked in a vernacular adaptation of Catholicism, one heavily influenced by local reaction to the centuries-long occupation by the British, further influenced by the Jansenism of late eighteenth-century French Catholicism, with its Ultramontane—read *severe*—sensibilities. Until lately, the Irish were dirt poor. The landscape had been denuded in the fifteenth century, the forests turned into fuel, now boggy lands that of their own composition grew little besides gorse and broom. Intensely rocky, windswept, green as the concentrated essence of that color, the climatic gift to Ireland of the daily rains that inundate the island.

Since the English occupation, and their seizing of lands, taking the best from the differently literate Irish, the local population have had plots little larger than oxcarts, sometimes held in lease agreements to ensure English sovereignty. The Irish made a valiant attempt to grow enough food for their families, the potatoes and the ubiquitous lamb being the major source of sustenance. Seaweed became both the fertilizer and soon, the soil, and later, the peat that warmed the houses and cooked the food harvested from the seaweed fortified soil—a model for twenty-first century *farm to hearth to table and return.*

During the English occupation, the Irish became fiercely loyal to the Roman Church—hierarchy, clergy, sacraments, devotions, as well as their heavily ruled and ritualized way of life. That fierce loyalty was deepened by the overlords forbidding the sacramental practice of the faith for several hundred years, what with their attempts to supplant it with the Anglicized Church of Ireland. The Anglo-Irish took the hauntingly beautiful Irish stone churches as their own, and then catered to the needs of the small colonial class of English who had immigrated to this neighboring island over the course of four hundred years.

There is a glowing shadow side to this Irish Catholicism, remnant of the pre-Patrician pagan Ireland, a Celtic sensibility imbedded in myths like that of the Irish hound *Cuchulainn*, in song and saga, in deep notions of the sacredness of the landscape and of the spiritual significance of particulars: trees, wells, rocks, rivers, mountains, animals, and the *little people*. The countryside—and really, all is countryside—was inhabited by these *little people*— fairies and gnomes and sprites—all with extraordinary powers to alter daily life. Akin to guardian angels, perhaps. I have used as a prayer book each day for the past quarter century *The Celtic Devotional*, a source book of natural and cosmic wisdom with a profound spiritual sensibility, written by Caitlin Matthews, who shares her deep appreciation for the natural religion inherent in us all, and keenly, in those many descended from the misty isle. My copy of the book is tattered, the spine long ago halved, the edges exposed, the binding loose. It's a most valuable and simple spiritual tome. Matthews has, with her resonant images, shaped me anew, encouraged me to a place apt for spiritual growth. Of all passages and prayers in this slim volume, organized into twice daily meditations, the following lines remain my favorites:

> *May I have the daring and audacity*
> *to travel my spiritual path to its very heart:*
> *to keep open the approaches,*
> *that the Beauty of the Universe may shine forth.*

These could have been penned by Teilhard, and the concluding prayer on Fridays in Samhain (winter), addressing the divine, the author prays,

> *Cunning Woman, Trickster and Clown,*
> *Keep me streetwise to the wiles of the world*
> *This winter day, till I come home to you.*

She identifies an extensive nomenclature for the divine that breaks out into new imaginings for word-wearied souls, like mine.

I have been to Ireland several times, once with Scott, once with my friend Mark Cloutier, and this time, significantly, alone. I am ever drawn to this evergreen place. Prior to this most recent trip, I made a retreat at Seattle University with my friend Jerry Cobb, a Jesuit and able spiritual companion. This was a standard eight-day Ignatian retreat. I knew I wanted to make another thirty-day retreat. I had done so as a Jesuit novice thirty years earlier. Recently, I had returned to seminary to complete my theological education, and something had stirred within me to again engage this long form of the Spiritual Exercises of St. Ignatius. I shared this idea with Jerry, who was enthusiastic in supporting me, though I would have no spiritual companion on this retreat. Rather, I would engage with the Spiritual Exercises alone—in Ireland.

I wanted a remote locale and located a cottage on Achill Island in the North Atlantic, off the coast of Mayo, and connected to the mainland by a causeway. The house I rented was a typical Irish stone cottage—restored, stuccoed, whitewashed—whose roof, once straw, had yielded, as did so many in the 1950s, to replacement by one of modern composition.

I made my plans and flew to London, then to Dublin, rented a car, and made my way west on the national auto road to County Mayo, a sparsely populated expanse of mountains, valleys, and fields with an intricate coastline. I wanted a rugged place, and I wanted to go in the winter, when I thought the weather would be most calamitous. My people, my ancestors, had come, some of them, from County Sligo next door, poor and perhaps illiterate, three generations ago, and I wanted to experience, at least in small part, some of the roughness and isolation of their daily lives, including the Atlantic coast in winter. My kin had left Ireland in two waves, the first during the devastating potato famine of the 1840s—the Harts, one Peter in particular, my great-grandfather. He eventually settled in eastern Iowa and engaged in farming and, not incidentally, in producing nineteen children—the fifteenth, my grandmother Elizabeth Anastasia. These were hardscrabble people, bringing their labors and their despised Catholicism to the *Know-Nothing* political landscape of the mid-nineteenth-century Eastern Seaboard. When they traversed the Appalachians and saw the gentle hills and black dirt of the Mississippi plain, they may have thought they had arrived in the promised land.

I spent my month on Achill Island, a large outcropping with several small villages and three distinct mountains. It is the westernmost scrap of land in Europe. I stayed in this suitable cottage, whose front yard yielded to the sea, with peaks on the distant mainland as the scape. The most significant natural feature was Slievemore, a flour sack of a mountain just to the north, in whose late afternoon shadow I dwelt for those many days.

The small cottage, two bedrooms, a living room with peat fireplace, and a modernized kitchen, was at the end of a lane with another dwelling nearby. On my initial drive down the lane, I promptly drove my rental car into the ditch, unnerved by passing other cars on narrow, ancient, rural roads. Fortuitously, my generous new neighbor saw this spectacle and came out—aged as he was—into the rain to pull me from the ditch with a hoist on his truck. He would barely accept my thanks, and soon went about his business, hidden from view by the ever-present hedgerows that mark much of the Irish roadscape. His wife became my local supplier of peat, by whose compacted flame I warmed myself, read, and sat and prayed for the next several weeks.

I make an annual retreat with the Trappist monks off a more pacific but somewhat rugged western Oregon coast, at the sublime Our Lady of Guadalupe Abbey in the highlands of the Willamette Valley in the *pinot*-growing regions southwest of Portland. I have repeated this pilgrimage for many years. As a Jesuit, I was ingrained with the rhythm of an annual eight-day retreat, and since my departure from the Society in 1979, have most years maintained that practice. Doing a long retreat in Ireland presented no significant challenge. But those weeks alone, not so many but enough, presented me with many of the challenges that solitude is designed to produce: an encounter with the Bright Mystery we feebly call God. I say feebly because it seems we exercise little imagination in trying to capture this *presence*, and we settle into a language that quickly becomes ossified. And this time alone in this ancient house tested me in ways that eight days with my Trappist brothers, and the silent company these devout and edifying men provide, never have. I am a Myers-Briggs INFJ (Introverted, Intuitive, Feeling, Judging) but close to the boundary between introvert, my deepest posture, and extrovert, which I overdeveloped to survive my complicated childhood and whose energies I have subsequently well-husbanded in my long career as a leader in the not-for-profit world. Still, I can be contentedly alone for long periods of time.

The retreat had the daily cadence I love. Each task of living received as much time as it required, unhurried and deliberate, whether it was preparing my simple meals, layering up and facing the elements each day for my ninety-minute walk on the island's main road, my five periods each day for prayer, or the other dailies: reading, gazing, writing extended notes on my laptop, sleeping long and hard, taking care of the lovely Irish cottage, managing the complex of awareness and feelings that arose over those days and nights. All soulful work, as Thomas Moore notes.

Walking the single road that traverses the island was a daily exercise in beauty, even in a drenching rain. The three mountains meet the shore with only a few yards of sand beach prior to the beginning of the steep climb, and the lowlands in between the peaks a mass of extended peat. There is an intact *famine village*, Slievemore, on the southern flank of the largest mountain, abandoned when death took most inhabitants and the few survivors fled to the mainland.

The locals, few that there are, inveterately wave at the walkers, whose return salute suggests goodwill and perhaps an acknowledgment of the stupidity of walking in the daily downpour.

From those retreat weeks, two events still hold me in their grip.

During the third week of the retreat, corresponding to the Third Week of the Spiritual Exercises of St. Ignatius (I used Jesuit David Fleming's fine translation), I had an encounter one evening in bed that shook me. My going-to-bed routine was to douse, if necessary, the remnant of flame from that day's peat fire, lock the two doors, and go into the back room, read for a while, and then fall asleep. I am an easy sleeper, and for most of the retreat, that remained true.

This night, Tuesday of that third week, I was caught in the grip of an intense and unexpected dread. So intense was it that I thought, perhaps, I was losing my mind. I felt panicky, deeply

alone, a bit paralyzed, and became acutely aware of my unac-
companied presence—or so I thought—in this little cottage
on a dark lane on a small island off the storm-ridden coast of
a remote section of Ireland. I had had a similar experience of
dread and panic on my vow retreat at New Melleray, the Trappist monastery in Iowa, thirty years earlier. I thought, *What have
I done? What is happening to me? Why am I here?* My attempt to
connect to some semblance of the divine within led only to more
fear and an overwhelming sense of abandonment. As well, a profound unworthiness swept through me. I grew very sad and felt
that perhaps some unforeseen calamity was upon me.

I remained in this state for some time when I realized: *This
is why you came here. This is why you're here. For this. If you cannot withstand this, what can you withstand? If God is not present
to you now, even if in a way you cannot ascertain or feel or in any
way know, when would God be present? How would God be present? What is this God with whom you made this journey if not in
this moment, in this fear, in this sense of sadness and near despair,
somehow present, somehow yet the Source?*

Slowly, calm returned. My plan to dress and get in the car
(yes, in the driving rain) and get to Westport—forty-five minutes away on the mainland—and find the one pay phone on the
main road I remember having seen and call Scott and what...tell
him I am afraid and sad and unknowing and filled with dread—
shelved. I came to know I had come here, among other reasons,
to have this very experience, to feel bereft and in some way dis-
integrating and abject, so that a deeper consciousness might
be unveiled, and to sit in some embodied trust beyond my own
machinations.

I slowly drifted back to sleep. Upon awakening, I was filled
with gratitude. I was *here*. I had not fled. I had allowed the suspension of my control to invite *presence* that I have intuited all
my life. And my mountain was still there, too. I opened the cottage door and greeted this holy mountain by name: "Good morning, Slievemore. And thank you."

The next week was my final one on Achill. During these Spiritual Exercises, I decided to revisit that desecrated friary, Rosserk.

The evening before I ventured on this day trip, I gathered some things from the cottage: a yellowish gold blanket, a squat candle and matchbook, the elegantly literate *Jerusalem Bible* that I had brought with me the day I entered the Jesuits some thirty years earlier, and my *Celtic Devotional*. What I could not find was *oil*, an oil special enough to use in ritual, an oil like the one I had used to bless and anoint countless friends as they were dying of AIDS. The next morning, again Tuesday, I loaded the car with these gathered items and, with extra layers of clothing, drove back on to the mainland and headed northeast, to County Sligo, to this hallowed place, Rosserk Friary.

The mountains of north County Mayo shone under a dusting of mid-winter snow, making the early morning trek enchanting. I made my way to the market town of Ballina and found a pharmacy on High Street where I asked the pharmacist if she had any oils: "Of course!" She offered me a pure oil, like the kind parents use to abate earaches in their children, one I found perfect for my healing purposes. With my new possession in hand, and a cup of coffee *to go* (a rarity in Ireland at that time), I headed out of town, following the River Moy southeast to Rosserk.

Though a place of haunting grace, and not so far from Ballina center, Rosserk was empty. A *national reserve*, the grounds are minimally maintained, and the open-to-the-heavens friary is kept in pristine, yet decayed form. The ecclesiastical structure accentuated the church at the friary's center, a chapel, really. Its altar is still entirely intact, although its surface heavily pebbled after centuries of exposure to the elements, the ground peppered with pea gravel, the holy water fonts to the left and right of the altar filled with rainwater, as if they were merely waiting patiently for believers to once more dip their fingers. To the right of the altar was a small vestibule, where the priest celebrating the Eucharist undoubtedly changed from his brown Franciscan robe into eucharistic vestments.

I placed my *Jerusalem Bible* on the altar and opened it to the first verses of Isaiah 61:

The Spirit of the Lord Yahweh has been given to me,
For Yahweh has anointed me.
He has sent me to bring good news to the poor,
To bind up hearts that are broken,
To proclaim liberty to captives,
Freedom to those in prison.

I then went into the vestibule where I took off my shoes and socks and shed my clothes and wrapped my *self* in the yellow-gold blanket from the cottage. I reentered the nave, approached the precincts of the altar, blessed myself as I had done with great regularity since perhaps my third year of life, now with the rainwater movingly held and blessed by the ancient stone fonts. I walked to the center of the nave and dropped the blanket to the ground.

I knelt, naked, and prostrated myself in front of the altar, which cradled the text that had driven my life since high school, Isaiah acknowledging for me the nearly unspeakable: "The Lord has anointed me. The command: to be present to those most in need, those poor, those captives, those brokenhearted...those just like me."

I began to weep. I lay there naked to the elements, naked to myself, naked in the presence of that which I had followed all the way here, and which I could barely describe or articulate any wisdom regarding. All this was mainly unknowable to me, although I had perceived it since a small boy, that *bright mystery* that brought me here, in its grip, for no purpose other than to experience *presence*.

After a time, I slowly rose and proceeded to the altar, where I took the oil that I had placed next to the scriptures, blessed the oil by praying simple words of intention over it, and proceeded to anoint myself: the crown of my head, my forehead, my eyes, my ears, my nostrils, my lips, over my heart, over my gut, on my genitals, my knees and my feet and finally my hands. I anointed those places on my person through which I knew life, those places on my person where I interacted with others, humans like me, where I had loved others, hurt others, taught others, forgave others, ran with others, been forgiven by others, healed others, denied others, and been present to others, over the course of a life, of my then half century of living. I continued weeping softly, as I reread the passage from Isaiah that had informed my life. As I finished reading these words, I kissed the altar and picked up a small fragment of stone that laid on top.

My marker. Something has happened here. This stone is my witness.

I returned to the nave, gathered up the blanket around my *again-as-is-always-being-blessed* body, went back into the vestibule, put on my clothes, gathered up my accoutrement, returned to the center of the nave and bowed to the altar and left this most sacred place.

I drove away from Rosserk that afternoon the same man I had been when I had arrived. But also—I departed an altogether different man.

15

SACRED PRECINCTS

Every day I add another piece to the religion that is
my own. It's built on years of meditation, chanting,
theological study and the practice of therapy—to me a
sacred activity.

—Thomas Moore

ONE RECENT SUMMER, we were invited on vacation with Scott's family for a ten-day sojourn to Umbria. We stayed in a beautiful villa on a gorgeous hilltop overlooking a vast Umbrian valley. To the north lay Perugia and eventually Bologna and Venice, to the south Spoleto, and eventually, Rome. Columnar Italian pines framed the region's vineyards and olive groves, and terra-cotta dwellings clung to hillsides above ancient villages.

Italy in person was quite like the Italy in my mind's eye, seen over decades of imagining—the angle of the light, the ease of the contours, the soft palette of colors, the languid pace of movement among the Italians, the smell of antiquity and garlic and earthy bread. It was not hard to imagine Roman soldiers marching on the lanes that became vias that later became highways, and eventually, modern thruways. Indoors or outdoors, an unnecessary distinction. I noticed immediately the temperate clime not dissimilar to that of Sonoma County, month for month. And the sea! Aquamarine, placid, becalming.

With Scott's family, we had gathered en masse on similar vacations, but on this trip I had an agenda, and I was perfectly happy to implement it alone. Assisi was my singular goal, and I told Scott that, on that first Monday, I would rise early and venture northeast to arrive in Assisi to attend Mass in one of the many churches at the heart of this medieval town.

I left before first light. Scott and his parents would join me for a late lunch. I had several luxurious hours alone! I parked below the *centro della città* where automobiles are consigned and walked up into Assisi as the sun was coming over the eastern horizon. Finding a small church on the main *via*, its door slightly open, I entered the dark vestibule and sensed Mass was about to begin.

Since 1988, going to Mass remained an elusive practice for me. I appreciated Jung's dictum that one could only stay in the shadow so long before the shadow eroded one's soul. After a decade post-Jesuit, worshipping with a good community, I accepted that—in essence—the church excluded me and so many others from several of its sacraments. I closed that door and did not look back. Or so I thought.

In Europe, where I seldom spoke the vernacular, I felt drawn to worship, oblivious to the particular words the priest might be saying, or what archaic version of the canon he would be reciting. Instead, I allowed myself to be filled with the sensuous elements of Catholic liturgy—and more significantly—to receive communion, without feeling the outcast. In Paris, at St. Sulpice, a favored church of mine, I discovered the congregation was mostly French-speaking West Africans, and the priests, either ancient Frenchmen, or immigrant Senegalese, or perhaps Mali, prayed in such a way that their energy invited me to relax and feel at home.

On two occasions, while visiting Paris, we have boarded the train at Gare du Nord and alighted sometime later in a small city in the French countryside to be in the presence of the shimmering magnificence of that ineluctable stone edifice, the Cathedral of Our Lady of Chartres, its sublime spiritual power penetrating me, accompanied by a sensual transfiguration.

In Assisi, I felt a similar peace being in this small church in the town whose streets *Il Poverrello* had trod. As in St. Sulpice, I felt at home. I have deeply appreciated for the past thirty-three years, that for gay persons, feeling at home in church is often unattainable, especially if we seek out churches of the denominations in which we were raised. And how many of these have been riven by gay sexuality: Catholic, Mormon, Presbyterian, Missouri Synod Lutherans, or the recently split Methodists. American churches have created well-known fault lines that deem some children of God not worthy of the church's sacramental or institutional life, like the post–Civil War split between those open to former slaves and those deeming them unacceptable for a place at the altar. While no longer a surprise, for literally millions, the spiritual wounds remain uncauterized. Karl Rahner, the deeply spiritual German Jesuit theologian whose work permeated the Second Vatican Council, seemed to anticipate this. After a lifetime of reflecting, he wrote, "The devout Christian of the future will either be a mystic, one who has experienced something, or he will cease to be anything at all." So much of what passes for contemporary Christianity seems so bereft of experiencing something, instead being so focused on maintaining power through dogmatic absolutism and the ultimately futile attempt of controlling others' bodies.

After Mass in Assisi that August morning, I left the church to seek out *un espresso* and some Italian pastry. The warmth of the morning was turning into real heat and the sun, now higher on its journey, beat down on the sienna-washed walls of the edifices that line the rough cobblestone streets of Assisi, as it has for millennia, and on me.

After Francis's death early in the thirteenth century, there was a stampede to recognize him, by both forces in the Vatican and forces within the nascent but booming Franciscan order. The grand churches of Assisi are a testament to that ardor. In the Upper Church of the Basilica de San Francesco d'Assisi, the frescoes of Giotto, known widely from their reproduction and their presence on devout calendars and Christmas cards, shortened my breath. The angle one's head and neck assume to appreciate them fully adds to their mystery, for they were, my memory suggests, like iridescent luminous wallpaper covering all available space on high. A muffled silence prevailed under the Giottos. One could only take in the frescoes for so long, feeling awestruck in their presence. I wondered what it would be like to be a parishioner in this artfully moving space and look up at these frescoes over the course of one's life, noticing the smallest of features that together created their whole. I felt privileged to be there, under this encompassing ceiling.

Two more treasures awaited me.

The tomb of Francis is in a dark crypt below the Upper Church, surrounded by kneelers where one can take time to be present and pray in whatever form that might take. I felt I *knew* my fellow devotees as we sat or knelt a few feet from the tomb of this one most often cited as the second person of Christianity, after Jesus (sorry, Paul!), in charismatic appeal and in exemplary holiness. Francis's manifestation of love still reverberates and models how this Love connects us, as we experience at any intense celebration or in the recognition over coffee that the other is fully present to us, and we to them. I prayed to be present to this thick grace, and I felt contained.

Upon leaving the crypt, I noticed a sign that said, *Museo*, with an arrow pointing down worn stone steps. I followed and entered a contemporary space in the church's bowels, where fragments of Francis's life were on display. To the right, hung on the wall, was a large octagonal Plexiglas box, perhaps six feet in diameter. Inside was the splayed, voluminously self-patched, brown robe Francis had worn. With hand stitching, Francis had continuously repaired, using scraps of brown cloth, the holes in the robe that time and work had worn way. The patches were primitive, and the effect of the liberally mended robe was overwhelming. I started to weep at its sight, and had to remove myself from the immediate environ, sobbing with joy and gratitude, and I did not know what else.

The Catholic penchant for relics intrigued me when I was young, and there is no accounting for it in the contemporary man that I would like to suggest I am. In the secular world in which

I often dwell, such an accounting makes no sense, and is generally the object of censorious, raised eyebrows. Nothing need be said. We moderns will have no truck with such enchantments. But more than superstition is going on. There is an unconscious interplay between symbol and psyche that extrudes the deepest of feeling, beyond the revered rationale, beyond the worshipped logical, beyond the realm of what the social sciences have yet been able to penetrate, what with their systems of classification and extrapolation based on external phenomenon and behavior, so often ignoring the interior phenomena that animate so many billions of lives. I was so glad to be in this room, so glad that in my life I got to see this garment, so glad to be in Assisi, and so glad to be right there, right then—with no place else to be, no other experience to be having, and no other desire present.

Other artifacts were also in the room in similar, smaller cases. I remember the contents of none. Perhaps a drinking cup, perhaps a spoon, an old hand-blocked copy of the Vulgate? The room was small, and I felt a need to make space for others coming in, so I left and went back outside into the Umbrian sun. I felt relieved. I felt present. I felt calm. And I felt blessedly alone.

I bought Franciscan sandals in a little shop filled with "Francisiana" that afternoon, which I only recently gave to the local homeless shelter for a living Francis who might abide there and, perhaps, in our Sonoma summers, need sandals to wear. I mistook their presence on my feet as maybe imparting to me some mirroring of this peerless saint. That proved not to be the case! To mirror him would require a very different set of behaviors from me, ones not induced by wearing similar footwear.

Over a delightful lunch alfresco, Dick, Mary, and Scott were all interested in my morning activities. Mary seemed particularly keen on what I had done and seen. I have always suspected that my mother-in-law had a place in her psyche in which ritual and sacramental life somehow drew her in, not that she mentioned this. Every year she put up her creche, in full view, perhaps not knowing that Francis himself established the first of these ubiquitous symbol sets. His, of course, contained live sheep and oxen, and perhaps a dog or two.

In our home, Scott is the creche-meister, and he has received tiny animals of various genera and species from friends over the course of our life together. Mary would give him a new addition to the menagerie each year, and when she came to our house at Christmastime, would always observe where Scott had placed the little creature. That day in Assisi, she had discreetly purchased another lamb to join our flock.

After we left Umbria, Scott and I had a few days in Rome. Like Carl Jung, who could not visit Rome, so overwhelming he knew the vast interwoven set of Catholic symbols would be— too much, and for him, the son of a conservative Lutheran cleric, whose religion's foundation was a rejection of the many add-ons of Roman Catholic culture, and who yet understood keenly the power of symbol and mystery. For my own separate reasons, not utterly divorced from Jung's, I, too, had not wanted to visit.

Most remarkably unremarkable was the heat. We stayed in a tiny *pensione*, and as one must, we ate avidly, amply, and often. We first ventured to the Pantheon, which a professor earlier in my academic career had described—a la Henry James—as the center of the center of the world. A Roman temple built on an Etruscan site, now a church, with the wide, circular oculus centered in the elliptical ceiling that allows the elements to penetrate the building and bring nature into this sacred space.

I decided not to go to Vatican City, and particularly not to St. Peter's, another kind of center of the center. The weight of the place was for me largely emotional, the place that the child I was thought to be the apex, now a place that felt exclusive and cold. The welcoming church of John XXIII had evolved into the defiant and harsh one of John Paul II and his aide-de-camp, Joseph Ratzinger, then the occupant of the chair of Peter.

But I hungrily went to the Gesu, the mother church of the Society of Jesus, with its grand and excessive Rococo-Baroque interior. Upon entering from the blazing hot *strada*, its gilt met my own, and it overwhelmingly won! I exhaled deeply, and my body was immediately centered in this glorious, symbolically rich church. It was, perhaps, my center of the center. The liturgy was soon to begin, and as at my beloved St. Sulpice in Paris, I eagerly took my place among the modest congregation, under-standing only the Italian that sounded like the Spanish I yet had available to me. I received the Eucharist, and for the second time on this Italian sojourn, wept.

After Mass, I lingered, inspecting all the side altars and the majestic, detailed ceiling. Above the high altar, Giovanni Battista Gaulli's stupendous vaulted ceiling is painted with the magnificent monogram of the name of Jesus, "I-H-S," with blinding rays of light emitting from its center. The monogram of his least society. I came upon the large altar over the tomb of St. Ignatius, a splendid Rococo-style space where I could imagine Inigo might have balked, but nonetheless, befitting one so storied and venerated. I had held no great devotion to Ignatius as a Jesuit, but rather to Francis Xavier and Matteo Ricci, who understood that to reach the Dowager Empress and begin his work in China, he needed to dress and speak like a Mandarin—and to my birth date saint, Peter Claver, who had ministered to the enslaved Africans in the slave market of Cartagena. Later, Alfred Delp came to embody what I valued in the Society. But I was glad to be here at Inigo's tomb. I knelt on the prie-dieu directly in front of the sarcophagus and bowed my head to acknowledge my desire to be present.

Immediately, without making any requests or even affirma-tions, I heard the word *Write!* And again, *Write!* And a third time, *Write!*

I did not want to write. I could not write. I shouldn't write. Who do I think I am to write? But I knew what the command "Write!" meant. It meant to write this, all of this, these chapters, these memories, these regressions, these sometimes humilia-tions, these graces, these intuitions, these connections, these epiphanies, these presences. At Ignatius's tomb, I was chastened, braced, and blessed all at once. I rose and I slowly made my way out of this homey church—homey for me. The sun still blazed. And I was upset. For I was sore afraid to write.

Some years later, Scott and I had the great joy of travelling to Istanbul with my nephew, Brian, and his wife, Dana, both Middle East-ern policy professionals. We went to, among other notables, Hagia Sophia. Again, a center of a center of a center. A magnificent museum in a former mosque in the ancient sacred building that began its life as the premier Eastern Catholic Basilica, now, recently, a mosque again. The intricate tile work with the many figures of Jesus as Christ Pantocrator, of Mary, and of numerous other saints, still embedded in the walls of the upper stories; below, the elegantly spare and breathtaking domed space in which devout Muslims for centuries had gathered to pray. In many mosques, unbelievers were not welcomed to stay for prayer, but in Hagia Sophia, which Kemal Ataturk, the founding father of the Republic of Turkey, transmogrified into a museum, that restriction did not apply. I sat somewhat removed from several fellow Abrahamic brothers and bowed before the Divine, whose presence here, as in so many sacred places on this earth, is a felt presence.

Leaving Turkey, we returned to Rome for our second visit. We had the luxury of a week, and we had the further luxury of autumn weather. We walked the seven hills and again ate our way through recommended *ristorantes* and *trattorie*. I revisited the Gesu, of course, and several other sacred sites. On this trip, I decided to forgo my resistance to visiting Vatican City, and we made a date with a private guide, a delightful—and connected—*professoressa*—whose services allowed us to skip the long lines already queued up at 8:30 a.m., the privilege of which, without batting an eye, I took full advantage. Our guide toured us through the Vatican Museum, chock-full of Renaissance fabulousness, and then led us into the already crowded Sistine Chapel. Having spent a lifetime in its broadly reproduced presence, it loomed large, and was. Craning my neck to take in the intricately painted Michelangelo ceiling, I found his painted images already burnished in my psyche. The hands touching, the finger of the Divine and the finger of the creature who emanated forthwith (some good theology), were stunning.

We exited into a lovely, perfectly manicured garden and *la professoressa* acquired *due caffè espressi* for us, a perfect time-out prior to entering St. Peter's. I thought the newly elected pope, the Jesuit Bergoglio, might any moment just happen by. That he had chosen Francis as his papal name heralded all he hoped to do in what might be a short tenure. We entered Bramante's,

Michelangelo's, Maderno's, and Bernini's magnificent and monstrous basilica through a side door. I was immediately in awe—in not such a good way. I felt overwhelmed, an experience I seldom have. The vastness struck me, as did the monochromatic polished pale sienna of the uncountable marbles and endless altars. I located St. Ignatius and St. Madelaine Sophie Barat, emotional touchstones for me, and happily, the tomb of the beloved John XXIII. There, on an available prie-dieu, I knelt and bowed my head.

Upon rising, I had to leave the basilica.

I skirted the cordoned-off area that now preserved *La Pieta*, heavily secured. I headed to the doors, and exited into the masterful *Piazza San Pietro*, and walked across the Vatican State's boundary to the first cafe I could find. Ah, another *café*.

I cannot ascribe my reactions to just one thing. They were not consciously driven. There was a dreamlike quality to my experience at St. Peter's, a feeling of vacancy, sterility, under the great Bernini dome, alien, as if in the museum of a culture whose heart I could not discern, whose aesthetic was cold, remote, somehow unforgiving. My own projections undoubtedly played their part, as did the heat and the crowds, mostly tourists, and perhaps some like me, untouchable.

I—sometimes with Scott, who has often, generously joined me—have visited churches ad infinitum throughout Europe, Argentina, Mexico, Turkey, rural England, and throughout Ireland, and even in Muslim Morocco. And synagogues—in the forsaken Jewish quarter of Toledo, Spain, the intact temple in the ancient holy city of Fez, the resplendent *Tempio Maggiore di Roma*, the *Synagogue de Nazareth* in the Marais in Paris, San Francisco's sublime Temple Emmanuel. And mosques, when appropriate, in Fez and the Hassan II Grand Mosque in Casablanca, the largest Muslim house of worship in Africa. Also, when visiting Istanbul—the Blue Mosque—and in Izmir, the old Greek city of Turkey on the Mediterranean, near Ephesus, where the simple House of Mary is located, high up in the hills, a house with a view if ever, where St. John the Beloved is said to have taken the mother of Jesus to live out her life. On the day we visited, no one else was there.

I am seeking something clearly, a place to feel close, but to whom? To a person, or persons, a community of persons? To my Self? To God?

My younger self was drawn to the silence, the smell, the distant memory of the close presence I felt when nestled in the pew of St. Margaret Mary Church in Omaha, Nebraska. Or the college church, St. John's, at Creighton, where I still drop in to pick up what scent I can of that sacred odor and that guileless time.

But to worship in them is challenging, and I am conflicted. I have taken on a lived posture in opposition to the dark work of Cardinal Ratzinger, who proclaimed homosexuals intrinsically disordered back in 1986, two years before my Folsom Street-induced exit. And in this I am profoundly not alone, but not exactly with others, either.

Queer people, whom I would assert without the requisite research to undergird my sense, but with forty years of ministry with them—are uniquely spiritually grounded seekers, having often been cast out from that which matters—family, church, community. Having to go inward to discover one's Self, queer people along the way discover how the divine is manifest, too, even if not acknowledged or understood via religious language. But the souls of queer folx, to adapt W.E.B. DuBois's intimate phrase, because of the experience of suffering that coming through on the way to coming out necessitates, have the capacity to be empathic and intuitive, that is, soulful, in ways that heal others, all others. Or so I have come to believe.

For those raised in Roman Catholicism, penance is the only one of the seven sacraments an out-gay person—living her whole life with integrity, including conscience-determined sexual integrity—can easily obtain if she was not willing to disavow her sexuality and its lived implications in her life. I have much sadness around this.

Not long after the "disordered-proclaiming" Ratzinger made his stand, the drawbridge was drawn up. That he later became pope sealed the doors, as was his wish. For millions of others, it became a fait accompli.

And yet, in Assisi, in the Gesu, at Hagia Sophia and the simple French cathedral in Casablanca and St. Sulpice and St. John's at Creighton, St. Agnes in San Francisco, St. Francis Xavier in New York City, all feel, in some way, "beyond the Pale"—that line the Anglo-Irish drew down the center-right of the country, believing those on the other side were wild, not amenable to civilization, British style. Those beyond-the-Pale counties to the west—Sligo, Mayo, and Galway, and Clare farther south—the tiny, stone wall-demarcated farmsteads my foremothers and fathers came from—those abject counties, my people most likely illiterate, not worthy of education, or land—but, as they would say, keeping the faith. Their contemporary counterparts, for me, these houses of worship remain pockets of grace, free zones, safe places, for me. Their light seems always on.

I find myself—with millions of others—sons and daughters, whose lives are required to be lived—if with integrity—just west of the Pale's border, a marker where the British hegemons sustained their dark reign of genteel terror lasting many hundreds of years.

On Achill Island off the Mayo coast, at the far western edge of the island—next stop, Boston—there is a large flat rock formation in the shallow bay that is only visible at low tide. The Achill Irish, all fishermen, knew the tides like they knew their children, maybe better. As low tide would be approaching, they fetched the otherwise masqueraded priest, and they would altogether celebrate the Eucharist on that rock, in violation of the civil authorities. The islanders, by the hundreds, would go to the isle's tip, and there, in darkness, after the sun set over the roaring North Atlantic, they would celebrate that presence in the way remnants had since that last supper in the upper room in another marginalized outpost of another empire long ago.

I love these places, these buildings, these oases in the often-vacant landscape of contemporary culture. And I find myself constantly on the search for that hidden flat slab, for that unexpected sacred site, for the presence of the holy, which often appears in places just beyond the Pale.

16

"TWO MEN KISSING"

Justice is really love in calculation.

—Martin Luther King Jr.

THE MASSACRE IN 2016 of people at Pulse, the gay nightclub in Orlando, that capital of Disney-curated happiness, got into my flesh, like fallout from a toxic explosion. Grief captured me and invited me to pay close attention...to many things.

He saw two men kissing in Miami recently, and it made him go crazy...a paraphrase of what the murderer's father relayed, as he reassured us that it was God's job—and not his son's—to punish the homosexuals. This most horrific massacre, done explicitly to queer people, gay men and women and their friends, by an individual who has the markings, among other traits and characteristics, of how the self-hatred of closeted gay people operates at the most primitive and destructive levels.

That it was accomplished by a weapon of war, a readily available assault rifle, a repeating death machine with no other identifiable purpose than the slaughter of human life. No honorable hunter would dream of using such a weapon on an animal nor would a sport shooter lug this death machine to a sporting event. Its purpose is clear.

Two men kissing....This most provocative of sights, this greatest affront, this enabler of deepest fear, for many, a most hidden longing. So forbidden, it is unspeakable. His victims were mostly Puerto Ricans in their twenties and thirties, salsa dancing, and happy to be in a place of refuge, which every gay bar in the United States is for gay people. Like church, only more joyful; like church, only inclusive; like church, only no clergy, and wild, and colorful, and embodied, and rhythmic, and sacramental, and communal, and life-affirming.

In Omaha, my hometown, the big gay bar, as in many cities, has no exterior sign, for the protection of its patrons. But once found, and safely ensconced inside, one finds a magnificent assembly of persons pulsing joyful life. Queer people, of course, but also straight, interracial couples, young adults who do not fit into the culture, tats and piercings and a variety of costumes abound. Our nieces, Staci and Laura, now suburban moms, took us to Omaha's big gay bar twenty-five years ago. They got atop the dance cubes and taught the assembly the Macarena. And being the hipsters they are, they knew where the bar was!

Every town and city has such spaces. Anderson Cooper said it clearly: Every gay man in America remembers the first time they went to a gay bar and how they felt. I would add the coda: *free.* For many, the only safe place on the planet. Queer women, too, have had bars and venues in most cities, and sometimes smaller towns, that were equally energizing. And for decades, these have been the site of bombings, arsons, gay bashings, stabbings, and mayhem—mostly unreported or unspoken.

Two men kissing...

In Orlando, a forty-seven-year-old mother was there with her beloved gay son, both to dance. She, a mother of eleven and he in his early twenties. She was slaughtered; he, somehow, was not.

Present also were three married gay couples, husbands dancing with husbands, souls deeply attached, slaughtered in each other's arms.

There was also the dashing Edward Sotomayor Jr., shot in the back as he shielded another from harm in what the beloved Teacher suggests is the highest human act of love, giving one's life for one's friends.

Sandy Hook also reverberates within me. Another slaughter of innocents, a town and a state and a nation stunned and aggrieved and disgusted. The press and the public said that this surely would be the turning point that would finally bring responsible control of weapons of mass destruction. We have had enough! But the potent gun lobby, the NRA, paying some senators more than two million dollars for their reelection campaigns—and that's real money—made sure not one iota of change occurred to America's gun laws. A political elite enthralled and in hock to a quite small—per capita—organization, a death factory.

Amanda Marcotte, a smart, literate reporter, said in her article in *Salon*, "'Bigotry is Bigotry, No Matter What Religion' put it most succinctly for me: homophobia, misogyny, toxic masculinity, and religious fundamentalism, in a noxious knot."

A few days before this massacre of gay persons in Orlando, one of those senators, the junior one from Georgia, one David Perdue, close by the horrific Charleston massacre at Mother Emmanuel Church of the summer before, had quoted Psalms suggesting that the quick demise of President Obama was to be prayed for...later attesting that he had been just joking, of course, his mouth dissembling his words so quickly one is amazed his gums did not render up his teeth. Not joking, his colleague, a Georgia representative named Rick Allen, recently suggested, as per his readings of Romans, gay people in the United States should be put to death. No post-Orlando apology forthcoming. You can YouTube what the homophobic Christian Republican lieutenant governor of Texas posted on his website the Sunday morning after the Pulse massacre, a passage from Galatians: "They shall reap such as they sow." Not intentional! Totally a coincidence!

Or you might YouTube the Baptist pastor in Sacramento who ranted in his hastily prepared sermon Sunday morning, the bodies in Orlando not yet cold, that the gunman ought to have lined up all the pedophiles at that nightclub and shot them all. But having fifty of them dead was better than nothing. I believe Southern Baptists consider themselves followers of Jesus.

Homophobia, having been its object for nearly eight decades, and having spent a considerable amount of time in its clutches and observing closely its admixture, is but a subset of misogyny, its doppelgänger if you will.

At the heart of this, and to the toxically gripped male, that most disgusting of human sights, is simply two men kissing. This must be annihilated! Denied. Beaten. Bashed. Legislated against. Condemned. AK 47-ed.

The National Conference of Catholic Bishops, in their moment-of-silence proclamation regarding Orlando, could not mention the word *gay* nor *queer* nor even the awkward acronym *LGBTQ+*.

Unspoken.

The Senate majority leader, Mr. McConnell, could not find these words in his vocabulary, either. Nor could the then governor of Florida, Rick Scott, in whose state this gay massacre occurred.

Unspoken.

In the United States Congress, then-Speaker Ryan asked for a moment of silence for the no-further-identified victims in Orlando.

Rep. Jim Himes, who represents the district that contains Sandy Hook Elementary School, could take no more. He walked out of the United States Capitol. He had had enough. He was joined by a few conscious others. Moments of silence, yes. Thoughts and prayers, yes. Legislative action, never.

Unspoken.

The love that dares not speak its name. The love like that of a woman.

Of course, you can YouTube violent extremists in the Middle East. ISIS, for example, during its tyrannical control of conquered territory, stoned gay boys to death in occupied Iraq, threw gay boys off the roofs on many-storied buildings to their deaths below in occupied Syria, and if you have not had enough, you can further YouTube the more civilized Iranians hanging two nineteen-year-olds "caught" in the act of making love.

Two men kissing...

As womenkind has battled to claim agency and person-hood, there is a perverse movement among some men who have perceived themselves to be its victims. The result is the current iteration of an ancient phenomenon now widely understood as toxic masculinity, a noxious brew of bravado, fear, isolation, resentment, and anger, with a steroidal emphasis on aggressive muscularity and control. It is certainly not all straight men—for many are indeed avatars of love, and my life is amply blessed with them—and it infects us all, women and men alike. When wrapped in a cocoon of dogmatic religion, it is—I would assert—the most destructive power in the world, and while it is a religion of brute force and coercion, of manipulative power and subjugation, its adherents often go by the name Christian, they go by the name Muslim, they go by the name Jew, they go by the name Hindu, and some even go by the name Buddhist.

For the interiorly minded, for the conscious adherents of these global faiths, for those for whom the sacred has context, content, and potency, the task of undoing this knot is paramount. Any system that privileges some by dint of gender or race or social location or sexual orientation helps maintain—if unconsciously—the global mechanism of massacre and death. The pattern of this toxic masculinity leads to enslavement, sexual trafficking and violence, authoritarianism, bullying, mass incarceration of Blacks, systemic racism, denial of the climate crisis—all manner of woes.

And yet, all the above being true, and daunting, and deeply sorrowing, what else struck me the days following the gay massacre at Pulse is the shattering experience of love and hope emanating from every quarter of the globe, people gathering en masse in the West and Middle East and Asia and the Latin world, in cities large and small, in places like Omaha's Memorial Park to London's Trafalgar Square to Taksim Square in Istanbul.

Spare but hopeful signs to me: former presidential candidate Mitt Romney offered generous words, as did Robert Lynch, the Roman Catholic bishop of St. Petersburg in Florida. The president of my university, the Jesuit Creighton University, Daniel Hendrickson, SJ, celebrated a memorial Mass on campus for the LGBT victims of this massacre. The Mormon lieutenant governor of Utah, Spencer Cox, gave a stirring, humble tribute to those slaughtered at a memorial service the night after the massacre in Salt Lake City. Imams from mosques throughout this nation, under the annihilating threat of the then presumptive Republican presidential nominee, reached out to gay folk to express sadness and solidarity.

Of course, Lady Gaga moved those gathered in New York to tears by her perennial assertion that she chooses to identify with the queer community and hence can only but share in its burdens, its sorrows, as she provided a large modicum of joy.

The incomparable Lin Manuel Miranda, when he accepted his Tony for Hamilton several nights later, shook the room with his sonnet embracing the victims of the Orlando gay massacre, ending this stunning, stirring piece with the words: "*...love is love is love is love is love is love is love is love, cannot be killed or swept aside...*"

In my ruminations over these decades, asking myself and the tentatively identified Divine Other, "Why do gay people exist?" "Why am I gay?" and "What is this for?" I have come to no final answers, though persistent with my questions. But I do think that in my over fourty-fourth year of being out, I sense that same-sex love is here, a thread in this human community, as an essential link in the membrane of consciousness undergirding the planet, to assert the primacy of love in this human community. For what every and each gay person has had to traduce simply to say, "I am gay, or lesbian or trans or queer"; what each gay person has had to traduce to find the ones whose lips they would but kiss; and for what long journey each gay person has had to travel to finally look into another's eyes and say simply, "I love you," and, like Mr. Sotomayor, be willing to form a human shield around another to protect her or him from life's many wounds, even its fatal ones, is testament to the absolute power of love.

It's testament to the absolute power of *Love* that it can defy the chains of normalizing culture that would bridle men into this toxic masculinity, that would warp religions of love into machines of dark and pernicious conformity and destruction—psychological, emotional, physical—that would alienate children from parents and parents from friends, that would regard women as somehow any less in any way to their male counterparts, and that would suggest that pigmentation of skin is, somehow, in the very genes a traiting of character.

Many on the planet, fellow citizens, rather, brothers and sisters, stood in reverent silence, small candles, actually or metaphorically, in hand, and acknowledged this profound pain, and in doing so, said, once more, never again. And should never not quite yet happen, these very citizens will keep saying it. And keep saying it in Newtown, Paris, Charleston, Las Vegas, Chicago, Nairobi, and in all the myriad places in which hatred and fear work hard to trump mercy and love.

It's testament to the absolute assertion that a human being is at heart and at the end, only ultimately a vessel for grace for the healing of the wounds of the others. We do so to continue the work of building the community of justice and love. Any other task is but a deviation from this human project. Queer people, among others, have acquired this complicated and costly knowledge because of our lived experience in the world. Those forty-seven women and men in Orlando hard won this knowledge at the moment of their deaths. They gave their lives for it. And though we queer people may fail to practice it fully in our lives, God knows, it is hardwired into our psyches, our souls. But this knowledge is for all of us, sexual orientation notwithstanding. And we are all called to be its missionaries.

17

A TRIPTYCH OF DREAMS

Since once again, Lord—though this time not in the forests of the Aisne but in the steppes of Asia—I have neither bread, nor wine, nor altar, I will raise myself beyond these symbols, up to the pure majesty of the real itself; I, your priest, will make the whole earth my altar and on it will offer you all the labors and sufferings of the world.

—Pierre Teilhard de Chardin, *Hymn of the Universe*

WHILE WORKING THROUGH the AIDS epidemic, I had a triptych of instructive dreams that illuminated the questions I have asked myself for forty years, usually beginning with the phrase, "What gives you the right?" or perhaps more accurately, "*Who* gives you the right?" My unconscious self, attending to the ongoing concerns of my waking psyche, offered me some sense of resolution. These dreams, which I have come to refer to as *the triptych*, are vivid within and have illuminated my path. As dreams do, they have invited me to be more my whole Self.

Dream One: I am looking forward to going dancing in the city—the city being San Francisco—but I find myself driving north—at night—on the Pacific Coast Highway. I turn into a wooded property, drive up a small slope, and park my car. I approach a darkened hillside and notice an opening. I enter a cave, illuminated by torches protruding from the rough walls, and am immediately struck by the scene. One ledge of the cave— perhaps twelve feet above the floor—is studded with a grouping of cells, like I would envision monastic cells might have looked like for the desert fathers in Egypt 1,800 years ago. Each is occupied by a gay man, legs crossed, still, alone, unaware of the other's presence but a few feet away. Isolated. Each man, with eyes downcast, is facing forward, their heads extended, as if waiting, expectantly. Perhaps waiting for death.

In the center of the cave's rough floor is an outcropping, maybe eight feet high, with a man sitting silently on top. I recognize him. He is a very successful investment counselor whom I know. I hear the words: It's not him. Walking into the cave more deeply, I encounter a man oddly dressed in Franciscan robes, complete with wide leather girder and sandals. He has the cowl over his head, and I only know it's him when he peers out at me: his eyes light up upon seeing me, and I finally recognize Gordon, my therapist. To my right, on the floor of the cave, is a tangle of naked gay men, writhing and interconnected but somewhat unconscious of their connection. They appear to be in some form of muted pain. I am aware I am in the right place and then I hear, *This is your work.*

Dream Two: Four months later, I dream I am about to be ordained (in more than half of all dreams I have dreamt over the past forty years, I am still a Jesuit). Again, it is nighttime, and again, I enter a cave, though a different one. This one has a rock formation in the center-rear of the expanse. The outcropping is reminiscent of the poured stark concrete interior of the chapel at the Paulist Father's Newman Center at the University of California, Berkeley, where I worshipped during the 1980s. In the worshipping space at Newman there is a striking, very large, extruded sculpture of Jesus emanating from the concrete, his muscled body beautiful, his face contorted in pain, arms down stretched. While worshipping at Newman over a ten-year period, I found great consolation in that corpus.

In the dream, my fellow ordinands and I are instructed to process in two rows, fourteen of us all told. (Coincidentally, there had been thirteen men, if memory serves, in my ordination class at the Jesuit School of Theology some years earlier). As I entered the assigned row, I felt resolute and handsome. We were dressed similarly in chasubles made of thick unbleached cotton, dyed rose and pale green, with the body of the garment in the shape of a Greek (equilateral) cross, and a similar smaller cross dyed into the fabric. I was joyful.

As we processed in, I was last in my line. I had been instructed to go to the left around the rocky altar. I knew the ones I loved were over to the left, so I was doubly joyful. As we processed in, the presiding priest stopped me as I was about to peel left. He announced that any of the men who had gone to the right could take my place and go to the left if they so desired, which meant I would have to go right. I was momentarily waylaid, and forlorn at the implication. But none of them wanted to, which surprised me, so I proceeded to take my place among those who loved me.

Dream Three: A scant week later, I dreamt I was in the ornate St. Francis Xavier College Church at St. Louis University, where I had studied philosophy and American Studies in the mid-seventies. When I was at SLU, I was often asked to read the first lesson from the pulpit, having pretty good pipes, though I found it a terrifying experience, the full meaning of which I did not understand for several years. In the dream, I was on the right side of the church, halfway back, where I often sit in churches. It was Sunday late morning and Mass was about to begin. I was now standing in the right aisle with two other Jesuits, amid a large crowd. As the Eucharist began, the celebrant interrupted the liturgy and came over to us—making us a group of four—

and spoke directly to me. The celebrant was my dear friend, Dick Howard. One of the other Jesuits was a man with whom I had had an intense friendship while in St. Louis; the other, the socius at the novitiate, the man who had once asked me a fated question: "Are you praying?"

Howie turned to me and blessed me, an action that I interpreted in dreamtime as consecrating me. He gave me what I was keenly aware was a most special gift. He handed me this round object of diaphanous material, like golden dry ice, its mysterious beauty ineffable, and incomparably light in density. The gift—in the manner messages are communicated in dreamtime—spoke to me: You must act on your words. I accepted it graciously and knew I was to leave the church building immediately, which I proceeded to do.

After dreaming this triptych of dreams, while spending significant time attending to the needs, both physical and spiritual, of our friends who were ill and dying, I had begun, at the request of friends, and then friends of friends, to develop a ministry sanctioned only by persons in need. The ministry resulted from those who desired spiritual conversation, sometimes confessional in tone. Later, some asked if I would ritualize the significant moments of their lives: their dyings, their deaths, their unions, their illnesses, their lives at moments of spiritual import; the moments when the membrane was thin. It was internally challenging for me, because I had left that path a decade earlier; nonetheless, here I was being invited to return, albeit in a different form. The issue of authority weighed heavily on me, but the unmet need weighed heavier still.

After many such entreaties, and not insignificant resistance, I invited people to come to our home on a given late Sunday afternoon. Near three dozen showed up and later, another dozen joined us. And so, we began to gather every other Sunday in the late afternoon, and we did so for the next seven years. We called ourselves "Spirit Group." In addition to our bimonthly gatherings, each December we retreated for a weekend at Santa

Sabina Retreat Center staffed by the Dominican Sisters in San Rafael. Santa Sabina's rooms and grounds were filled with icons that bespoke the presence of the divine in nature, in the feminine, in the other. It felt like home to us motley seekers.

I have been on group retreat teams many times in my life, but rarely have I experienced a community like the one I experienced with these women and men of Spirit Group. The desire for the Holy was palpable, regardless of the various labels individuals used to describe the hunger within. On every other Sunday, we sat together in silence, developed simple rituals, and prayed aloud what was in our hearts. I would typically offer a reflection from one of the scriptures, Hebrew or Christian or another, and we would read prayers from the great religious and spiritual traditions of the world. And we sang. We found lyrics that spoke of God in inclusive language and evocative symbols. I had placed a basket of smooth Japanese river stones near the entrance, and as we came into the space, we would each take one and hold it for the duration of that holy hour. At its conclusion, we would randomly place the stones on the centering table, releasing our intentions, hopes, fears, and loves into the ether of the room. We would conclude by offering each other robust embraces that spoke to our mutuality.

In so many ways, the experience was sublime. The openness of the individuals in the group was manifest. Wisdom and comfort were easily shared, tears were often shed in both joy and grief, acknowledgments of our individual and collective humanity, our warts and all, were spoken. Mainly, we were people raised in Christian churches, but there were also Jews and active Buddhists present, and persons of no identifiable faith tradition. The universality of the deeper truths all religions contain was lived out in our living room month after month.

Doing this work, I decided to return to seminary—at the multidenominational Pacific School of Religion, the oldest seminary in the West, and a constitutive part of the Graduate Theological Union, to finish the master of divinity degree I had started as a young Jesuit twenty years earlier. I was on the cusp of turning fifty. My spouse, Scott, was then president of PSR's board of trustees. As I finished my academic work, folx from four differ-ent denominations inquired as to whether I might be open to ordination within their traditions. I was both honored and non-plussed but felt a commitment to those who had shaped my min-istry, those who for many reasons were outside the walls. As a blessed bon mot, I was given the annual award for distinguished preaching by the seminary.

While a student, I was invited to enroll in a course called Congregational Leadership, as the only student leading a non-traditional community, a house church. The challenges of these communities were made apparent to me by Speed Leas, the sage professor, who had been a consultant to churches in crisis for his career. He highlighted what I might expect as we contin-ued to meet as Spirit Group. He told me the average life of such groups—house churches in the vernacular—was about three years. Speed spoke of eventual infighting, petty jealousies, issues of authority, other matters that sounded not at all applicable to my experience up to this point in Spirit Group.

Spirit Group met bimonthly, and the sense of community deepened over time even as vaguely understood challenges emerged. The group, at the annual retreat some years in, asked if I would accept a stipend and commit to remaining the group leader for the foreseeable future. After consulting other pas-tors of small congregations, I agreed, and in turn, the group formed a steering committee. And from these two aspects of the group—money and power—small differences began to emerge. As individuals began to express these differences, the group, as happens to most house churches, began to splinter. This was in the fall of our seventh year. It happened very quickly and caught us all, I suspect, unawares.

I had employed the servant leader model for my work with this group, and that model stretched me thin. Combined with my full-time work in the epidemic, my small private practice, and this, the stress suddenly felt enormous. Without an effective structure to move us into the future, the structure we had cre-ated became a significant source of tension. I knew, too, because of my complex relationships with individual congregants in the group—some who had been close friends before Spirit Group, and some newer members whom I did not know as well, some of whom wanted more of me than I could give. In truth, I did not have the wherewithal to mend the breach, and I was not sure it was mine to mend. I felt my time of service was ending. It wrenched me and left me with great sadness and a sense that I had failed the group. But I knew, too, intuitively, and from my professor's warnings, that Spirit Group's time had come to an end. My head and my gut reminded me that in the end I am in charge of nothing, and nothing is set in stone, even if hallowed by Japanese river stones.

Several months later, still grieving this loss, I went to visit my old congregational leadership professor to share with him my experience and perspective on what had transpired with Spirit Group. I asked for his insights. He suggested that all that happened was built into the process on the first day Spirit Group met many years earlier, and that nothing I, nor anyone else, could have done would have prevented its demise. He went into some detail as to how house churches end, which I found consoling. I also found his comments sobering, and in some critical ways, relieving. Nonetheless, the spirit that this lovely group generated is still available to us when we see each other in all the overlapping milieus in which we live and work. Friends still express gratitude for those years and for what transpired in our small but potent gatherings. As do I.

My triptych of dreams led me to embrace what call I have always sensed. The AIDS epidemic conspired in my less-than-conscious self to demand that I see what was right before my eyes, and to respond with what I knew to do. I thought I had buried this ancient call, for which I felt no authority to engage. But the world in which I lived proffered its own authority, and the specter of death and the keen desire for connection with the Divine demanded that I give up my resistance and work generously with each with my gifts and my deficiencies. My graced experience at Rosserk Friary sealed my commitment.

Jung has taught me to trust the efficacy of my dreams and to invite the right brain to meet its culturally endorsed partner, the left. The sense that I had as a young boy of this nascent call— not knowing exactly what it meant—has been enacted over the course of my adult life. It is still not fully clear exactly what it asks. And in this lies a further invitation:

What is our secret entry into Your heart?
We find it on the path of letting go of what we
Thought we knew, arriving at the place where we
Know nothing of knowing beyond every notion of Love.

—Meister Eckhart

18

A DARK WOOD

Even in our sleep, pain we cannot forget
falls drop by drop upon the heart
until in our own despair, against our will, comes wisdom,
through the awful grace of God.

—Aeschylus

WE LIVE ON OUR homestead just shy of two acres of oak-studded land in Sonoma County. A century ago, in addition to orchards and now celebrated vineyards, the vast landscape of Sonoma County, half again as big as Rhode Island, was cattle country, with generations of steers compacting the soil, which was already tough clay. The land more recently pastured horses, adding to the clay's density and resistance. And we are in gopher country, where critters, which I originally looked upon as a scourge, but have of late begun to consider the natural inheritors of the land. Scott and I are somehow their guests. They have a singular capacity to break up the ever-dense clay soil.

In our sixteen years on our large rectangular parcel, we have planted over one hundred trees. We have planted several Autumn Blaze sugar maples—more redolent of the Midwest, but an emotional necessity for me—three dozen Leland cypresses, to provide a privacy screen to the south, and many others: Monterey cypresses, Hollywood junipers, some pine. A dozen Japanese maples huddle together in the slash of shade, under which sits a seated Buddha, covered after many years with moss. St. Francis stands in repose close by. Off the patio, a cedar from the Atlas Mountains of the Maghreb, planted to honor the Trappist monks, wantonly slain at Tibhirine in the rough Algerian desert, their simple witness too much to bear for religious fundamentalists. The surviving monk transplanted his solo monastery to Morocco, a site we recently visited, paying homage to his confreres.

In the back meadow, we are fortunate to have a grove of seven ancient live oaks, deciduous, majestic, with canopies that in summer create total cover, and in the winter, myriad windows to the twinkling of stars in our dark sky. At the base of the grandest oak sits a statue of St. Jude, my childhood patron and, coincidently, the patron of hopeless cases. I aptly chose Jude for my confirmation when I was but ten. When our good friends, Jude Sharp and Jack Jackson, moved nearby, we gave them their St. Jude as a garden-warming present. After several years of raking up the immense oak leaf drop, I found out it best for the trees to leave their leaves in place. I learn. And we have a pomegranate laden with fruit enough for the winter holiday table.

Our pride is a grove of two dozen redwoods, some now in their fourteenth year, nearly twenty feet tall and on their way to seeming infinity. I planted them with the intent to create an inner space, a ten-foot round where I have placed an old, unpainted Adirondack chair—a place to be still and to sit still in the woods. Near perfect. And it was here, amid all these natural companions, that I entered my own dark wood.

Standing on the chip-sealed drive one morning fifteen years ago, in my late fifties, I was overcome with dread, a sense that I did not want to live. My elan vital, the engagement and vigor with which I lived my life, was draining away. I did not want to die, nor did I feel in any way as if I were considering ending my life. I was not even depressed in the clinical sense. But I was very aware that something vital within me was ebbing, and I became ever increasingly and profoundly sad.

The sadness was to last several years and much about it remained mysterious.

As with all such encounters, my dark wood was filled with a light so bright that like a black hole, nothing could emit from it.

For the previous thirty years, the public life that I had created and to which I had responded, had been very fulfilling. Opportunities had allowed me foundational experiences that matured me. Predicated on both sobriety and coming out, the bandwidth had been both circumscribed and deep.

I kept this darkness to myself. After several months, I decided to share some of this with Scott. He listened carefully, then said, wisely, "I trust you. You'll know what to do." Perfect, really, and insightful and spacious.

Later into this duskier time, I called my physician. I had ended therapy several years before, and my intuition told me this was not a therapeutic question, exactly. My doctor, Gregory Nunez, several years younger than me, was both measured and empathic. We met, and I told him my predicament. He responded that sometimes such situations occur because there had been a neurological event, a small, almost—to the untrained eye— imperceptible stroke perhaps. "Would you mind if I put you through some simple tests to determine if perhaps this was the case?" Of course, I agreed, and he proceeded to ask me several recall questions, counting backward, gestures intended to see if I could follow his movements, and so on. I passed easily. He suggested that I might see a staff neurologist to which I readily agreed. So he arranged for me to meet with his colleague the next day.

I arrived for my appointment with an avuncular older Irish doctor who felt familial. Dr. John Cassidy was a widower, as he shared with me, and near the end of his career. We had an unhurried visit. He, too, put me through a more rigorous set of tests in his office, and then spent considerable time asking me questions about my life. I shared with him that, since my childhood, I had had a recurring, daily anxiety—experienced as dread—that occurred around 2:00 in the afternoon. It would grip me, and I would feel panicky, like I wanted to exit my body to escape its clutches. It would intensify until around 3:30, then begin to abate, and by 4:30, it would be gone. I would again feel like myself, present, even calm. These visitations affected me more acutely in my adult life, especially when I was alone, as I often am. If I was seeing clients, it would wait for their exit from my office to descend on me. If I were on vacation or otherwise engaged with people, it would rarely haunt me.

In my early therapy with Mario, we had identified this as an anticipation of the onset of the cocktail hour at home, which would commence most days at 4:00 p.m., awaiting the emotional exit of my parents. That the dread would continue to grip me throughout my life—despite all the therapeutic work I had done—was its own sadness. I had suffered two debilitating panic attacks in the summer of 1972 as I prepared for taking vows as a Jesuit. Both events had occurred while on summer holiday in Omaha, but I was never again so immobilized. But these daily dreads have accompanied me ever since.

Dr. Cassidy shared that he observed three neurological events in me, distinct parts of a generalized anxiety disorder, though I had yet only spent the better part of an hour with him. He suggested that I might be aware, with my clinical background, of all three, and he acknowledged these complications had undoubtedly haunted me since childhood. "You have a little OCD" (a little, you think! I thought) and "You have several tic disorders" (of which I knew, having managed my body and its involuntary movements since I was a young boy). Then he said, "You have a slight case of Tourette's." I was not dumbfounded, for even though I had intuited this, I thought that I had completely masked it. I asked him how he ascertained that diagnosis.

He told me that he had been practicing neurology for forty-five years and had a pretty keen eye and ear. I granted him that. I had been making a certain noise, not at the level of phonetic articulation, since childhood, a guttural sound that was rewarded by Sr. Yvonne boxing my ears in second grade, after I persisted noising after several warnings. My tic disorders had also gotten me in trouble in later elementary school, again with teachers, who believed they might jar this behavior out of me with their practiced disciplining. Only decades later did I understand how their technique reinforced rather than eliminated the involuntary jerky noises and movements.

"You undoubtedly know," he continued, "you developed these symptoms, as you have developed this daily dread response, to manage anxiety, to deal with trauma. And the symptoms we develop early on get hardwired, they don't ever fully go away." This I already knew, only too well. As children, the maladaptive behaviors we take on, both consciously and unconsciously, provide a masquerade, a limited self-presentation that hides the truer, often more wounded person beneath.

Reading my chart, he noted that I described myself as an alcoholic in longtime recovery, and that like many other alcoholics, I had grown up in an alcoholic household. He asked about my homelife when I was a boy, which I shared in some detail, acknowledging both the salutatory and highly dysfunctional aspects. After an hour talking, he stopped asking questions. Then he said starkly, "You know that you raised yourself, don't you?"

With his words, a terrible truth was revealed, one I had known but could never say, not really claim nor fully acknowledge. I'm not sure what scales on the eyes are, but I know that day they were removed. His question ionized the air, not only in his office, but back over the many chapters of my life. It was not a literal statement, exactly, but it bore a literal truth, and the developmental implications for me were staggering. Though a therapy veteran on both sides of the couch, this wise man's simplicity of word felt fresh, as if I had never considered such a thing. And that's because I hadn't, exactly. The nascent implications of his question, a statement really, rushed in on me. It woke me up.

So similar in import to my experience with Mario in 1984, shared in an earlier chapter, when Mario's insight into my dad opened me up to a universe of further knowledge and growth. Like Mario's then, this new declaration hit me profoundly. I told Dr. Cassidy, a neurologist and healer, that I appreciated his insights. As our time together ended, he said that he would be happy for me to visit again, if I so chose, and asked if I would be interested in going up the ladder and speaking with a psychologist.

Of course, wanting to know all that I could about this dark wood, I again agreed, hoping for it to ease and that my journey through it might end.

At my next appointment of inquiry, I met the head of the psychiatry department, another warm and empathic man, and we had an engaging conversation for about an hour. He knew I was a therapist, so we could move to a more substantive plane with the ease and economy that a mutual vocabulary provided. At the end, he said that he didn't think my predicament was psychological, and that I had more experience than his counseling staff. Additionally, he didn't think that I would gain much from reentering therapy. I readily agreed. He then offered me some psychotropic relief. I told him that, while I was not averse to meds, I did not believe that displacing this suffering with antidepressants was the solution to my dilemma. Ironically to me, he concurred and said that his door would always be open should I want to come back to talk. I thanked him, departed, slowly reentering the wood from whose engulfment I had hoped I might escape. This was not to be, at least not yet, but was bolstered by the presence of my husband Scott, who reaffirmed that I would know what to do.

I set aside my spiritual practice, finding no consolation there, with some faint resentment that it failed to uplift me.

Some months later, I called the intuitive, Laura, who I had been seeing annually for many years. I would come to her office with some thorny questions that I could not easily work through, or see my way through, or more often, fully understand. We would begin by sitting in silence for perhaps ten minutes, after which time she would share what she had just experienced, psychically. Then she would ask if any of it made sense. She spoke in complex metaphors that often resonated with me.

Laura is a highly spiritual woman, a lesbian, a Jew, and a practicing Buddhist. She had worked with many current and former Jesuits over the years and had a very good working knowledge of my life and path. Her wisdom was always helpful, insightful, and dynamic, if not clear. I told her about the dark wood. I added that I had stopped praying, stopped meditating, and discounted what I had come to know and see: the knowings. I shared with her that I had stopped my interior conversation with the Divine. She said, "Great. Keep stopping. But don't take down or move the images and icons on the altar in your study." She had known about my prayer space.

My altar, a squat antique Japanese butcher's chop block, raised perhaps six inches off the floor, has served as the platform for my sacred tableau: a small icon of the Christ Pantocrator—sovereign of the cosmos and a beloved Orthodox image—that I had purchased in a religious goods store in Paris. In addition, there is a small terra-cotta skull from Mexico, painted blood red with black markings and brilliant white teeth, which reminded me, as I was taught as a young Jesuit, to daily remember my death—memento mori. I kept a tiny, gilded frame with a photo of my nine-year-old self in a posture of tentative openness, and the disembodied leg and foot of one of those twelve-inch flexible artists' models of the human body, which captured how I had felt disembodied and alien from my sexuality. I had encircled it with an Irish claddagh ring that my dear friend, David, gave me shortly before he died, a symbol of so many similarly lost friendships. I had added a golden globe reminiscent of a sacred dream I had had, representing my work in leaving the edifice of the church to bring what gifts I have into the street, into the world. Lastly, there is a small rough piece of stone taken from the altar of the desecrated Franciscan chapel in Rosserk Friary in Ireland, the site of my own experience of being blessed to do the work I have felt called to do.

Laura advised that each day, instead of sitting or praying or meditating, just slowly walk by these objects, and allow them to be present to me. I asked her for how long? She said, as she usually did, "You'll know."

As I left her office, I felt I was taking away not answers, but deeper questions, the ones I had initially come to discover. This is how I typically leave Laura's office—with more, not less, to ponder. I continued to dwell in the dark wood, though in it I was slowly realizing more, slowly beginning to see refractions of light.

My final journey of discovery soon found me on an airplane to Chicago, and in conversation with my friend Robert Thompson. I had known Robert for several years. He was the pastor of an eclectic, unaffiliated, very progressive Protestant church in Evanston, and a friend to my old and dear friends, Art and Jo. They had intuitively hosted a dinner a year earlier so that Robert and I could meet. I'm not sure that we connected that night, but over the ensuing years, we connected deeply, as Scott and I did with Robert's gracious wife, Judy Langford. My admiration for and intuitive trust in Robert was clear. I knew some of his own path, which included a large dollop of suffering and equally sharp lessons of humility.

On the night I visited, Judy was travelling, developing national policy for the needs of children. Robert and I sat at their kitchen table until late into the evening. I told him of my experiences of late and of my search for understanding, if not relief. The dark wood I had entered had persisted now for several years. While not altering the pattern of my days, it did cast a pall over my consciousness, my interior life, my heart, and my head. It was as if I moved at a moseying pace, through gauze, so as not to distract myself in any greater way. I lived with a weight, a sadness, an unknown constriction, not quite evident to others in my everyday life. I had, after several years, grown accustomed to it. Winston Churchill remarked that all his life he had been accompanied by a black dog, his depression. While not sensing this predicament as depression, it clearly had a black dog quality to it.

After our hours-long conversation sharing this spiritual malaise, Robert got up from the table and meandered into his study. He returned with a small paperback and handed it to me. It was his friend's (Mirabai Starr) elegant and accessible translation of *Dark Night of the Soul* by St. John of the Cross.

I was not pleased.

He said, "This is what you are to read, and this is what you are to understand about what you have been going through." Robert is a man without sharp edges. He does not express himself in absolutes (as I am wont to do). Ordinarily, he isn't highly directive. But his clarity was stunning, and his adamant instruction startling. I took the volume from his hand and pawed it. "I read John of the Cross in the novitiate," I said, with a perhaps less than gracious tone, to which he replied, "Well, you're not in the novitiate anymore."

In this spiritual classic, John of the Cross offers an extended meditation on how the human being experiences the absence of the divine, and the purposefulness of that absence in a purification of desire to invite a deeper intimacy ultimately with the Beloved. With Robert's retort, I was humbled. I thanked him for the recommendation, the gift, and the other gifts he offered me. I flew back to California with the knowledge that Robert had been discerningly clear about what I needed to do.

It took me a year—slowly—to read and internalize the contents of this thin volume, focused on John of the Cross's experience, his movement toward grace, and his foreboding knowledge of the spiritual life. On some days, a paragraph was what I could muster. I came to know that my dark wood was neither neurological nor psychiatric. Though I described it as a wood, it too felt like a desert, one I had been invited into for reasons profound and searing, reasons that I could not intellectually understand. And yet, while I was willing to be led, only mere glimpses of what I would encounter were available on the horizon.

How have I come to understand all of this?

Let me speak both clinically and in the language of the spirit, with a metaphor from aeronautics as a way of explaining what I have come to know.

Around the age of two—for parents, the terrible twos—we experience the early vital thrust of the ego in launching us into the world—without which we could not begin nor sustain early life phases. It is like a booster rocket that is necessary in powering us ultimately to attain higher reaches of the atmosphere—a fully lived life. Over time, it is necessary to master the ego in some direct proportion to its seemingly benign reign of very satisfying terror. But if the booster, the ego, does not ultimately recede, we will not fully achieve becoming our richly complex selves, becoming persons. The ego controls all that it can. It sees its main job as protecting us from all of what it regards as danger. It has a seemingly endless capacity to extend its reach, not only to overfill our shadow selves, but to spill into those parts of our lives lived in the light. Our spiritual selves, our soulful selves, are prime targets for the ego's desired hegemony.

The ego is, of course, necessary, for without it we would not move through the developmental stages of our lives to attain a sense of spiritual maturity: equanimity, generosity, balance, perspective, self-awareness, tenderness, humility, and, ultimately, graceful self-transcendence—the vocabulary of spiritual growth and interior movement. But the ego is insufficient. In his book *Prisms: Reflections on This Journey We Call Life*, James Hollis, an elder in the Jung community, extrapolates from Jung:

> Whenever our ego frame collapses, we're in the presence of...the large, radical Other. Whenever we are obliged to radically alter our sense of self and world, we are in the presence of mystery. Whatever calls the ego to consciousness to encounter its limitations and open to the reframing of understanding is...a religious encounter.

As the ego maintains its pervasive grip on us, we simultaneously experience the nascent movement of the soul toward its full realization, a quieter and subtler movement for sure. Necessary skirmishes ensue and produce suffering. It is a long and arduous task, and one we would escape, not realizing its necessity nor having a glimpse of its beneficent outcome. In our culture, the alternatives to this suffering are many and readily available. We grow to rely on them, and finally, we become inured to them.

Their efficacy begins to wane, suffering again emerges, and so we titrate the numbing agent.

But our remedies ultimately fail us. We are not so powerful nor is our genetic inheritance so determinate. Eventually, our intellect falters, our accomplishments decay, our will fades, and our glories tarnish. We cannot power our way to internal peace, contentment, and joy. We strive harder, grow manic, and become more controlling. We try to assert the learned powers we thought effective and find them wilting at our feet. We suffer.

Carl Jung's insight into this dilemma and its formidable task describes how we individuate (*become one's self*). Jung ennobled this destination by capitalizing it, "the Self." The Self is akin, I assert, to the apex of the mystical experience in which the Divine is realized within—an inner light, an inner knowing, an inner awareness, an inner presence. The mystics of many traditions describe this journey to *individuation* in exquisite religious language. The prolific writer-monk Thomas Merton approached this subject—exemplified in his life and in his life's work and described in his immense written output, from *The Seven Storey Mountain* through *New Seeds of Contemplation* and *Thoughts in Solitude* through his voluminous correspondences to the *Asian Journal*, this last volume penned at the end of his too brief life— ultimately in his search for solitude.

A contemporary writer, Thomas Moore describes this journey lovingly in *Care of the Soul* and its accompanying *Dark Nights of the Soul.* As does Richard Rohr, whose opus, *The Universal Christ*, takes the Christic event and extrapolates it, and us, into the cosmos, understanding the interior journey as the rubble-strewn path toward this universal realization, in language that Teilhard de Chardin would appreciate.

The contemporary poet Christopher Wiman writes with lucidity and grace his own memoir of desolation and spiritual individuation in *My Bright Abyss.* Simone Weil's brilliant intellect and spiritual ardor informed her most profound writing, *Waiting for God*, which continues to be a beacon eighty years after her death.

In the Middle Ages, Teresa of Avila and her confrere, John of the Cross, Meister Eckhart, Catherine of Siena, Marguerite

Porete, and many others described the arduous apophatic—an awareness of the divine experienced through negation—as the mystical path. Reformation and Enlightenment modes discounted this profound mode of spiritual experience, only to have them mushroom up in the current postmodern, techno-driven, mass culture moment in which we find ourselves.

One of the truths I have come to sense clearly is that what we hold as spiritually true must also be psychologically congruent, and vice versa.

As a young man, I found alcohol, many an Irishman's good friend. It was a no-brainer. It ameliorated the shame and trauma that I had settled into in my early adulthood. It also allowed me to downplay any gifts I might have been given, and it almost killed me.

After the grace of sobriety at the age of twenty-nine, I had thirty seemingly formidable years. I had plenty of elixirs, for sure, but none so toxic or addictive as the chemicals. But the blandishments of the ego—of course—were ever at hand. Those thirty years found me engaged in good work, even heroic work, Joseph Campbell might say, and greatly satisfying. My contributions were valued by others and often acclaimed. I found it meaningful, sometimes exhilarating, and always consistent with my values and self-image. During these years, I had an attenuated spiritual life, shrouded in advancing mystery and marked by an inadequacy of language, both of which I found confounding. And then—rather suddenly, or so it seemed—the dark wood. The spiritual miasma. The painful unknowing. The failure of will and effort. This desert amid the fecundity of our small, treed plot of Sonoma County. I experienced this aridity while being loved by many and tenderly espoused. This gray mist enveloped me.

This dark wood.

I realized slowly after entering this wood, that I was not in charge of much in my life. I had suffered several significant defeats, though I sensed that these setbacks were not the sole cause. I entered this wood after thirty years of relative achievement and enviable success. But I had suffered these defeats in late middle age, as the life-horizon became more faintly apparent in the distance.

Three events—among many—stood out to me, all of which bore the marks of trauma: fear, feelings of helplessness, a sense of loss of control, and isolation from one's community.

Spirit Group that I had organized and into which I had poured my deepest energy and from which I drew such joy and received such grace, ended, sadly, if necessarily.

Shortly thereafter, Mark, my closest friend in California, and I had what appeared to be an irreconcilable misunderstanding, a breach impossible for me to have predicted. In short order, he left my life, as did most of our shared posse. I was profoundly bereft.

At the same time—a shiny bauble—a deluxe position to which I had been recruited at a major San Francisco philanthropic institution, one I had trepidatiously accepted, became a nightmare in no time. After less than two years, I extricated myself from that toxic environment, and from the prestige and benefits the position had offered.

I felt like a failure and, in a significant way, alone.

This trifecta inflicted a wound to my exhilarated ego, an accumulation I could not clearly see, only feel. For a long time, I could not put the pieces of this tripartite puzzle together. I faulted myself for not being able to understand what I was experiencing. True to my ingrained self, and my highly attenuated perfectionism, my Enneagram Oneness, the presence of the inner critic who had been working to protect me—he had believed since experiencing childhood trauma—self-blame became the go-to option.

Nonetheless, I am not a bystander to my life, as we never are. Even though my conscious Self had done the best it could adjusting to this cumulative loss, my best could not prevent the collapse that came from their combined weight: the loss of my spiritual community, of that vital friendship, of this high-profile, career-capping professional position, and mostly the pervasive conversation the inner critic engaged in. God knows what else filtered in during those days. I had a large if unwitting ego-investment, and I could not imagine, nor tolerate, failure. And at the end of the day, I felt abandoned.

In addition to this shadowy trifecta, another significant phenomenon—in ways more powerful than these recounted events—seeped into me. I became increasingly filled with an awareness of the environmental crisis our utterly beneficent planet was experiencing, one of human manufacture. I read voraciously. The writing necessarily had a dystopian quality to it. Over time, I was gripped by this existential dread. It seemed to complement the woundings that had accompanied my personal life, perhaps overtook them.

Scott and I began to address the challenge of the climate crisis on a personal level, making changes in our behavior and environment. Though the shifts we made were not inconsequential, they seemed insufficient, infinitesimally small, considering the data and the dystopian forecasts. I felt powerless. Though I believe we can be part of the change necessary to bring about the beloved community, a just society, I could not extend this hope to the climate crisis.

That hope would come slowly. Again, it required of me to acknowledge and own the limits of the ego. I could not square the possible end of human existence—as I understood one potential outcome—with the presence of the divine, with the animating grace of the Spirit. I could not understand this in the same ways that I grappled with the Holocaust, the Middle Passage, and chattel slavery. I could not integrate it into any available construct. I knew that humans in our greed and fearful projections had created these profound tragedies, and I knew they were ours to undo.

I had been leeched decades before of a belief in a god who relented if petitioned enough, of a god who would swoop in and save humanity from its delusional behavior. But more intimately, I could not countenance the personal God with whom I had this particular and vivifying relationship. Had I manufactured this

God? Was I in my own way delusional? Were the underpinnings of my faith merely an illusion?

I could not answer these questions with any absolute clarity. I had reached the limits of reason. My need to control had hit ego-bottom.

As I had come to know from the wisdom of the 12-step programs, bottom is a place of hope, for we are invited to do the only thing left possible for us...to surrender. My flight to Chicago had been, importantly, my bottoming out. My asking for help—from my friend Robert—was an unarticulated acknowledgment that my ego was finally spent.

I was not in charge of the universe nor of little else. In giving me the John of the Cross text, a shoot of hope unwittingly poked through.

I came slowly to appreciate the absolute limits, and nonetheless, the large effects, one person can have. The equilibrium necessary to allow me to respond as only one individual, fully aware, can, began to rebalance my life. In doing my part and learning how to fully do this, I learned anew: this is what I can do. Alone, I cannot reverse the climate crisis, but neither is despair an adequate response. Furthermore, we are not alone in our efforts.

I began to take all of this into that quiet hour early in the morning when the many imponderables I face I offer for the Utterly Imponderable to receive. And I began the slow, unconsciously grounded path to reengage in life, as life is and not as I would like it to be or tried to make it, to create it. My teacher Bob Egan had written, "The woods are autobiographical revisions. Something about our past is being undone, and we are being unraveled from memory. The dark is mothering and fathering us again."

My interior life and its practices that had been repugnant to me—unfocused, unsatisfying, and dry—took on a freshness. I had been loath to sit and pray. I could find slight consolation, little succor, no joy. And yet, from the Source, or, as my friend

Grace would say, from Love, consolation, succor, even joy, were returned to me.

Thanks to Scott and Gregory, John, Laura, Robert, Mirabai, Juan de la Cruz, and others, I slowly began to return. Some of the trappings of the ego that I had so successfully navigated the previous thirty years began to fall away.

The darkness slowly departed, or, as Tule fog does here in California, so utterly opaque when in it is present, it finally lifted. Or did its work and receded. Or went into hiding until next it might be needed. I was slowly but surely restored and newly opened to the presence of the divine in the countless ways the divine presents. The inner critic grew softer. I began once again to sit in the morning at my little butcher block of an altar, peacefully, patiently. Humor returned. So did music and dancing and vibrancy and succor and, in some modicum, joy. In retrospect, what I experienced was another death of the ego, as we encounter a series of these dyings over the course of a lifetime. I had had such a death as a closeted man. And again, as an active alcoholic. And as a traumatized and shamed human being. Like the other deserts, this dark wood was pervasive. It asked for but one thing: *Let go*. These words echoed through the interior:

> *I am here. Let go and give up your beneficent control. Love your broken self. Embrace your errant sexuality. Hold your imperfect body with tenderness. Cry your dammed-up tears. Be with each moment as it is, not as you would have it be. Forgive your dad now. And several others, too. Let Scott love you. Let the divine in, not as the idol you have so effectively crafted as a God-look-alike. Believe that I dwell within you. Stop thinking every spiritual truth is metaphor. Did I say let go? Yes, that again. And trust. Always. I am here.*

Scott witnessed me throughout, never asking me for more than I could say, always and subtly assuring me of his presence.

Spirit Group had to end. With no cohesive, commonly held system of belief, no universally recognized sacred text, and no transforming symbol(s), that we lasted seven years was a testament to the spiritual hunger and goodwill of its many members. Seven years for this house church was a profound blessing. The grace of our experiences together still redounds in our lives as do many sweet friendships these many years later.

My friend Mark came back into my life seven years after his departure, and the experience we had of mutual forgiveness marks my life. Out of this came a renewed and clearer friendship, one in which our mutual intimacy is alive.

The institution that I left slogs along, as institutions do.

Regarding the climate crisis, we are slowly, and hopefully in time, creating the necessary mass consciousness to allow the planet to continue to be our ever-graced abode. I retain some hope.

As for me, I more than slog. A life now, and again, fully engaged and endlessly blessed. Grateful, as they say in Ireland, for *the all of it.*

19

A WADI IN THE DESERT

What it is that dwelleth here I know not but my heart is
full of awe and the tears trickle down.

—An eleventh-century Japanese sage

MY EARLY, ROBUST, and rather naïve faith was built on the
foundation of a mid-twentieth-century Irish Catholicism, along
with a multitude of forms: a metaphysical assurity, moral
absolutism, perfectionism, Jansenism, a bellicose Old Testament
deity, an unquestioned clericalism, all of which contributed to
an airtight worldview. Much of this has been detailed in this
book. The second half of life, as described by developmental
psychologists and astute spiritual directors, and informed by the
experiences of those of us fortunate enough to be living fully into
it, has had a different purpose—or task. This time of my life has
simplified my knowing that the Divine is present.

This awareness came through the dark wood. We are invited
to trust, to simplify, to embrace solitude, and to live a life that is
blessed. My previous efforts to manage, define, understand, and
to manipulate the Divine, while so human, were for naught.

As the thirteenth-century Meister Eckhart, yet most contemporary of mystics, observed: *Once we have said something*

definitive about God, we have said nothing. The universe is an immensity we can barely glimpse. As my eloquent friend Bob Hotz wrote, "We always seem to hogtie mystery."

When I was young, I had a sensation one night, while lying in bed, of a presence. I was shown things—ways, effects, more presence. As you can see, I have no adequate words to describe this, even now, decades later. I trusted the sensation and knew intuitively that these "knowings" were to be held close, that they were not—at least then—to be shared, even though I knew no reason for that. You, dear reader, may well have had such experiences, and may well have contained your experience inside.

Jesus said, "Unless you change and become like children" (Matt 18:3). Wise teachers from other traditions have spoken similarly. We grapple at each stage of life, each developmental hurdle, with God, with the divine, the numinous: some abandon the project as futile, unworthy of our efforts, regarding the project as immature, unsophisticated, banal; others drift away, without giving it much thought. Yet others, burned by the moral absolutisms that substitute for life in the spirit, wither, and some fight a long time and leave exhausted. All so easily understandable.

As the assistant novice master asked me, querulously, in 1971: *Bill, are you praying?*

Well, kind of. My physical response was swift. Thereafter, I was in the chapel at 6:30 a.m. sharp, kneeling at one of the prie-dieux for the full half hour, right next to my friend, Jim Bretzke, who was always there first. Jim became a moral theologian. Prayer, thereafter, became a part of my daily life, a ritualized time spent attending to the matters of the interior, in and with whatever tools I had available at each developmental stage of my life. Yes, my mind wanders mercilessly, the orchestra inside a blaring cacophony; it, too, a significant part of prayer. Reading Isaiah, the Psalms, Mark, John, Ephesians, and my Celtic sages, I find both solace and challenge. And the habit of prayer became one I leaned into.

As Jesuits, we made an annual eight-day retreat, in addition to the thirty-day retreat made shortly after entrance. In the summer of 1974, while on one of these yearly spiritual exercises at the old Jesuit retreat house in Oshkosh, Wisconsin—a hot and muggy place in July—I had an experience during one of the many prayer periods of a retreatant. I was in the large, amply windowed day room overlooking beautiful Lake Winnebago. That afternoon, I was not particularly focused, a little drowsy. In a moment that seemed longer, the unclothed arms of Jesus, larger somehow than mine, reached down from above me and grasped my forearms as I grasped his. He pulled me up and said, *I will never let go of you.*

I felt absolute serenity. A preternatural calm came over me, and an effortless joy immediately filled me. I felt transported into myself and knew that this communication was singular, essential, and gratuitous.

When later sharing this experience with the retreat director—an obligation as I understood it—he immediately dismissed it as a mirage, a flight of emotional fancy, a confabulation that many young religious on the spiritual path imagine themselves having. He further suggested the evil one presents such manifestations to draw the penitent away from the harder work of self-examination or reflection. I was not a penitent at that time, and I did not regard prayer as merely self-examination. I left his room and did not return. The experience, which I did not speak of again, has never left me, even as I traversed the dark wood. I do not know its full meaning, for it seems to be starkly clear. What remains with me forty-six years later is the clarity and simplicity. The image, or affect, or presence was palpable, physical, tactile. Whatever it was, it was a gift. An enduring one, and a vital one: *I will never let go of you.*

And I have not yet been let go.

For the past thirty years, I have continued to make an annual eight-day retreat. For the past dozen years, the locale has been the Trappist Abbey of Our Lady of Guadalupe in the rolling hills of the Willamette Valley near the Oregon coast. The abbey's buildings sit amid a thousand forested, hilly acres. The care that the monks have taken in constructing their home is inspiring, particularly the spare and evocative abbey church and the unusual Zendo, with two-story windows that fill the length and breadth of the north wall, looking out into the sublimely lit forest beyond, are inspiring. I spend most days in the Zendo, sitting on a zafu, the round, tufted Japanese cushion often used in Buddhist meditation (and by Trappist monks!) while in the redeeming silence. I am often the only one in the large room.

Ten years ago, after decades of praying, I would ask with humility, *Let me find the divine within.* I could add, as I write, *finally.* The prayer had overtones of exhaustion, pathos, and self-pity. And arrogance. For I was wedded to my own lack of worthiness, a defensive trope memorized in early childhood, not easily abandoned, which in my interior life stumbled up against the enormous grace that I had been provided since birth. In the Zendo, I sit on the same deep purple zafu, left center, next to a load-bearing post. I am closer to the vast window than to the rear of the room. While sitting in silence that evening, with only a candle illuminating the room, a swoosh, as one might hear from a bird released from a cage, came down from the uppermost back right corner of the room and impregnated my psyche with the words *I am in you.*

And then silence. An interior silence, complemented by the serenity of the Zendo, of the forest, of the night. I experienced a deep peace. And a divine assertion, fully taken in. I sensed *the within.*

Three years ago, at Guadalupe, I arrived with my usual, updated agenda—just shaving off a few sharp imperfect edges, just a few reformations to make myself somehow more acceptable to You...I mean, just a better man. And then: *I am here. I am here.* There was a literal quality to it. And yet, there was more....

In prayer, the "I" is a challenge to understand. We are shy to say the source of the I. *I am here* resulted in immediate and spacious calm. It cleared the air, and swept through my psyche, like a gust of wind, opening me up and settling me down and inviting presence, mine and not mine. Yet only *I am here.*

I made this retreat a few months prior to turning seventy. I knew the time was right for me to retire from my work as a psychotherapist. I had loved my work, and, as I suspect all committed therapists do, I loved my clients. Their humanity, which they presented with humility and hope each week, was a gift to me, no matter how complex the complications, no matter how resistant the defenses. These individuals bared their souls bravely, and at times, awkwardly. Yet, after thirty-five years, I knew I had other work to do and that I had completed this work.

Francis Thompson, the English Catholic poet who lived at the turn of the nineteenth century, described fleeing *the hound of heaven down the night and down the days, down the arches of the years.*

I have also and to no avail. Yet that *Hound* precedes us at every turn. For me, in the men at San Quentin State Penitentiary, the monks at the Trappist Abbey of Our Lady of Guadalupe, my friends dying at Davies Hospital in San Francisco, my students at Mercy and Marquette High Schools, my friends on Holy Hill in Berkeley, my friends practicing these principles at an AA meeting, my friends called Glenns, and my non-Glenn friends who have qualified me for a life with their love.

All of us want peace, even if our feeble means of attaining it are contraindicated. As my professor Larry Palmetier, a former Maryknoller, told me one evening after a clinical psyche class, *Each person is doing the best they know how to do today.*

Late in the first decade of this new century, while at Guadalupe, after decades of resistance, I experienced a surrender to the divine presence within. In that moment and subsequently, the divine presence has still been bound by my limitations, as all experience is. And yet, the experience is alive within me. I have been attending to the One who was at the heart of that experience for a long time. The awareness—sometimes dim—remains.

At the heart of my journey are the Beatitudes, the *koans* Jesus articulated on a mountain side two millennia ago. For me, the Beatitudes embody the philosophy of so many teachers, so many bodhisattvas. Important for me are the following:

- the recently deceased Boston physician Paul Farmer, MD, and his *Partners in Health*, carrying medicine up the deforested mountainsides of Haiti to heal the sufferings of the most abject of human beings;
- the clear-eyed Bryan Stevenson and the staff of his *Equal Justice Initiative* freeing those, usually Black, falsely imprisoned in the South, one man at a time. In his spare time, Stevenson puts up markers at the lynching sites of Black men;
- the queer folx at *The Trevor Project* who work arduously to stem the tide of queer youth suicide, another hidden plague of ours;
- Jacques, my Dutch émigré friend and mentor, who carries on his holy work at San Quentin, inviting men to transform their anger into real power in the program *GRIP—Guiding Rage Into Power*;
- Rikki Moreno, a nurse and friend from Continuum days, who travels to the *Kino Border Initiative* at the Mexican-U.S. border, tending the needs of immigrants;
- the tireless Bill McKibben, reconstructed Methodist, Isaiah-like, who is prophesying on behalf of the beleaguered planet, and the movement at *350.org*, a call to citizen action.

Jesus's first words in the Gospel of John are *What do you want?* We know what we want, and that it's going to cost us. There is always a whiff of suffering involved. Choose suffering, or at least a pinch of it. *God*, the commonly referenced word to capture something beyond even the imagination and the limits of the limitless universe, appears to have endowed this evolving creature Homo sapiens, (ah, *sapientia*, wisdom) with a capacity to feel deeply this knowing of empathy, of relatedness, of love.

In his startlingly beautiful *Sophia: The Hidden Christ of Thomas Merton*, Christopher Pramuk shares a story of Merton finally meeting, in the summer of 1964, his longtime correspondent, the esteemed Zen master D. T. Suzuki, who was responsible for bringing awareness of Zen to the West. Their Christian-Buddhist dialogue had engaged them both—delicately yet deeply—for a decade, and their meeting was profoundly moving for Merton, as it no doubt was for Suzuki. As they were taking their leave of each other, the ninety-four-year-old Suzuki said, *The most important thing is Love!*

In this Love must our wisdom lie. It is contrary to imposed suffering, injustice, war, violence, exclusion, shame, and power. We may know just a smidgen about Love, but the yeast of that smidgen is enough. From it, the bread of love will rise. We can trust it, and we can gain our fill. What else offers such hope, possibility, insight, vision, and splendor?

Some years ago, Scott and I, along with our travelling companions, my nephew, Brian, and his wife, Dana, visited Morocco, a completely intriguing land. During our stay, we traversed the Atlas Mountains—the alpine spine that runs the eastern length of the country—to camp at the edges of the vast Sahara Desert. Dana had found a wadi, an oasis to host us. Since childhood, I had wanted to experience this sandy expanse, an apt metaphor for aspects of the spiritual life, and my desire was renewed my reading *The Monks of Tibhirine*. Their presence and service among the nomads, eventually leading to their suffering and slaughter, is exemplary. (The film made from this evocative book, *Of Gods and Men*, is a religious experience in and of itself.) I have come to see their lives as a wadi, akin to those places—and persons—with whom we find respite and restoration. It is in my wadi, my daily sitting cross-legged and still that renews and reengages me with the mystery at the heart of my life. And it is in my wadi that the One I have been seeking—or maybe the One who has been seeking me—is present.

Curiously, subtly, and creatively, as I observe the horizon of my life, I realize that the mystery of Jesus remains the locus of my seeking. I have not written much about the centrality of this person, this mystery. I sense a real, present, and authentic Jesus—the corporeal embodiment of the Cosmic Christ—present since the beginning, and irrepressibly moving us toward the future by engaging each of us in the work of building the earth, as Teilhard fashioned the task. He illuminates our connections to all other human beings and to all creation, inviting us to cocreate the realization of Love. This Love completes the divine self-emptying, the kenosis, by which our own completion and path to consciousness becomes realized. This Love is present, not confined to any socially constructed nomenclature or symbology, including the grand ones of my own inheritance.

For me, the mystery of Jesus—this Sophia, this Wisdom, this Love, regardless of one's stance on faith—becomes a vital and durable model of what it means to be a human being. Roger Haight, the silenced Jesuit, in his resplendent eponymously named volume, calls him *The Symbol of God*. Wisdom is the compelling draw, the existential magnet pulling us to the Divine. With authenticity and clarity, with his peculiar kind of power, Jesus, this Sophia, this Wisdom, the embodiment of this Love, this symbol of God, draws and welcomes, if our souls are seeking.

Jesus remains at the heart of my profound spiritual quest, pointing to and mirroring for me what God might be, enunciating the highest of human values, and the deepest mythological truths. Incorporating utterly those values and truths in his life, Jesus, a *person* transformed.

He lived a life of fullness and died a death of pathos and singularity, seemingly defeated, as a result of his decision to be present to himself and to all of life around him—at any cost. The Buddha would recognize Consciousness in this Nazarene; the Prophet, the presence of the Holy; Confucius, wisdom; shamans, deeply abiding mystical strength; Druids, the utterly natural; Jungians, wholeness. Alan Watts, the perceptive Christian Buddhist polymath of the mid-twentieth century, beautifully describes Jesus as *having had at a young age an experience of overwhelming Cosmic Consciousness*, which led him to his profound identification with the divine.

For those drawn to Jesus, to Sophia, to You, for those of us schlepping through ordinary lives, we know these things about him in the most subtle, mundane, and compelling ways. His story has created a story the rest of us can live by, one that draws untold numbers of humans. Regardless of intellect or station, he appeals to us who know deeply our own spiritual need and who want to feed that spiritual hunger.

Several years ago, my friend Michael Kelly—of happy memory—was engaged in doctoral studies in mystical theology in Melbourne, Australia. He constructed a dissertation project interviewing a half dozen gay men, whose spiritual journeys were of interest to him. There are few books on the particular and peculiar interior journeys of gay people—journeys that had previously been regarded as irrelevant or even impossible. Given our history, years of mutually exploring our inner lives with each other, we spent many hours together on this project, Michael interviewing me, asking me to expand on my responses, patient with me as I struggled with words. I spoke with what clarity I could about Jesus, about this One, who has utterly shaped and infused my life. About this I am often self-conscious, living in the postmodern world, in a deconstructing *milieu*, and a landscape that identifies the word *Christian* so closely with values and a *persona* that would have been anathema to the Jesus whom I have come to know, with a Jesus whom the fundamentalists of all stripes have assured me would not abide my presence.

Michael Kelly appreciated my struggle. In it, I was far from alone. His book, *Christian Mysticism's Queer Flame: Spirituality in the Lives of Contemporary Gay Men*, in which he identifies me by my middle name, David, is about the experiences of other men of deep spirituality, men representing perhaps millions of others, whose life experiences would not otherwise have been recorded. How bereft mystical theology would be without these queer experiences of the divine.

For it is in the human margins that we all inhabit that so much of the work of the Spirit occurs. Unlike Thoreau, observing men living lives of quiet desperation, a deeper truth suggests that multitudes, despite or perhaps because of the suffering life imposes, are living vibrant lives of beauty, kindness, and untold generosity. These attentive humans—with the light this One provides—go about repairing the torn fabric of life.

This mysterious Jesus spoke so elegantly and clearly that his words are incontrovertible as images, as instructions, as lights for living fully human lives. His words are so powerful and piercing that they become indistinguishable from Jesus himself. They surpass conventional wisdom, which elevates their status to *true words*. They go against the grain, upset authority, redesign history, impact human relations, strip power. They wipe away human distinctions, contest the law, contradict the elders. They set the old on its ear and demand a new way, a revolution of the heart, a restructuring of behavior, a reordering of relationship, an intimacy with God.

These words of Jesus are available to all, always, regardless of caste, class, fortune, power, or distinction.

In the surviving texts, Jesus placed his hands on people, their wounds laid bare, and they were healed. He spoke beyond the pale of the authorities, with nothing but his ancient scriptures and his prayers formed by that inner voice, and he spoke with authority. He was no scribe, no priest, no Pharisee, no Zealot. He spoke in parables, little conundrums meant to encourage pause, little *koans* for the rote-soaked mind. He spent time together with sex workers, with men apparently unmarried far past the appropriate age. He knew women, which made him suspect as a male of his time and place. He defied the law, those codified statutes that regulated—and sometimes strangled—his religious culture. He chose to be with those who lived on the margins of society, those outside of power. He was brazen in his affections and offered everyone the prospect of human—spiritual—freedom.

Meister Eckhart says, *You do not hesitate toward me, since You are all love and only love, and when You love You love without measure, and when You love me in this way, I find out who I am and who You are, which is all and ever only love.*

Jesus's core message was lived out in the flesh. The reign of God is at hand, not there, or over there, but here, within me and within you. He demanded attentiveness and presence as he was attentive and present. He invited each person to be herself, himself. He preached that true life is found through a heart of forgiveness and compassion and when one knows incontrovertibly that one is loved. He invited his listeners to love their enemies, for only then could they love themselves. And to forgive others their wrongs, for only then could they know that they had already been forgiven. The reign of God was realized in his presence, in his person.

This Jesus haunts my journey. I have known Jesus, the Jesus of my childhood, of my youth, of my adolescence, of my apostasy, of my novitiate, of my addiction, of my closet, of my shadow, of my liberation, of my marriage, of my work, of my mess, of my loves, of my alienations. He, too, is the Jesus of my darkness, and the Jesus of my light. He is persistent, insistent, subtle—and not—silent but deafening. He is unremitting, not caring about my age, my orientation, or my ego. I sense he does not care about the external approbations, but about the reasons of the heart.

That is the Jesus on whose life I stake my claim, the embodiment par excellence of the presence of the Cosmic Christ to whom I bear witness. That is *Sophia*, the Wisdom we require. Jesus's current flows right out of his hands into mine, into my body, into my heart. He clarifies my mind, reforms my intellect, liberates my will, saying fiercely,

Be alive, Billy, Be alive! There is nothing else to be! I am with you, and I will never let go of you. You are made—just as you are—in the image of the One who loves you. You are a priest in the world. Do not worry about the *hows*, or the *whos*, and do not worry about the *wheres*. All shall be revealed in time. These are not your concerns. *You are simply to be who I made you to be. For I am in you.*

He calls me to sit each day. He dissipates my fear. He entices me to breathe. He cajoles me to play. He holds me and lifts me up. He sends me these spiritual *compañeros*: my humble clients; my blessed friends; men in prison; fellow travelers; therapists and spiritual directors; sages; my many beloveds; my dear husband; my reliable family. I behold animals domestic and wild, the birds that eat at our feeders and bathe in our baths, nature as present on our land and in the world, the plains, deserts, and mountains, the unfathomable seas, and the broad nighttime heavens, resplendent with stars.

I cannot say *no* to him anymore. Though I yet scramble for it, that word has left me, dropped from my vocabulary, buried in the heap. I claim all this as the source of my life. For me, there is no other. In these pages, I have endeavored to share a life, mine, one of grace, in both its dark and its light emanations. Grace has crept into my crevices, has led me into the world, has brought me face-to-face with immeasurably gifted friends and some sketchy characters, all of whom have been my teachers. Perhaps the remainders from the sketchy characters have been the more sublime. I have been significantly a Glenn, a Catholic, a Jesuit, a gay man, an addict, a teacher, a psychotherapist, a husband, and a friend. Each of these are all in all. You cannot pull the addict from the psychotherapist, nor the gay man from the Catholic, albeit a very complicated one. You can take nothing out of the Glenn.

I came here seeking a person. Over the course of time, I have been granted keener insight into just who that person is. My grappling with the language and symbols worthy of the divine has invited me, as if I were on a very long retreat, to go inside—anew—as if starting from scratch, to be present to the One who is ever present to me.

I am aware that many memories from my life have potent feelings yet attached to them. In writing, these feelings have returned with what seems like renewed vigor: affection, grief, anger, sadness, thrill, tenderness, hope, and joy.

When I got sober and came out, life became fully technicolor for me. Though those highly saturated hues can be garish, they are also vivifying. Think ruby slippers! I work to subdue the garishness, and time leeches it as well. But I am ever grateful for the vividness. I am living a full life. Moving toward the end—now on the horizon—I am, quite remarkably, after all, a member of the least society of Jesus, that society of wisdom, of kenosis, of trickster, of absence, of presence, of healing, of service, of joy, of darkness, and finally, of Love.

Thank you, beloved reader, and companion, for taking this journey with me, for becoming part of this journey.

SELECTED BIBLIOGRAPHY

For the past twenty years, I have circuited an annual list, "Books and Media, Soulful and Spiritual," recommending books that I had read and viewed of particular interest—books and films that have held me up! When I am reading, I jot in the margins and dog-ear pages. My books are marked up in black and red ink, tones of yellow neon highlighter. I have selected the more than fifty most impactful books and films from my teen years to now. For those authors whose whole *oeuvre* have been important to me, I have highlighted with an asterisk, and I have selected one or, at times, two books to represent their work and impact on me. I have sought out the most recent translations or revised publication dates for older volumes.

Some of you, perhaps one of you, will find a nugget here that shifts your life as they shifted mine.

Baldwin, James. *Giovanni's Room*. New York: Dell, 1956.*
Becker, Ernst. *Denial of Death*. New York: The Free Press, 1973.
Bonhoeffer, Dietrich. *The Cost of Discipleship*. New York: Touchstone, 1995.
Boswell, John. *Christianity, Social Tolerance and Homosexuality*. Chicago: University of Chicago Press, 1980.
Brinton Perrera, Sylvia. *The Scapegoat Complex*. Toronto: Inner City Book, 1986.

Buber, Martin. *I and Thou*. Translated by Ronald G. Smith. New York: Charles Scribner's Sons, 1958.

Camus, Albert. *The Stranger*. New York: Vintage Press, 1989.

Christie, Douglas. *The Blue Sapphire of the Mind: A Contemplative Ecology*. Oxford: Oxford University Press, 2013.

Coates, Ta-Nehisi. *Between the World and Me*. New York: Spiegel and Grau, 2015.

Delp, Alfred. *Advent of the Heart*. San Francisco: Ignatius Press, 2006.

Diaz, Miguel H. *Queer God De Amor*. New York: Fordham University Press, 2022.

Endo, Shusaku. *Silence*. Translated by William Johnston. New York: Taplinger, 1980.

Freeman, Laurence. *Jesus the Teacher Within*. New York: Continuum, 2006.

Fromm, Erich. *The Art of Loving*. New York: Harper & Row, 1956.

Garrow, David. *Bearing the Cross: Martin Luther King, Jr., and the Southern Christian Leadership Conference*. New York: Vintage Books, 1988.

Goffman, Irving. *Stigma*. Englewood Cliffs, NJ: Prentice-Hall, 1963.

Greene, Graham. *The Power and the Glory*. New York: Penguin Classics, 2015.*

Grumbach, Doris. *The Presence of Absence*. Boston: Beacon Press, 1999.

Haien, Jennifer. *The All of It*. New York: Harper Perennial, 2011.

Haight, Roger. *Jesus Symbol of God*. Maryknoll NY: Orbis Books, 1999.

Hammarskjöld, Dag. *Markings*. New York: Alfred A. Knopf, 1968.

Hansen, Ron. *Mariette in Ecstasy*. New York: Harper Collins, 1991.

Harper, Ralph. *On Presence*. Philadelphia: Trinity Press International, 1991.

Hesse, Herman. *Siddhartha*. New York: Bantam, 1982.

Hopkins, Gerald Manley. *Selected Poetry*. Oxford: Oxford University Press, 1986.

Houselander, Caryll. *Essential Writings*. Maryknoll, NY: Orbis Books, 2005.

John of the Cross. *Dark Night of the Soul*. Translated by Mirabai Starr. New York: Riverhead, 2002.

Jung, Carl. *Memories, Dreams, and Reflections*. Translated by Richard and Clara Winston. New York: Vintage Books, 1963.*

Kazantzakis, Nikos. *The Last Temptation of Christ*. New York: Bantam, 1960.

King, Martin Luther, Jr. "Letter from the Birmingham Jail" (speech). Read by D. Graham. Mission Audio, 2013.

Kung, Hans. *On Being a Christian*. Translated by Edward Quinn. Garden City, NY: Doubleday & Company, 1976.*

Marsh, Charles. *Strange Glory: A Life of Dietrich Bonhoeffer*. New York: Alfred A. Knopf, 2014.

Matthews, Caitlin. *Celtic Devotional*. New York: Harmony Books, 1996.

McNeil, John. *The Church and the Homosexual*. New York: Pocket Books, 1976.

Merton, Thomas. *The Asian Journal of Thomas Merton*. Edited by Naomi Burton, Brother Patrick Hart, and James Laughlin. New York: New Directions, 1975.*

————. *New Seeds of Contemplation*. New York: New Directions, 2007.

Metz, Johannes Baptist. *Poverty of Spirit*. Mahwah, NJ: Paulist Press, 1998.

The Mission. Directed by Roland Joffe. Written by Robert Bolt. United Kingdom: Columbia-Cannon-Warner Distributors, 1986.

Monette, Paul. *Borrowed Time: An AIDS Memoir*. New York: HBJ, 1988.

Moore, Sebastian. *Let This Mind Be in You: The Quest for Identity through Oedipus to Christ*. New York: Harper & Row, 1985.*

Moore, Thomas. *Care of the Soul*. New York: Harper Collins, 1992.*

Moran, Martin. *The Tricky Part*. New York: Anchor Books, 2006.

Morris, David J. *The Evil Hours: A Biography of Post-Traumatic Stress Disorder*. Boston: Houghton, Mifflin, Harcourt, 2015.

Of Gods and Men. Directed by Xavier Beauvois. Written by Étienne Comar. France: Mars Distribution, 2010.

Pramuk, Christopher. *Sophia: The Hidden Christ of Thomas Merton*. Collegeville, MN: Liturgical Press, 2009.

Rohr, Richard. *Quest for the Grail*. New York: The Crossroad Publishing Company, 1999.*

Rumi, Jalal al-Din. *The Soul of Rumi*. Translated by Coleman Barks. San Francisco: Harper San Francisco. 2001.

Shakespeare, William. *King Lear*. New York: Simon & Schuster, 2004.

Silence. Directed by Martin Scorsese, Martin. Based on the novel by Shusaku Endo. World: Paramount Pictures, 2016.

Teilhard de Chardin, Pierre. *The Divine Milieu*. New York: Harper Torchbooks, 1965.*

————. *Hymn of the Universe*. London: Collins, 1961.

Tolson, Andrew. *The Limits of Masculinity*. New York: Harper & Row, 1977.

van der Kolk, Bessel. *The Body Keeps the Score*. New York: Penguin Books, 2014.

Weil, Simone. *Gravity and Grace*. London: ARK Paperbacks, 1987.

Wilde, Oscar. *De Profundis*. London: Methuen & Co. Ltd., 1911.

Wiman, Christian. *My Bright Abyss: Meditation of a Modern Believer*. New York: Farrar, Strauss, and Giroux, 2013.*

Wolff, Hanna. *Jesus the Therapist*. Oak Park, IL: Meyer-Stone Books, 1987.

ABOUT THE AUTHOR

A former Jesuit, William D. Glenn spent his career as an educator, psychotherapist, and community leader in the San Francisco Bay Area.

Glenn is currently the chair of the board of trustees of the Graduate Theological Union in Berkeley, is a cofounder, with his husband Scott Hafner, of the Center for LGBTQ and Gender Studies in Religion at the Pacific School of Religion, and past president of the San Francisco AIDS Foundation. For nine years, he cofacilitated a group for lifers at San Quentin State Penitentiary.

Glenn holds three master's degrees: a master of divinity from the Pacific School of Religion, where he was awarded the Paul Wesley Yinger Award for Distinguished Preaching; a master of arts degree in clinical psychology from the University of San Francisco, and one in American Studies from Saint Louis University.